Intergroup Relations

Intergroup Relations

Walter G. Stephan and Cookie White Stephan
New Mexico State University

WestviewPress
A Division of HarperCollins*Publishers*

Social Psychology Series
John Harvey, Series Editor

Empathy: A Social Psychological Approach, Mark H. Davis

Violence Within the Family: Social Psychological Perspectives,
Sharon D. Herzberger

Social Dilemmas, Samuel S. Komorita and Craig D. Parks

*Self-Presentation: Impression Management
and Interpersonal Behavior*, Mark R. Leary

*Experimental and Nonexperimental Designs in Social
Psychology*, Abraham S. Ross and Malcolm Grant

Intergroup Relations, Walter G. Stephan and Cookie White Stephan

Published in 1996 in the United States of America by Westview Press, Inc., 5500 Central Avenue, Boulder, Colorado 80301-2877, and in the United Kingdom by Westview Press, 12 Hid's Copse Road, Cumnor Hill, Oxford OX2 9JJ

Stephan, Walter G.
    Intergroup relations / by Walter G. Stephan, Cookie White Stephan.
        p.   cm.
    Includes bibliographical references and index.
    ISBN 0-8133-3008-4 (pbk.)
    1. Small groups. 2. Interpersonal relations. 3. Social
psychology.   I. Stephan, Cookie White. II. Title.
HM131.S8155   1996b
302.3'4—dc20   96-414
                                                              CIP

The paper used in this publication meets the requirements of the American National Standard for Permanence of Paper for Printed Library Materials Z39.48-1984.

10   9   8   7   6   5   4   3   2

CONTENTS

PREFACE

As we were writing this book we saw headlines such as the following:

Swastikas Deface Anti-Racism Fliers

Prejudice Polarizes College Campuses

Race Riot follows Acquittal in Beating of African American Motorist

Serbs Launch Campaign of Systematic Rape Against Moslems

Thousands Killed in Ethnic Violence in Burundi

Rising Tide of Illegal Immigrants Threatens Border States

21 American Soldiers Killed in Attack in Somalia

Religious Fundamentalists Kill Tourists in Egypt

Rival Black Political Factions Massacre Each Other in South Africa

Homes of Turkish Workers Burned in Germany

Palestinians Attack Jewish Settlers in the West Bank

Israeli Soldiers Kill Hundreds During Infitada in Gaza

More Than One Hundred Thousand Iraqis Die in Gulf War

IRA Bomb Kills 12 in Belfast

New York Trade Center Bombed by Terrorists

We live in a world saturated with hostility and violence between groups. Intergroup hostility and violence are so common that we encounter evidence of them every day of our lives. But it takes the juxtaposition of a set of headlines such as the preceding to drive home the horrific magnitude of the problem. The hostility and violence range from international disputes between Arabs and Israelis to interethnic disputes between African Americans and Whites to domestic disputes between women and men. At the root of this hostility and violence are stereotyping, prejudice, and discrimination. To reduce this hostility and violence and improve relations between groups we must ask: Why do people stereotype one another? Why do members of different groups hate one another? Why do people discriminate against others who differ from them?

Finding answers to these questions is of vital importance in our modern global village. As cultures and subcultures come into greater contact with one another, it becomes increasingly important to understand the sources of the difficulties that impede fruitful interactions among groups. If we are to live in contact with people who differ from us, we will need to become more tolerant of group differences and better able to deal with them without conflict. Yet there is evidence all around us that intergroup conflict may be a greater problem now than ever before. Racial, ethnic, and religious tensions in the United States and elsewhere around the globe are persistent issues that are far from being resolved.

Intergroup relations can be analyzed from many different perspectives. A wide variety of disciplines, including anthropology, political science, sociology, economics, history, and psychology, have yielded important insights into an array of issues concerning intergroup relations. Here we restrict ourselves to a psychological analysis of intergroup relations. In fact, our focus is even narrower, since within the possible psychological approaches we will focus only on a social psychological analysis.

Social psychologists study individual behavior as it is affected by the thoughts, feelings, and behavior of others. Our focus will be primarily on the stereotypes, prejudices, and discriminatory behavior of individuals and the manner in which these cognitions, feelings, and behaviors affect others and are affected by them. Our primary interest will be in relations among individuals as they are affected by their own group memberships and the groups to which others belong. The issues that concern us are how group members perceive themselves and one another, what their attitudes toward other groups are, and how these perceptions and attitudes affect their behavior. We will also be concerned with the measures that can be taken to improve intergroup relations. In particular, we will examine techniques for eliminating stereotypes and reducing prejudice, paying particular attention to the ways in which intergroup contact can best be managed to achieve these ends. We will also discuss the ways in which group members can most effectively approach intergroup conflict situations.

The social psychological approach with its emphasis on the individual is only one among many approaches to the study of intergroup relations. Ultimately information from many different disciplines and approaches within disciplines will need to be integrated to create a comprehensive picture of relationships among groups, their causes and consequences, and techniques for improving them. Such an integration is beyond the scope of this book, but we do hope to provide you with a look at the rich bounty of knowledge that social psychologists have harvested. We believe this knowledge can enrich the lives of individuals by helping them combat their own biases and preconceptions, improve interpersonal relations among members of different groups, and make a significant contribution to our ultimate understanding of intergroup relations.

The Organization of the Book

We start by discussing stereotypes in chapter 1. We examine the nature of stereotypes, how they are measured, and the mechanisms by which they operate. We analyze the manner in which stereotypes bias our perceptions of others and our behavior toward them in ways that function to maintain stereotypes. In the last section of chapter 1 we present methods of changing stereotypes. The second chapter examines prejudice and racism. We focus primarily on relations between African Americans and Whites in the United States. This choice was made in part because relations between these groups have been a central issue in intergroup relations historically, and in part because, for that very reason, they have been studied more extensively than other types of intergroup relations. We discuss the most prominent theories of prejudice along with the research that supports them. The basic argument made by these theories is that racism and prejudice have changed in the last half of the twentieth century and have become more subtle, although not necessarily less damaging, than in the past.

The third chapter analyzes the contact hypothesis. This hypothesis concerns the conditions under which intergroup contact can promote positive intergroup relations. We use an extended example, the case of school desegregation in the United States, to illustrate the utility of the contact hypothesis. The fourth chapter addresses issues of social identity and the role that social identity plays in intergroup relations. The fundamental premise of theories of social identity is that the groups to which we belong provide a basic element of our identities and predispose us to favor these groups over others.

The fifth chapter examines the unique problems that arise in interactions among people from different cultures. Problems such as culture shock and ethnocentrism, as well as solutions to these problems, are presented in this chapter. The final chapter discusses techniques for resolving intergroup conflicts. After discussing the origins of conflict, techniques such as deterrence, negotiation, mediation, and unilateral de-escalation are analyzed. These techniques often involve interactions between representatives of their respective groups, but the principles typically apply to interactions among individual group members as well.

Acknowledgments

Many people made contributions to this book. Galen V. Bodenhausen, Patricia Devine, Felicia Pratto, and Charles Stangor made valuable comments on earlier versions of the manuscript that resulted in many improvements. John A. Harvey invited us to write this book; we are glad he did so. We hope you find it informative and useful.

Stereotypes

> To consider every member of a group as endowed with the same traits saves us the pains of dealing with them as individuals. (Allport, 1954, p. 169)

Rwanda is a small republic in central Africa. In 1994 the presidents of Rwanda and the neighboring republic of Burundi were killed under mysterious circumstances in a plane crash at the airport outside of the capital of Rwanda. Their deaths touched off a bloody civil war in Rwanda. Even the most conservative estimates of the resulting carnage indicate that more than 200,000 lives were lost. The antagonists in this civil war were two ethnic groups, the Hutu, who are the majority group in Rwanda, and the Tutsi, who are the minority group. Like most such struggles, this one has a long history, but its modern antecedents can be traced to the period just before and after Rwanda achieved independence from Belgium in 1962.

For most of the colonial period the two ethnic groups lived together relatively peacefully. In the years immediately prior to independence, two political organizations existed in Rwanda, one controlled by the Tutsi and one controlled by the Hutu (Kuper, 1977). Both organizations were ideologically moderate. For instance, a Hutu manifesto in 1957 declared that, although the principal problem of the country was the domination of one group by the other (the Tutsi are economically dominant), both groups shared a common ancestry and in this sense were brothers. The Tutsi-dominated party (Union Nationale Rwandaise [UNAR]), although elitist in defense of Tutsi privilege, expressed a commitment to fight against ethnic hatred.

As independence approached, ethnically based political tensions escalated. Increasingly, the common ground between the two groups diminished, and an accentuation of group differences occurred. The increasing use of repression by the economically dominant Tutsi minority led to a fear of aggressive retaliation by the Hutu. The aggressiveness imputed to the Hutu was used to justify additional repression. The spark that ignited this highly flammable mixture was the beating and rumored murder of a Hutu subchief. The response was a peasant uprising in which Hutu tribesmen burned thousands of Tutsi homes and killed some Tutsies. The Tutsi reaction consisted of the summary arrest, torture, and execution of Hutu leaders. Fear and suspicion gripped the country. Each group increasingly perceived the other group in dehumanized terms, as bloodthirsty barbarians. Each group blamed the other for aggression against its members.

Elections just before independence brought the Hutu majority to power in 1961. Tutsi were removed from positions of authority, many were executed, and UNAR was eradicated. The Tutsi mounted military raids against the Hutu, who countered with massive reprisals. According to de Heusch (1964), "From then on every Tutsi, in the interior as well as the exterior, whether or not supportive of these military adventures . . . [was] considered an enemy of the country" (Kuper, 1977, p. 193). The categorical process was complete. All differentiation among the Tutsi was obliterated.

The next atrocity was committed by the Hutu in response to an invasion by the Tutsi from neighboring Burundi in 1963. "Hutu, armed with clubs, pangas and spears, methodically began to exterminate all Tutsi in sight, men, women, and children'' (Kuper, 1977, p. 196). An estimated 10,000 people were slaughtered before the massacre ended. The hatred created by this massacre continued to seethe beneath the surface of Rwandan life for the next three decades. Incidents of violence gradually increased until the explosion into civil war in 1994.

The descent into social chaos in 1963, which set the stage for the bloody civil war of 1994, illustrates the role of group perceptions in intergroup relations. From an initial stance of some common goals, tempered with expressions of reservations and suspicion, the groups came to attribute hostility and aggressiveness to each other. Outgroup members were perceived as hated barbarians, a view that was ultimately used to justify genocide.

Of course, outgroup perceptions are usually not as negative or overgeneralized as those between the Tutsi and the Hutu, nor are the consequences this tragic. Nonetheless, our views of other groups, especially our stereotypes of these groups, are often negative and overgeneralized, and they do have important effects on our behavior toward them and on their reactions to us. What are stereotypes and how can they come to have such destructive effects?

Defining Stereotypes

Journalists often do more than report on society. They also provide valuable insights into its fundamental nature. Walter Lippman, one of the great journalists of the twentieth century, gave us the concept of stereotypes (Lippman, 1922). He argued that "the real environment is altogether too big, too complex, and too fleeting, for direct acquaintance. We are not equipped to deal with so much subtlety, so much variety, so many permutations and combinations. . . . We have to reconstruct it on a simpler model before we can manage with it'' (p. 16). Stereotypes are one of the simplifying mechanisms people use to make a complex social world more manageable. But Lippman also recognized that a stereotype ''is not merely a way of substituting order for the great blooming, buzzing confusion of reality. It is all these things and more. It is the guarantee of self-respect, it is our projection upon the world of our own sense of value, of our position, and our own rights. The stereotypes are . . . highly charged with feelings that are attached to them'' (p. 96). Thus stereotypes serve many functions, including helping people to maintain their self-esteem and justify their social status (cf. Jost & Banaji, in press). To serve these functions, our perceptions of the traits possessed by other groups are often distorted.

The early literature on stereotypes typically condemned them as unduly negative, overgeneralized, and incorrect (cf. Brigham, 1971). Later theorists, however, argued that stereotypes were no different from generalizations about nonsocial categories (e.g., the characteristics of birds) (Brigham, 1971; McCauley, Stitt, & Segall, 1980; Stephan, 1985). All generalizations organize and simplify the world. By stressing the similarity of generalizations about social groups to generalizations about nonsocial stimuli, the newer definitions avoided condemning stereotypes as morally wrong and pointing an accusatory finger at people who possess them. In accord with the newer definitions, we will define stereotypes as the traits attributed to social groups.

Stereotypes are frequently useful in everyday social interaction and often perform a valuable function. They can provide us with sets of guidelines that shape our interactions with physicians, nurses, waitpersons, accountants, professors, infants, schizophrenics, depressed people, shy people, and so on. For instance, knowing that someone is schizophrenic and that schizophrenics are likely to have delusions and hallucinations and that their affect may be flat or inappropriate prepares one for interaction with that person.

For intergroup relations, however, stereotypes are important primarily when they are negative, overgeneralized, or incorrect, because then they have detrimental effects on intergroup interactions. Stereotypes have detrimental effects because of the expectations they create concerning the behavior of others. When these expectations are negative, they lead us to anticipate negative behaviors from outgroup members. When the expectations are overgeneralized, they lead us to anticipate that most outgroup members will behave in similar ways. They make it less likely that we will treat outgroup members as individuals—each with his or her own unique qualities. And when stereotypes are incorrect, they can cause suffering to those who are misperceived and lead to misunderstanding and conflict.

The next section surveys techniques of measuring stereotypes, after which their origins, their implications, and how they can be changed are discussed.

Measuring Stereotypes

Three techniques for empirically measuring stereotypes have achieved considerable acceptance. The first is the original technique devised by Katz and Braly (1933), the checklist technique (before reading on, take a minute to read box 1.1). This technique is used to uncover the consensus in one group's views of another by asking respondents to indicate the traits that characterize the other group. Respondents select from a large list of trait adjectives those that they feel characterize a given group. The stereotype consists of those traits that are nominated by the greatest number of respondents. For instance, in a study of college students in Russia, the respondents were given a list of 115 traits and asked to indicate the 15 that best characterized Americans (Stephan, Ageyev, Stephan, Abalakina, Stefanenko, & Coates-Schrider, 1993). Table 1.1 on page 7 lists the 10 most frequently nominated traits. Is this list different from your own stereotype of Americans? If so, why do you think these differences exist?

The second technique, the percentage technique, is the most widely used. The percentage technique is used to determine the prevalence of a set of traits in a given group (Brigham, 1971). Respondents are given a large list of traits and asked to indicate the percentage of group members who possess each trait. The stereotype consists of the traits perceived to be possessed by the highest percentage of group members. In the Stephan et al. study cited, a second sample of Russian students was asked to indicate the percentage of Americans who possessed each of 38 traits. The 10 traits with the highest percentages are also listed in table 1.1. Notice that though the two techniques yield similar results, there are also some differences.

The third technique, the diagnostic ratio, is used to determine the traits that uniquely distinguish a given group from people in general (Martin, 1987; McCauley & Stitt, 1978). As in the percentage method, respondents are asked to indicate the percentage of group members who possess each of a list of traits. Then they are asked to indicate the percentage of people in general who possess these traits. A diagnostic ratio indicating the degree to which the group is perceived to differ from people in general is then calculated for each trait. This is done by dividing the percentage of group members who possess the trait by the percentage of people in general who possess the trait. The stereotype consists of those traits with the highest ratios. The Russian students were also asked to indicate the percentage of people in general who possessed each of the 38 traits. The diagnostic ratios that were calculated from their responses appear in table 1.1. The stereotypes emerging from the diagnostic ratios are somewhat different from the stereotypes using the checklist and percentage techniques. There is only a 60 percent agreement with each of the other

Using the following list, select the 10 adjectives that best characterize Americans. Then select the 10 adjectives that best characterize Russians.

Optimistic	Friendly
Aggressive	Independent
Outgoing	Tough
Patient	Secretive
Wasteful	Humorous
Dignified	Passive
Restrained	Irresponsible
Materialistic	Truthful
Oppressed	Confident
Serious	Kind
Competitive	Ambitious
Conservative	Expert
Spontaneous	Sociable
Patriotic	Hospitable
Disciplined	Progressive
Energetic	Industrious
Proud	Strong
Emotional	Obedient
Adaptable	Enterprising

Later you will have an opportunity to compare your answers to those of Russian and American students.

techniques. The reason for this difference is that some of the traits that appear using the checklist and the stereotype techniques (e.g., sociable, ambitious) are traits that Russian students think characterize people in general—that is, they are not unique to Americans.

Studies comparing techniques of measuring stereotypes suggest that most techniques yield similar results. However, as it was intended to, the diagnostic ratio does provide a different view of the content of stereotypes (Jonas & Hewstone, 1986; McCauley & Stitt, 1978; McCauley, Stitt, & Segall, 1980; Stephan et al., 1993). All techniques of measuring stereotypes have in common an attempt to assess the traits associated with social categories. But do all social categories

TABLE 1.1 Russians' Stereotypes of Americans

Checklist Technique		Percentage Technique		Diagnostic Ratio Technique	
Ambitious	70%	Ambitious	81%	Spontaneous	1.95
Competent	70%	Spontaneous	78%	Independent	1.87
Enterprising	64%	Dignified	75%	Enterprising	1.77
Competitive	64%	Competent	75%	Dignified	1.77
Independent	62%	Energetic	75%	Outgoing	1.76
Self-Confident	59%	Enterprising	75%	Competent	1.68
Spontaneous	58%	Competitive	74%	Energetic	1.60
Dignified	58%	Patriotic	73%	Competitive	1.57
Emotional	53%	Independent	72%	Confident	1.57
Sociable	53%	Sociable	72%	Optimistic	1.56

Source: Stephan et al., 1993.

have stereotypes associated with them? Aren't people more apt to stereotype some groups than others? These questions are examined next.

Categorization

> If perceptual experience is ever . . . free of categorical identity, it is doomed to be a gem, serene, locked in the silence of private experience. (Bruner, 1973, p. 9)

The cognitive basis of stereotyping is categorization. In fact, stereotypes, as defined here, are an almost inevitable consequence of categorization. To create social categories, we focus on the characteristics that make the people in that category similar and that distinguish them from other people. Categories such as "disabled person," "Protestant," or "Caucasian" all refer to qualities that make the people within these categories similar—their physical abilities, their religious beliefs, or their race. When we categorize people by using a group label, we are highlighting the similarity of people within the category and the way these people differ from other groups. Simultaneously, we also tend to de-emphasize the many differences among the people within a given category.

There is, of course, an almost infinite array of social categories. We have categories for jobs, social roles, recreational interests, age, social class, race, religion, gender, political affiliation, mental health, physical health, and so on. Stereotypes can be associated with any of these categories. However, some of these categories are used more frequently than others in everyday social interactions, especially during initial interactions. Why is this so?

Rosch (1978) has suggested that some categories are more likely to be used than others because they are more basic to information processing. Rosch theorized that when a set of categories can be logically organized into a hierarchy from less inclusive to more inclusive, there will be levels within this hierarchy that are basic to cognitive processing. For instance, at the highest level we can categorize people as being members of the species *Homo sapiens*. At a lower level we might have nationalities (American, Russian). Below that level might be the social roles in each society (banker, wife). The social roles could then be classified according to whether they are achieved (physician) or biologically based (female). Within the achieved and biologically based roles we could have various subtypes (cardiologist, brunette, etc.). With a little effort you can probably think of further distinctions within these subcategories.

Rosch's position is that certain levels of such hierarchies are more likely to come to mind and be used than other levels. These *basic categories* tend to be those at an intermediate level of abstraction, neither too inclusive nor too exclusive. In the hierarchy just described, social roles might be a basic category—one we would naturally use when interacting with someone we did not know. Another important set of basic social categories concerns visible features that tend to be immediately encoded upon meeting people, such as their sex, age, and race (McArthur, 1981). A recent study indicates that people do indeed spontaneously categorize others on the basis of such readily apparent physical features (Stangor, Lynch, Duan, & Glass, 1992). This study found that certain physical features come to be considered "informative" because they are associated with stereotypes. Physical features that are not informative, such as hair color or eye color, are not used as often to categorize others. For instance, in a racially homogeneous society such as Japan, race is unlikely to be used to categorize others. Since nearly everyone belongs to the same race, the physical features associated with this race are not informative. In contrast, in a racially mixed society such as the United States, racial categories are likely to be used because race has been historically important and, as a result, racial categories are associated with social stereotypes.

Stangor's research suggests what types of categories are most likely to be basic (e.g., physical appearance categories associated with stereotypes), but it does not tell us anything about the content of the associated stereotypes. One answer to this question is that stereotypes are derived from the history of the relations between members of the social groups. As the role of historical factors is discussed it will become clear that cognitive and motivational factors also play an important role in shaping the content of stereotypes.

Historical Origins of Stereotyping

The social roles commonly held by any two groups that coexist, particularly their positions in the dominance hierarchy, are especially important in determining how each group views the other (Campbell, 1967). The master-slave relationship between African Americans and Whites in the South before the Civil War furnishes a clear example of a situation where two groups occupied specific social roles. It was inevitable that the master-slave relationship would shape how each group viewed the other. Consider the working and living conditions of the slaves. They were forced to work under threat of punishment; their maintenance was provided for only in the most minimal ways; it was actually illegal to educate slaves before the Civil War; and slaves could be severely punished for any signs of rebellion. It should come as no surprise to find that Whites viewed African American slaves as lazy, dirty, and ignorant and that they often believed that the slaves were content with their lot. The residues of these stereotypes have persisted even into the present day.

Correspondingly, the historical views of Whites held by African Americans were partly due to the positions occupied by the Whites with whom African Americans came in contact. In most societies, businesspeople and those from the upper classes tend to be seen as grasping, haughty, competitive, domineering, ambitious, progressive, and intelligent (LeVine & Campbell, 1972). The traits attributed to businesspeople and the upper classes have left their marks on the stereotypes of Whites held by African Americans. This stereotype includes the traits deceitful, sly, intelligent, industrious, selfish, conceited, and cruel, among others (Stephan & Rosenfield, 1982).

Once created, stereotypes become a powerful force supporting the status quo. The traits attributed to African Americans as a consequence of slavery have continued to have a negative impact on their treatment in American society. The problem, as Allport (1954) noted many years ago, is that stereotypes can be used to justify discriminatory behavior. As the following quote indicates, attributing negative traits to the slaves made it easier for Whites to justify treating them as less than human.

> Calling various African peoples all one racial group and associating that group with evil, sin, laziness, bestiality, sexuality, and irresponsibility, made it easier for White slave owners to rationalize holding their fellow humans in bondage, whipping them, selling them, separating their families, and working them to death. (Spickard, 1992, p. 15)

The modern legacy of these extreme forms of discrimination occurs when Whites use the traits they attribute to African Americans as an excuse for discriminatory behavior, such as refusing to sell them houses or insurance or to hire them. What applies to African Americans also applies to other social groups in subordinate positions. Negative stereotypes are used to justify discrimination and to maintain current relations not only between racial and ethnic groups but also between the social classes and the sexes (Jost & Banaji, in press).

One of the remarkable things about the stereotypes of African Americans in the United States is that, despite the vast changes that have occurred in relations between the two groups during this century, changes in stereotypes have not kept pace with these changes (Karlins, Coffman, & Walters, 1969). Many of the traits in the older stereotypes endure (Dovidio, Evans, & Tyler, 1986). How can this possibly be the case? One answer lies in the low levels of contact between the groups. In the absence of contact, the historically derived stereotypes are passed from generation to generation through socialization. A second answer is that there are fundamental psychological processes operating to maintain stereotypes, even in the face of changing intergroup relations. Several of these processes are discussed next.

Biased Labeling

The labeling of group differences and similarities is a complex process subject to interesting and important distortions. When considering group differences, people tend to emphasize traits that allow them to regard the ingroup (the group to which they belong) as superior to the outgroup (Brewer, 1979). Ingroup members tend to choose a positive label when describing a trait possessed by the

TABLE 1.2 Biased Perceptions of the Same Traits in Ingroups and Outgroups

Ingroup	Outgroup
Assertive	Pushy
Neat	Compulsive
Cautious	Cowardly
Patriotic	Clannish
Confident	Conceited
Flexible	Wishy-Washy
Steadfast	Rigid
Easygoing	Lazy
Hard-working	Driven
Reserved	Snobbish
Devout	Fanatic
Tough	Mean
Innocent	Naive
Smart	Cunning
Inquisitive	Nosy
Brave	Foolhardy
Tactful	Insincere

ingroup and a negative label when describing the contrasting trait in the outgroup. For instance, when Americans describe themselves, they say they are friendly and outgoing. The English, describing these same behaviors, say that Americans are intrusive and forward. The English describe themselves as being reserved and respectful of the rights of others. Americans, however, think of the English as cold and snobbish (Campbell, 1967). This biased labeling process contributes to the formation of positive stereotypes for the ingroup and negative stereotypes for the outgroup.

Even when two groups share the same trait, biased labeling can lead to the trait being described favorably for the ingroup and unfavorably for the outgroup (see table 1.2 for some hypothetical examples). For example, both African Americans and Whites view themselves as intelligent, a positive trait. African Americans also acknowledge that Whites are intelligent, but in labeling intelligence-related behaviors in Whites they use negative traits such as slyness and deceitfulness (Stephan & Rosenfield, 1982). When a trait comparison does not favor the ingroup, its importance tends to be downplayed in group stereotypes.

Biased labeling is not restricted to the labeling of entire groups; it also occurs when people interact with individual outgroup members in specific situations. Several studies have shown that there is a bias in the attributions used to explain the behavior of ingroup and outgroup members (see fig. 1.1). When an ingroup member does something good, the behavior is typically explained by some positive underlying personality trait, such as possessing the appropriate skills or abilities. If an outgroup member does equally well, the behavior tends to be explained by situational factors, such as the ease of the task. The opposite occurs for negative behaviors. Here it is the outgroup member's behavior that is explained by internal personality traits, whereas the ingroup member's behavior is attributed to situational pressures (Hewstone & Jaspars, 1982). This set of biases is known as the *ultimate attribution error* (fig. 1.1) (Pettigrew, 1979b).

A similar bias is prevalent when groups differ in social status (Foschi & Takagi, 1991). Members of higher-status groups are expected to perform well while members of the lower-status groups are expected to perform poorly. When the performances match the expectations, internal attributions are made (i.e., the high-status group member's success is attributed internally as is the low-status group member's failure). When the performances disconfirm the expectancies, external attributions are made (i.e., the poor performance of the high-status group members is explained away, as is the good performance of the low-status group members). The result is that stereotypes of high-status groups are likely to be more positive than those of low-status groups.

To illustrate, one study found that when an African American student performed well on an extrasensory perception (ESP) task, prejudiced White students believed it was due to luck, but when a White student performed well, the prejudiced White students believed it was due to ESP abilities. In contrast, when an African American student performed poorly, White students said it was because of a lack of ESP abilities, but when a White student performed poorly, it was seen as being due to bad luck (Greenberg & Rosenfield, 1979). For the White students in this study, the African American students are both outgroup members and members of a lower-status group, so both the ultimate attribution error and status biases combine to create attributions denying them credit for success and blaming them for failure.

	Ingroup	Outgroup
Positive performance	Internal attribution (e.g., high ability)	External attribution (e.g., good luck)
Negative performance	External attribution (e.g., bad luck)	Internal attribution (e.g., low ability)

FIGURE 1.1
Ultimate attribution error.

It is ironic that the categorization of others, which is originally undertaken to understand other groups and interact with them more effectively, can ultimately lead to negative stereotypes of outgroups. The next section turns now to an examination of how stereotype information is represented in our minds and how information related to stereotypes is processed. This discussion will make it possible to understand another property of stereotypes—their self-sustaining nature.

The Structure and Processing of Stereotype Information

The Structure of Stereotypes

In describing the structure of stereotype information in the mind, we will adopt an associative network model (cf. Anderson, 1983; Rumelhart, Hinton, & McClelland, 1986). In associative network models, it is assumed that discrete pieces of information, called *nodes*, are linked together to form networks. The links between the nodes can vary in strength with the result that some pairs of nodes in a network are more strongly associated with one another than others. For example, in a stereotype there may be a strong link between the group node and the node for a particular trait (e.g., Americans are

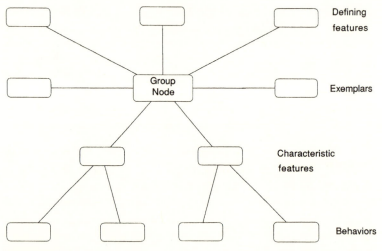

FIGURE 1.2
Network model of stereotypes.

materialistic), whereas there is only a weak link between the group node and some other trait node (e.g., Americans are restrained). Three basic types of information represented by the nodes in stereotype networks—defining features, characteristic features, and individual exemplars (see fig. 1.2)—are discussed next.

The *defining features* of a category consist of the criteria used to define group membership (Smith, Shoben, & Rips, 1974). What are the defining features of the category "American"? To be defined as an American a person must be born in the United States, be born of an American parent, or be naturalized through a legal proceeding. The *characteristic features* do not define the category, but they are associated with it. The most important characteristic features of stereotypes consist of the traits associated with the category. For American students' stereotype of Russians, the characteristic features consist of such traits as disciplined, hard-working, strong, proud, obedient, and serious (Stephan et al., 1993). The defining and characteristic features of social categories are qualitatively different. To be identified as a category member, an individual must possess at least some of the defining features. However, an individual may possess none of the characteristic features of a category and still be a category member. A Russian who is not disciplined, hard-working, strong, proud, and so on is still a Russian, albeit not a stereotypical one.

Exemplars consist of individual members of the category a person has directly or indirectly encountered—for instance, the particular Russians one has met, seen in movies, or read or heard about. Category exemplars are important in stereotyping because they may be used in forming stereotypes or making judgments about groups. If you visited Costa Rica, you would develop an image of the Costa Rican people as you encountered more and more individual citizens (exemplars).

Processing in Stereotype Networks

A node in a network can be activated by stimuli that are perceived in the external environment or by internal stimuli, such as your own thoughts. The node for "Italian" could be activated by seeing an Italian movie or by thinking about a friend who is Italian. When a node in a network is activated, the activation spreads outward along whatever links exist to other nodes. For example, activating the node for Italian may activate the nodes for the traits "emotional" and "expressive." The flow of activation through networks is often completely automatic (Bargh, 1984, 1988). Thus when a given node in a stereotype is activated, it can in turn automatically activate the other nodes in the stereotype. This is a passive process; it does not necessarily involve conscious awareness. Of course, it is also possible for people to exercise active control over the processing of stereotype information. Devine (1989) has suggested that people who are low in prejudice often exercise control to prevent their stereotypes from affecting their behavior (see chapter 2).

Processing in stereotype networks typically begins with activation of the nodes for the defining features. Activation then spreads automatically to the group node and the person is identified as a member of a given group. For instance, the presence of such defining features as a bearded face, masculine clothing, masculine nonverbal behavior, or large physical size may activate the node for "male." Activation then spreads from the group node to the stereotype-related traits. Thus the group node for "man" might activate the traits aggressiveness, coldness, lack of emotional expressiveness, and competitiveness in a person holding the traditional male stereotype (Spence & Helmreich, 1978).

A study by Banaji and her colleagues found that activating a stereotype-related trait, by having subjects unscramble sentences concerning trait-related behaviors, affected later judgments of members

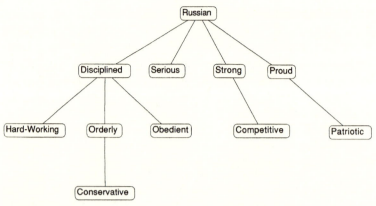

FIGURE 1.3
Network diagram of Americans' stereotype of Russians.

of the stereotyped group but did not affect judgments of members of another group (Banaji, Hardin, & Rothman, 1993). In this study it was found that activating the trait "aggressive" subsequently led to more extreme ratings of men on this trait, but it did not affect the ratings of women. Presumably, initially activating the stereotyped trait activated the group node and when a group member was subsequently rated, this activation was added to the prior activation of the group and trait nodes leading to an amplified judgment.

The strength of the links between nodes depends on the frequency with which the links have been activated (Bargh, 1988; Smith & Lerner, 1986). In the study of American stereotypes of Russians referred to earlier, the strength of the links in this stereotype was measured by asking subjects to indicate the frequency with which the nodes in the Russian stereotype occurred together. The group node was most strongly associated with the traits disciplined, serious, strong, and proud. But it was also found that the traits themselves were sometimes interlinked. For instance, the trait "disciplined" was linked to "hard-working," "orderly," and "obedient"; "orderly" was in turn linked to "conservative" (see fig. 1.3). The hierarchical organization of the traits in this stereotype is consistent with other research indicating that traits are often organized into hierarchies with the broad, abstract traits (e.g., good) forming the highest levels and the more narrowly descriptive traits (e.g., charitable, generous) forming the lower levels (John, Hampson, & Goldberg, 1991).

Affect Associated with Stereotypes

The cognitive nodes in stereotype networks are also linked to affective reactions (cf. Bower, 1980; Clark & Isen, 1982; Fiske, 1982; Fiske & Neuberg, 1989; Fiske & Pavelchak, 1986, Isen, 1982, 1984; Posner & Snyder, 1975; Stephan & Stephan, 1993). Any type of affective reaction, including hate, liking, fear, and happiness, may be associated with the various types of cognitive nodes in stereotypes. Indeed, more than one type of affective reaction may be associated with a single node. For instance, the ambivalence theory of intergroup attitudes suggests that attitudes toward stigmatized groups (e.g., the disabled) consist of simultaneous feelings of aversion and sympathy (Katz, Wackenhut, & Hass, 1986).

The affect associated with group labels is of special interest. If the affect is predominantly negative and leads to a negative evaluation of that group, then the person may be said to be prejudiced toward that group. Obviously, affective reactions can vary in intensity. We have strong positive feelings about some groups and strong negative feelings about others and, as Katz has suggested, sometimes we have both positive and negative feelings about the same group.

When a cognitive node for a category is activated, it activates both the cognitive and affective nodes to which it is linked. In one study supporting this idea, White subjects sat before a video screen on which the word "white" or "black" was briefly flashed in order to activate racial categories (Dovidio, Evans, & Tyler, 1986). A series of adjectives was then presented and the subjects were asked to determine whether or not each adjective could ever be true of the category presented initially (white or black). The speed with which these decisions were made was recorded. Some of the words were taken from the positive stereotypes of each group (e.g., ambitious, musical) and some were taken from the negative stereotypes (e.g., conventional, lazy). It was found that presenting the word "white" on the screen facilitated the processing of positive traits in the White stereotype, whereas presenting the word "black" facilitated the processing of negative traits in the stereotype of African Americans (as measured by the reaction times). Thus, activating racial categories by presenting categorical labels facilitated the subsequent processing of affectively consistent stereotyped traits. Similar effects have been found after the group labels "old" and "young" were presented to young people (Perdue & Gurtman, 1990) and for words commonly used to label the ingroup (we, us, ours) and the outgroup (they, them, theirs) (Perdue, Dovidio, Gurtman, & Tyler, 1990).

In some of these studies the group label was presented so quickly that it could not have been consciously recognized by the subjects. This suggests that the facilitating effects of the group labels were entirely automatic. Thus the activation of the group label can automatically activate traits that are affectively consistent with the evaluation of the group (Neidenthal, 1990). The group label was presented as a written word to the subjects in the Dovidio studies, but briefly presenting faces has a similar effect (Baker & Devine, 1988). Taken together, the implication of these studies is that during intergroup interaction, traits that are affectively consistent with the evaluation of the group will be automatically activated and will be available to be used as a basis for expectancies, attributions, behaviors, and subsequent judgments. For an anti-Semitic person, the negative traits she or he attributes to Jews are likely to be readily accessible whenever the category "Jews" is activated. The anti-Semite will probably expect behaviors consistent with these negative traits and is likely to make judgments and attributions that are consistent with these traits.

There is also a bias toward the recall of information that is affectively consistent with one's prior judgments (Dutta, Kanungo, & Freibergs, 1972; Higgins & Rholes, 1978). For instance, in one study English Canadian subjects read lists of traits that were attributed to English Canadians or French Canadians (Dutta, Kanungo, & Freibergs, 1972). They subsequently recalled more of the positive than the negative traits that were attributed to the ingroup and recalled more of the negative than the positive traits attributed to the outgroup. These retrieval biases tend to increase over time (Higgins & King, 1981). Thus, it appears that people tend to remember bad things about members of disliked groups and good things about members of liked groups.

Mood Associated with Stereotypes

In general, when people are in a positive mood, it facilitates the processing and retention of positive information (Bower, 1980; Mayer, 1989; Mayer & Salovey, 1988). Likewise, negative moods facilitate the processing and retention of negative information, although research suggests that this effect may not be as powerful as the one for positive moods. The differential processing of mood-congruent information can influence subsequent recall, evaluations, and other judgments (Esses, Haddock, & Zanna, 1990; Mayer, 1989; Mayer, Gayle, Meehan, & Haarman, 1990). For instance, Erber (1991) found that subjects in positive moods believed that other people were likely to engage in positive trait-related behaviors, whereas subjects in negative moods made negative behavioral predictions. In a study by Forgas and Bower (1986), subjects were put in a positive or negative mood through the use of false feedback on a personality test and then asked to read a series of positive and negative descriptions of individuals. Subjects in a positive mood made more positive and fewer negative judgments about the stimulus individuals, whereas subjects in a negative mood made more negative and fewer positive judgments. One implication of these studies is that when people experience positive or negative affect during intergroup interactions, they may process mood-congruent traits and behaviors more easily than mood-incongruent traits and behaviors. Thus people in a negative mood may attend to and recall the negative behaviors of others, which could facilitate the creation and maintenance of negative stereotypes.

Bodenhausen (1993) has argued that the effects of mood on stereotyping depend on two factors: (1) the ways in which a particular mood affects processing capacity, and (2) the motivation to process information systematically. Moods that produce high levels of arousal (e.g., fear, anger) and those that produce a sense of well-being (e.g., happiness) can reduce either the capacity or the motivation to process information systematically. When moods create nonsystematic processing (sometimes referred to as heuristic processing), stereotypes tend to be relied upon. However, for negative moods that people wish to escape (e.g., sadness), there may be a motivation to engage in effortful, systematic processing. In studies supporting this view, subjects who were made to feel either happy or angry through a mood induction procedure made more stereotyped judgments of other students than subjects who were induced into a sad mood (Bodenhausen, Kramer, & Susser, 1993; Bodenhausen, Sheppard, & Kramer, in press). Although the results of studies of the effects of mood on encoding, recall, evaluation, and judgment are complex, it appears that when either positive or negative moods detract from systematic processing, they have detrimental effects on intergroup relations.

Associative Network Models and Expectancy Confirmation

> The self-fulfilling prophecy is, in the beginning, a false definition of the situation evoking a new behavior which makes the originally false conception come true. The specious validity of the self-fulfilling prophecy perpetuates a reign of error. (Merton, 1948, p. 195)

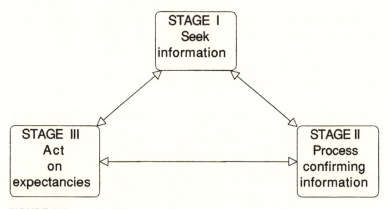

FIGURE 1.4
Three-stage model of stereotype processing.

Actively processing social category information can set in motion a sequence of related events that confirms the existence of the stereotyped traits associated with the group. This expectancy-confirmation sequence has three stages, beginning with the collection of confirming information, proceeding to the biased processing of confirming and disconfirming information, and ultimately leading to behavior that will cause stereotype-based prophecies to be fulfilled. These three stages describe a temporal sequence, but they do not constitute an invariant sequence and any one of them may occur without being accompanied by the others (see fig. 1.4).

Stage I: Information Acquisition

The first stage consists of acquiring information about the traits possessed by members of another group. When people are trying to determine the traits possessed by others, they rely on two information-seeking strategies: (1) They seek the information most relevant to deciding if the other person possesses a trait (diagnostic information) and (2) they seek information that confirms their preconceptions (Bodenhausen & Wyer, 1985; Devine, Hirt, & Gehrke, 1990; Duncan, 1976; Skov & Sherman, 1986; Snyder & Swann, 1978; Trope & Bassok, 1983; Wilder & Allen, 1978). The tendency to seek diagnostic information is likely to lead to sound judgments about the traits of others, but the tendency to seek expectancy-confirming evidence can lead to biased beliefs concerning the traits of others, that is, to beliefs that support stereotypes.

Many of the studies dealing with information acquisition employ a paradigm in which subjects are asked to formulate strategies to test hypotheses about the traits possessed by another person. Under these conditions, people often choose to solicit information that will confirm their hypotheses rather than pursuing evidence that could disconfirm their hypotheses (for a review, see Snyder, 1984). The reason that people seek confirming information appears to be that it is cognitively more efficient than seeking information that disconfirms expectancies (Skov & Sherman, 1986).

It is important to note that people are probably unaware that they are gathering information in a biased manner. Even when people are offered a reward for gathering unbiased information, they still tend not to do so. In a study illustrating this idea, subjects were asked to test the hypothesis that their conversation partner was an introvert (Snyder & Swann, 1978). They were then given a list of questions they could use during the interview. Many of the questions were designed to elicit information related to introversion (e.g., ''What factors make it really hard for you to open up to other people?''), and many were designed to elicit information related to extraversion (e.g., ''In what kind of situations are you most talkative?''). Both types of questions could have provided information relevant to determining whether the other person was an introvert. The subjects were offered a reward of $25 if they could select the questions that would best test the hypothesis that the other person was an introvert. Despite the reward, the subjects chose to ask questions oriented toward confirming, rather than disconfirming, the hypothesis.

In the case of stereotypes, when a group node is activated, the information in the nodes linked to the group is more easily accessed than information from other networks. In particular, the characteristic features of the group will be activated. These traits will create expectations. When attempting to determine whether individual group members possess these traits, people will try to gather the best information they can, but their capacity to do so may be compromised by the tendency to seek out information that confirms their expectancies.

Stage II: Information-Processing Biases

> Confident expectation of a certain quality or intensity of impression will often make us sensibly see or hear it in an object which really falls far short of it. (James, 1890, p. 424)

The second stage consists of the effects of expectancies on the cognitive processing of observed behavior. In the first stage, the process of actively seeking out information that confirms stereotypes was discussed, whereas in this stage the more passive process of observing others or receiving information about them is discussed. When the activation of social categories creates expectancies (Deaux & Lewis, 1984; Jackson & Cash, 1985), people typically attend to and encode expectancy-confirming information to a greater extent than disconfirming information (Bodenhausen & Wyer, 1985; Wyer & Martin, 1986). This confirming evidence is then readily accessible to be used as a basis for subsequent judgments (Higgins, Rholes, & Jones, 1977; Rothbart, Evans, & Fulero, 1979). For instance, in a study by Darley and Gross (1983), it was found that students viewing a videotape of a child's academic performance rated the child's ability as above grade level if they had been told she had a high socioeconomic background, but they rated the child's ability as below grade level if they were told she came from a low socioeconomic background. Similarly biased judgments have been found in a number of other studies (e.g., Bodenhausen, 1988; Duncan, 1976; Sagar & Schofield, 1980).

When stereotypes are activated, attention tends to be allocated to the processing of stereotype consistent information, with the result that people see what they expect to see. In one intriguing demonstration of this effect, students were told that the person they were about to interview was either sociable or unsociable (Major, Cozarelli, Testa, & McFarlin, 1988). If they were told that the interviewee was sociable, they were actually assigned to interview another student who was unsociable, whereas if they were told that the interviewee was unsociable, they were actually assigned to a sociable interviewee. Nonetheless, at the end of the interview the interviewers' ratings reflected their expectancies more than the interviewees' actual traits. For instance, subjects who expected the other person to be sociable rated their interviewees as more sociable than those who expected their interviewees to be unsociable.

One consequence of this differential attention is that expectancy-confirming information is generally better remembered than expectancy-disconfirming information. Expectancy-confirming information is most likely to be recalled when it concerns traits (rather than behaviors) and when it concerns groups (rather than individuals) (Stangor & McMillan, 1992). This is one of the many reasons why stereotypes are so hard to change—confirming evidence about the traits of groups is so easily encoded and recalled (cf. Hamilton, Sherman, & Ruvolo, 1990). An American who expects Italians to be emotional and encounters some emotional Italians and some non-emotional Italians may pay more attention to the emotional ones. Later the American will have these confirming exemplars available in memory for use in making judgments about Italians.

Although it is not entirely clear why expectancy-confirming information is differentially encoded and recalled, two factors have been frequently discussed. The first factor is that stereotype-based expectancies are rarely expected to apply 100 percent of the time, which means that disconfirming evidence may be discounted. Some ''exceptions to the rule'' are probably anticipated and such exceptions may not necessarily be taken as disconfirmations of the group stereotype (cf. Srull, Lichtenstein, & Rothbart, 1985; Stern, Marrs, Cole, & Millar, 1984). For a male manager who holds a traditional stereotype of women, an assertive female employee is just the exception that proves the rule.

The second factor is that stereotype-based expectations often concern traits that are difficult to disconfirm (Hilton & von Hippel, 1990; Rothbart & John, 1985). For negative traits like aggressive, superstitious, deceitful, and selfish, it is usually clear when they have been confirmed but not when they have been disconfirmed. For instance, if people stereotype members of an outgroup as untrustworthy, many behaviors, including both being honest and being dishonest, can be interpreted as confirming their expectations. That is, even an outgroup member's honest behavior may be seen by an ingroup member as an attempt to set her or him up for some later situation in which the outgroup member would benefit from betraying the ingroup member's trust. For ambiguous traits, such as being untrustworthy, it is difficult to determine what behaviors would disconfirm them, so disconfirmations may not be recognized as such.

However, if the expectancy is very strong and susceptible to disconfirmation, disconfirming evidence is likely to affect later recall (Srull, et al., 1985). When expectancies are strong, it appears that the unexpected information is processed more elaborately (at a deeper level) than expected information (Hemsley & Marmurek, 1982; Srull et al., 1985; Stern et al., 1984). The deeper encoding appears to involve creating more complex links between the items of disconfirming evidence and other items of information previously associated with the social category node. Suppose a professional football player acts in a clearly submissive manner. This unexpected behavior will draw attention and the observer may attempt to relate this information to various aspects of the stereotype of football players with which it conflicts. Doing so makes this information easier to retrieve later and thus it will be more accessible for use in subsequent judgments.

It appears that disconfirming information is encoded at a more concrete level than confirming information (Maass, Salvi, Arcuri, & Semin, 1989). Confirming information is encoded in terms of traits, but disconfirming information is encoded in terms of the specific actions or behaviors displayed. The result is that confirming information directly supports the existence of stereotypes by strengthening the link between the group and the associated trait, whereas disconfirming evidence has less effect on stereotypes because it is encoded at the behavioral, not the trait, level. If a physician makes an unintelligent investment decision, it is the behavior itself that is likely to be encoded (she made a poor investment on that time-share apartment), but if the physician makes a sound investment decision, it is likely to be encoded in terms of the stereotyped trait (she's really intelligent).

Despite the more elaborate and concrete encoding that expectancy-disconfirming evidence receives, behavior that disconfirms expectancies is often attributed to situational factors rather than to factors within the person (Crocker, Hannah, & Weber, 1983; Kulik, 1983). The person who observed the football player behaving submissively may decide that he did so because of external pressures (e.g., the coach threatened to have him traded if he did not behave more civilly off the field), not because he is a submissive individual. If disconfirming evidence is attributed to the situation, the disconfirming evidence will not contribute to stereotype change, since it is not attributed to a trait possessed by a group member. Even in those studies indicating that disconfirming evidence has been better remembered than confirming evidence, the impressions of the other person remained congruent with the initial impression (e.g., Hastie & Kumar, 1979; Hemsley & Marmurek, 1982). An explanation for this finding is that a trait linked to a group node will be weakened only if an internal attribution is made to account for the disconfirming evidence (Crocker, Hannah, & Weber, 1983).

In addition, we tend to dislike people who disconfirm our stereotypes (Costrich, Feinstein, Kidder, Maracek, & Pascale, 1975; Deaux & Lewis, 1984; Jackson & Cash, 1985, but not Jackson, MacCoun, & Kerr, 1987). In one study, females who acted in masculine ways were evaluated less positively than females who behaved in feminine ways (Costrich, et al., 1975). Another study found that women who performed well in gender atypical jobs were unfavorably evaluated by male supervisors (Reskin & Padavic, 1988). These findings suggest that even when people from a stereotyped group are successful in counteracting a stereotype, they may create or reinforce negative attitudes toward themselves or their group.

Most of the preceding studies of expectancies have examined the effects of disconfirming information on subsequent judgments of the same person about whom the information was provided. A small number of studies have examined the effects of disconfirming information on judgments of the prevalence of the trait in the stereotyped group. For instance, would seeing one nonaggressive, warm, emotional, noncompetitive man change the stereotype of a woman who held a traditional stereotype of men? Although some studies suggest that providing disconfirming individuating information may change the original stereotype (e.g., Hamill, Wilson, & Nisbett, 1980), people seem to be very conservative in allowing disconfirming information to influence judgments of entire stereotyped groups (Grant & Holmes, 1981; Rasinski, Crocker, & Hastie, 1985). Taken together, the studies on expectancies reflect a general tendency to process information in ways that support preexisting stereotypes, even when disconfirming information has been encoded (Stangor, 1986; Wilder & Shapiro, 1991).

Stage III: Self-Fulfilling Prophecies

Expectancies frequently lead to self-fulfilling prophecies. That is, people's expectancy-based behaviors lead to reactions on the part of the other person that confirm the expectancies (Harris, Milich, Corbitt, Hoover, & Brady, 1992; Snyder, 1984, 1992; Snyder, Tanke, & Berscheid, 1977). For example, an individual who expects Costa Ricans to be friendly may act in such an outgoing and receptive manner that Costa Ricans respond by being friendly (cf. Fazio, Effrein, & Falender, 1981; Snyder & Swann, 1978). In one study White interviewers sat at a greater distance from African American interviewees, made more speech errors, and terminated the interview more quickly than when they interviewed Whites. In a follow-up study it was found that these negative interviewer behaviors led to lower performances by interviewees (Word, Zanna, & Cooper, 1974).

Snyder (1992) has shown that self-fulfilling prophecies are more likely to occur when people are in the process of acquiring information about others. In one study of this phenomenon (Snyder & Haugen, 1994), subjects were led to believe that the person with whom they were conversing on the telephone was either obese or of normal weight (the conversation partners were actually randomly assigned to one another so these labels were not valid). In one condition the subjects were asked to use the interaction to get to know the other person; in a control condition they were not given these instructions. The stereotype of the obese as unfriendly, reserved, lazy, boring, and sad created expectancies that were self-fulfilling, but only among subjects instructed to get to know the other person. In this condition the subjects whose conversation partners were labeled as obese treated their partners in such a way that the partners behaved in unfriendly, reserved, and unenthusiastic ways, compared to the partners who were not labeled as obese.

The rather gloomy conclusion that can be drawn from the studies of self-fulfilling prophecies is that there is a tendency to make one's negative expectancies come true. However, the next section demonstrates that this outcome need not always occur.

Changing Stereotypes

Stereotypes can be changed by modifying the components of the networks that comprise them (cf. Crocker, Fiske, & Taylor, 1984). To create more favorable stereotypes, links between a group node and a positive trait can be strengthened or created. Similarly, to reduce the impact of a negative stereotype, links between a group node and a negative trait can be weakened. Also, new subtypes can be created or people can be encouraged to use alternate categories that have fewer negative traits associated with them. Further, it may be possible to relabel negative traits with more desirable labels.

Strengthening or Creating Positive Links

Because the links between groups and traits are the basic elements of stereotypes, they will be the primary focus. Links between the group node and positive traits can be strengthened by the presentation of confirming instances. The activation of related positive traits may also strengthen group/trait links through the process of spreading activation. Creating positive moods in intergroup interactions may also strengthen existing positive group/trait links (Mackie et al., 1989). In addition, creating positive moods may increase the probability that information relevant to positive traits will be preferentially processed and recalled, and the processing of information relevant to negative traits may be inhibited. The possibility also exists, however, that positive moods will simply lead to a reliance on preexisting stereotypes.

New positive traits can be added by acquiring information about the group from others or through direct experiences with group members. To add new positive traits through direct experience, it is necessary for the trait-related behavior of group members to be encoded, for internal attributions to be made for that behavior, and for the trait to be linked to the group node. The behavior is most likely to be encoded if it is salient (vivid) in the situation (McArthur & Post, 1977; McArthur & Soloman, 1978). Internal attributions must then be made for the behavior. Attributional inferences depend on such factors as consensus, distinctiveness, and consistency information (Kelley, 1967). An internal trait attribution to a group is most probable when many group members consistently behave in a distinctive way that is not commonly displayed by members of other groups. To link the trait to the group node, the group node has to be activated either through automatic categorization or conscious processing. For instance, if most Costa Ricans consistently behaved in a distinctively friendly way toward foreigners, this could lead to the perception of Costa Ricans as friendly.

Weakening Negative Links

The process of weakening links between the group node and negative traits is more complex than strengthening positive group/trait links. Although it seems paradoxical, stereotypes may have to be activated through either automatic or controlled processing if the negative group/trait links are to be changed. This idea was supported in a study where subjects were covertly primed with traits consistent with mental retardation (words such as "dull" and "dumb" were presented on slides), or no primes were presented. Then the subjects read about a person who was labeled as a retardate or was not labeled in any way. It was found that explicitly labeling the group and priming traits consistent with this label subsequently led to greater recall of information inconsistent with expectancies regarding the group than in any of the other conditions (Skowronski, Carlston, & Isham, 1993). These results suggest that activating the outgroup label and its stereotype can facilitate the retention of stereotype-inconsistent information.

For stereotypes to be modified, people must have sufficient cognitive resources available to process stereotype-related information (Gilbert & Hixon, 1991). That is, the situational context should not place heavy processing demands on the individuals. The situation probably should not involve difficult tasks or create high levels of arousal or anxiety (Stephan & Stephan, 1985).

To weaken negative group/trait links, the tendency to seek out and prefer confirming evidence must be overcome. One technique that is effective is to lead people to consciously consider traits opposite to those that are expected (Lord, Lepper, & Preston, 1984). Also, if people are encouraged to seek evidence that disconfirms their expectations, they will do so (Snyder & White, 1981). In addition, it has been found that situations in which ingroup members are dependent on outgroup members increases both the effort that goes into processing information about the outgroup (Borgida & Omoto, 1986; Erber & Fiske, 1984) and the chances that disconfirming evidence will be encoded (Darley, Fleming, Hilton, & Swann, 1986).

If the disconfirming information is encoded, it will not have an impact on eliminating the group/trait link unless the disconfirming evidence is attributed internally (Crocker et al., 1983). Rothbart and John (1985) have argued that disconfirming behavior is most likely to weaken stereotypes if it clearly disconfirms the stereotype and occurs frequently in a variety of settings. The processing of disconfirming evidence is further facilitated if the outgroup members who engage in the disconfirming behavior are perceived as otherwise typical (Rothbart & Lewis, 1988) and if the disconfirmations are strongly associated with the group label (Rothbart & John, 1985). In addition, the disconfirmations should be dispersed across a number of different group members (Johnston & Hewstone, 1992; Weber & Crocker, 1983). For instance, in one study subjects were presented with information on the performance of a group of 10 African American college students who were competing to represent their college in a mathematics contest with a rival college (Mackie, Allison, Worth, & Asuncion, 1992). When it was reported that these students had recently performed very well, African Americans as a group were rated as being more intelligent than they were in a control condition. Thus in this study stereotype-disconfirming information about a number of different outgroup members generalized to the group as a whole.

Other factors that lead to the controlled processing of disconfirming information should also facilitate the weakening of group/trait links. For instance, having people actively consider the response options open to the other person (Langer, Bashner, & Chanowitz, 1985), asking them to form accurate impressions (Neuberg, 1989; Srull et al., 1985; Stangor & McMillan, 1992), and creating low processing demands (Pratto & Bargh, 1991; Srull, 1981; Stangor & Duan, 1991) have all been shown to promote the controlled processing of trait information. Furthermore, if the disconfirming evidence is positive in nature, it may be more likely to be attended to, encoded, and recalled by people who are in a positive mood.

Attempts to change stereotypes are inhibited by the tendency to create self-fulfilling prophecies. Fortunately, self-fulfilling prophecies are not inevitable, as indicated in a study by Hilton and Darley (1985). If the people about whom the expectancy is held are aware of the other person's expectations, they can successfully counteract the expectancy. They are particularly likely to counteract the expectancy if they are certain that they do not possess the expected trait (Swann & Ely, 1984). Also, people can be successfully trained to explicitly behave in disconfirming ways (Cohen & Roper, 1972). Thus, to change stereotypes it may be valuable for people who are stereotyped to be aware of the associated expectations so they can counteract them.

One study suggests that the effects of negative expectancies can be offset when the people holding the stereotype are trying to get others to like them (Neuberg, Judice, Virdin, & Carillo, 1993). In this study subjects were asked to conduct a job interview with another student. They were either provided with information about the applicant that created a negative expectancy concerning job-related skills (the applicant was not sociable or good at problem solving) or with no expectancy. Half the subjects were instructed that successful interviewers try to get applicants to like them and they should try to do so, too; the other half of the subjects were not given instructions on this topic. The results of the interview revealed that interviewers who tried to get the applicant to like them treated the negative-expectancy applicant more favorably than interviewers in the control condition. The negative-expectancy applicants responded to this more favorable treatment by acting in more positive ways. The more positive behavior of negative-expectancy applicants, in turn, led the interviewers to have more favorable impressions of them. The results of this study are encouraging, because the implicit norms of many social situations encourage people to try to get along. Thus the implicit norms in these situations could have the effect of undermining negative stereotypes (cf. Snyder, 1992).

Subtyping and Activating Alternative Categories

In addition to modifying the internal links within the stereotypes themselves, it is also possible to reduce the use of stereotypes by adding new subtypes to a category or by substituting superordinate social categories. Breaking down a category into subtypes is promoted by the presentation of information that is inconsistent with current stereotypes and that is concentrated within a relatively small number of individuals (Weber & Crocker, 1983). Subtyping is also facilitated if disconfirming behavior occurs among group members who are not representative of the group in other ways (e.g., are atypical in terms of demographic characteristics) (Weber & Crocker, 1983). Subtyping may be particularly likely if members of a disliked group engage in disconfirming behavior that is unusually positive. They may then be grouped together as "exceptions to the rule" (Pettigrew, 1979b). For example, older men who are active in public affairs may be subtyped as "elder statesmen" (Brewer, Dull, & Lui, 1981).

One problem with creating subtypes is that they leave the original stereotype unchanged and thus do not benefit the people who continue to be categorized as members of the larger group. Also, subtyping may not be beneficial if the subtypes that are created have stereotypes that are no more positive than the previously existing stereotypes. Kanter (1977) found that women in organizational settings dominated by men were subtyped into groups such as "seductress," "pet," and "iron maiden," all of which were associated with negative characteristics. Another study found that young Whites' subtypes of African Americans, such as "ghetto Blacks" and "welfare Blacks," were viewed at least as negatively as the group as a whole (Devine & Baker, 1991).

Substituting superordinate categories for categories lower in the hierarchy may be useful in reducing the impact of stereotypes (Sherif, Harvey, White, Hood, & Sherif, 1961). When superordinate categories (e.g., the human race) are evoked, former outgroup members (e.g., people from other countries) become members of a more encompassing ingroup. In effect, this reappraisal converts the entire outgroup into a subtype within the superordinate group. Cooperative interaction involving members of different subgroups has been shown to produce identification with the larger group (Gaertner, Mann, Dovidio, Murrell, & Pomare, 1989; Gaertner, Mann, Murrell, & Dovidio, 1989). To illustrate, reminding ethnic subgroups that they are all part of one national group may reduce the tendency to use ethnic stereotypes, if the national affiliation is important to all the ethnic groups.

Altering Biased Labeling

When acknowledged differences between groups exist, the stereotype cannot be changed by eliminating the links between the category and the associated traits. In instances such as these, however, the labeling of the trait can be changed. For instance, the British might have fewer problems interacting with Americans if they could view the Americans' behavior as friendly and sociable, instead of intrusive and forward. In a similar vein, if the affect associated with a particular trait can be changed from negative to positive, the stereotype is likely to create fewer difficulties in intergroup relations. If Americans could learn to like and appreciate the reserve displayed by the British, interactions between the two groups might be smoother.

Stereotypes can and do change. The process is not mysterious, but it is complex. The conditions under which stereotypes can be changed that have been outlined provide room for cautious optimism about the future of intergroup relations. With careful attention to the conditions necessary for change, it is possible to design programs that will promote changes in negative stereotypes. The topic of techniques of improving intergroup relations is so important that it is discussed at the end of each chapter.

Summary

This chapter has argued that stereotypes are a basic product of the categorization process. Categorization emphasizes similarities within categories and differences between categories. Intermediate levels of hierarchically organized structures of information are most likely to be associated with stereotypes. The content of social categories is determined in part by the history of relations between members of the groups. For instance, the stereotypes of African Americans and Whites are still influenced by the historical roles they occupied in the past. Biased labeling also plays a role in the creation of negative stereotypes of outgroups. In addition, the ultimate attribution error leads people to attribute the positive behaviors of ingroup members and the negative behaviors of outgroup members to internal factors.

Stereotypes are structured into networks consisting of interlinked nodes of defining features, characteristic features, and exemplars. Activating any one of these nodes, through either automatic or conscious processing, activates the other nodes to which it is linked. The strength of the links depends on the frequency with which they have been activated. The nodes in stereotype networks can also have affective and emotional responses linked to them. Moods can influence the processing of mood-related information. Typically, positive moods facilitate the processing of positive information, whereas negative moods facilitate the processing of negative information.

When stereotypes are activated, they can lead to self-fulfilling prophecies through a three-stage process. First, there is a bias that can lead to seeking information that is stereotype-confirming. Second, people attend to and encode stereotype-confirming information, unless disconfirming evidence is strong and unambiguous. Even when stereotype-disconfirming evidence is encoded, it is unlikely to be attributed to internal factors, and it may lead to disliking the person who disconfirmed the stereotype. Thus there is a general tendency to perceive that one's stereotypes have been confirmed. Third, stereotype-based expectancies influence behavior, which can increase the chances that outgroup members will respond by fulfilling these expectations (prophecies).

Changing stereotypes can involve adding positive links to established stereotypes by presenting new information that is highly distinctive, consistently displayed by many members of the group, and infrequently displayed by members of other groups. Stereotypes can also be changed by weakening negative links. This requires that disconfirming evidence be encoded, attributed internally, and linked to the group. Creating positively viewed subtypes of the group and encouraging people to use superordinate categories may also reduce stereotyping. In addition, relabeling negative traits should reduce negative stereotyping.

Theories of Prejudice

CHAPTER OUTLINE

In recent years racial incidents have become increasingly frequent in the United States. Moreover, they are no longer created solely by a small number of hate groups whose views most Americans reject. Surprisingly, university campuses have become a focus for racial incidents: Racist episodes were reported at more than 300 colleges and universities between 1986 and 1991. For instance, at the University of Maryland-Baltimore, one in five African American students reports some form of racial harassment (*Newsweek,* 1991).

Race is becoming an increasingly divisive issue in politics, and it was a dominant issue in the 1988 and 1992 national elections in the United States. Further, a 1991 Congressional debate over a proposed civil rights bill provoked heated charges of reverse discrimination and quotas from one side, countered by charges of barely disguised racism from the other. In 1992 rioting in Los Angeles followed the announcement of the verdict in the trial of four White policemen charged in the videotaped beating of African American motorist, Rodney King. In 1993 the verdict in the King case and the verdict in the trial of the two African American men accused of beating a white truck driver, Reginald Denny, during the Los Angeles riots dominated political discussions.

How can racial incidents such as these occur with such frequency in the 1990s, 30 years after the major battles for integration in the United States were fought and won? What do these incidents mean in a society in which most people believe that the attitudes of American Whites toward African Americans have changed in a markedly positive direction in the past 50 years?

This chapter examines theoretical explanations for current race relations in the United States. It first defines prejudice, attitudes, discrimination, and racism. Then it discusses traditional explanations of prejudice. Finally, it examines arguments that traditional prejudice directed against racial and ethnic minorities has been replaced by a new type of prejudice and discrimination, which has been given many labels and which we will call covert racism.

Prejudice, Attitudes, Discrimination, and Racism

Prejudice is typically thought to be an attitude (e.g., Newcomb, Turner, & Converse, 1965; Secord & Backman, 1964; Sherif & Sherif, 1956). Rigidity, irrationality, overgeneralization, and injustice are components often included in the definition of prejudice (Ackerman & Jahoda, 1950; Allport, 1954; Kelman & Pettigrew, 1959; Simpson & Yinger, 1985). Although many definitions exist, we prefer the relatively simple definition of prejudice as ''a negative attitude toward members of socially defined groups'' (Stephan, 1983, p. 417).

Prejudice is thought to foster, promote, and justify discriminatory behavior, although often individuals' levels of prejudice are not strongly associated with their behaviors (e.g., Ajzen & Fishbein, 1977; Brigham, 1971). Situational constraints, multiple determinants of behavior, differences in level of specificity of attitudes and behaviors, and low accessibility of prejudicial attitudes in memory are among the factors that can lower the association of prejudicial attitude and discriminatory behavior (Ajzen & Fishbein, 1977; Chaiken & Stangor, 1987; Fazio, 1986; Wicker, 1969).

Attitudes themselves have been defined in many ways. For example, attitudes have been viewed as evaluations (e.g., Eagly &

Chaiken, 1992; Olson & Zanna, 1993), as affect (Breckler & Wiggins, 1989; Greenwald, 1968), as cognitions (e.g., Kruglanski, 1989), and as including cognitive, affective, and behavioral components (e.g., Secord & Backman, 1964). We believe that, with respect to intergroup relations, it is most useful to think of attitudes as affective reactions (Duckitt, 1992a, 1992b; Stephan, 1983). This definition is consistent with social psychologists' recent emphasis on prejudice as an affective reaction (Brewer & Kramer, 1985). As Mackie & Hamilton (1991) argue:

> the history of intergroup relations is rich in evidence of intense
> emotional, even passionate, forces guiding the thoughts, feelings,
> perceptions, and behaviors of group members. Some intergroup
> contexts in and of themselves seem to generate affective reactions that
> can disrupt ''normal'' social interaction. Moreover, if our self-
> identities are wrapped up in our perceptions of our own and other
> groups, then the stereotypes we hold of outgroups are destined to be
> affectively laden. (p. 3)

Whereas prejudice is an attitude, discrimination is typically defined as negative behaviors directed toward members of socially defined groups because they are members of this group. Racism is the term commonly applied to prejudice and discrimination directed at racial or minority groups.

Traditional Explanations of Prejudice

Social psychological explanations for prejudice have varied over time (see Duckitt, 1992a, 1992b, for excellent reviews). In the 1930s and 1940s the predominant explanations were individual-level psychodynamic explanations (e.g., projection, scapegoating, frustration, hostility displacement) (Ackerman & Jahoda, 1950; Dollard, Doob, Miller, Mowrer, & Sears, 1939). In the 1950s efforts to explain the success of Nazi ideology led researchers to explain prejudice as a result of an authoritarian personality (Adorno, Frenkel-Brunswick, Levinson, & Sanford, 1950).

Beginning in the 1960s and 1970s, sociocultural explanations replaced individual-level explanations of prejudice. There is a sad history of racism in this country. The genocide and subjugation of the American Indians; the institution of slavery; the forced annexation of parts of Mexico; the importation of foreign workers, beginning with the Chinese in the 1850s, and the eventual restrictions on their immigration; the expulsion of Mexican American citizens during the Depression; the internment of Japanese Americans during World War

II; the legal segregation of public facilities that existed until the 1960s; and the growing anti-immigration feelings in the 1990s, to give only a few examples, demonstrate the pervasiveness of prejudice and discrimination in the social structure of the United States. Prejudicial norms and conformity to them, learned as a part of childhood and adult socialization, were used to explain the deep-rooted racism in the society (Duckitt, 1992a, 1992b). These past conditions were believed to have left a residue of current discriminatory practices and patterns in all institutions of American society. For example, segregation is no longer legal, but segregation is rampant in housing in most cities in the United States. Equal treatment is mandated by law, but discrimination is readily apparent in political, legal, and educational institutions, and socioeconomic inequality among ethnic groups remains. These vestiges of intentionally discriminatory policies are thought to communicate to citizens of the 1990s that prejudiced views and discriminatory practices are still tolerated in United States society today.

Individual-level and societal-level explanations of prejudice are not mutually exclusive. On the contrary, individual and societal forms of prejudice reinforce each other. Faced with massive inequality, many people find it easy (as well as comforting and self-serving) to view the world as just and to assume that people receive the life consequences that they deserve (Lerner, 1980; Lerner & Miller, 1978). Racial inequality is thereby blamed on the victims of prejudice and discrimination (Ryan, 1971).

It is sad that many individuals from disadvantaged groups themselves accept the existing discriminatory societal arrangements and negative stereotypes directed toward their own group. Karl Marx, among other theorists, noted this phenomenon, labeling it false consciousness. Marx argued that the control of material production allows for the control of mental production (Marx, 1843/1967). Recently a similar concept of system justification has been proposed. System justification is seen as a psychological process contributing to the preservation of existing social arrangements even at the expense of personal and group interest (Jost & Banaji, in press). Stereotypes, it is argued, justify the exploitation of certain groups and explain the powerlessness or poverty of these groups in ways that make differences in life chances among groups seem legitimate or natural, even to the members of the stereotyped groups. Justification of the system, in which all members of a culture have been socialized to engage, frequently appears to be more important to negatively stereotyped groups than justification of their own group characteristics and interests. For example, in the United States, many women as well as men subscribe to negative stereotypes of women; Whites and African Americans have been shown to have similar racial stereotypes (e.g., Sagar & Schofield, 1980); abused women and rape victims often feel responsible for their victimization; and many lower-class individuals believe strongly in the myth that anyone in the country can become anything she or he desires to be.

The myth of America as the melting pot—that all people who came from or to the United States were assimilated into one harmonious cultural group—is alive today. This myth, and the actual assimilation of White ethnic immigrants into the Anglo-American majority, create the image in the minds of some that inequality no longer exists in the United States. From this perspective, attempts by the United States government to remedy institutional discrimination through equal opportunity programs constitute reverse discrimination. The empirical data, however, show that government policies not only are not conferring advantage but also are not consistently increasing minorities' quality of life, relative to Whites. As one can see in tables 2.1 to 2.3, minority life expectancies have increased, and minority infant, maternal, and neonatal mortality rates have declined but have not reached Whites' levels; for the last 20 years, percentages of minorities below the poverty line have remained unchanged.

TABLE 2.1 Expectation of Life at Birth, 1970 to 1990

	White		Black		All Nonwhite	
	Male	*Female*	*Male*	*Female*	*Male*	*Female*
1970	68.0	75.6	60.0	68.3	61.3	69.4
1975	69.5	77.3	62.4	71.3	63.7	72.4
1980	70.7	78.1	63.8	72.5	65.3	73.6
1985	71.9	78.7	65.2	73.5	67.2	75.1
1990	72.6	79.3	66.0	74.5	65.3	73.6

Source: U.S. National Center for Health Statistics, *Vital Statistics of the United States*, 1993.

TABLE 2.2 Infant, Maternal, and Neonatal Mortality Rates,* 1970 to 1990

	1970	1975	1980	1985	1989
Infant deaths					
White	17.8	14.2	11.0	9.3	8.2
Black	32.6	25.2	21.4	18.2	17.7
All nonwhite	30.9	24.2	19.1	15.8	15.2
Maternal deaths					
White	14.4	9.1	6.7	5.2	5.6
Black	59.8	31.3	21.5	20.4	18.4
All nonwhite	55.9	29.0	19.8	18.1	16.5
Neonatal deaths					
White	13.8	10.4	7.5	6.1	5.2
Black	22.8	18.3	14.1	12.1	11.3
All nonwhite	21.4	16.8	12.5	10.3	9.6

*Number of deaths per 1,000 live births.

Source: U.S. National Center for Health Statistics, *Vital Statistics of the United States*, 1993.

TABLE 2.3 Percentage of Families Below Poverty Level, 1970 to 1990

	White	Black	Hispanic
1970	8.0	29.5	NA
1975	7.7	27.1	25.1
1980	8.0	28.9	23.2
1985	9.1	28.7	25.5
1990	8.1	29.3	25.0

Source: U.S. Bureau of the Census, *Current Population Reports,* 1993, Series P-60, No. 175.

Noting the tenacity with which prejudice and discrimination are embedded in the fabric of the society, during the 1970s some theorists argued that self-interest must underlie continued prejudice (Duckitt, 1992a, 1992b). One of the most popular of the theories making the argument regarding prejudice as a result of the interest of one's group is realistic group conflict theory. The next section turns to a detailed look at this explanation of prejudice.

Realistic Group Conflict Theory

Realistic group conflict theories of prejudice argue that self-interest lies at the heart of prejudice and discrimination against many groups, whether racial, national, sex, or religious. It is assumed that greater intergroup competition for scarce and valued resources intensifies prejudice among these groups. This intergroup competition is known to elicit hostility (Sherif & Sherif, 1967), the most extreme outcome of such competition being warfare.

Certainly many different groups are in direct competition for social and natural resources (LeVine & Campbell, 1972). To take one important example of competition, only a certain number of skilled jobs exist, and the number of qualified applicants exceeds the number of jobs. Members of each ethnic group are in direct competition for these jobs. These direct conflicts lead ingroup members to denigrate members of the outgroups. Realistic group conflict theorists also believe that the competition among groups is invariably unfair. The majority group can define the prevailing resource inequalities that benefit the group as just and right and engage in discriminatory behavior to protect its privileged position (van den Berghe, 1967).

Considerable research supports these basic premises. Rising competition has been shown to produce exclusionary laws, immigration quotas, and labor force competition restrictions (Olzak, 1992). Intergroup competition also promotes violence. For example, in a recent reanalysis of lynchings in the South over a 50-year period, a significant positive association was found between the number of lynchings and economic indices based on the value of cotton (Hepworth & West, 1988). In a study of U.S. ethnic incidents between 1877 and 1914, Olzak (1992) has shown that ethnic conflict increased when barriers to free competition in economic and political arenas broke down. Ironically, then, integration in these arenas *promoted* rather than ameliorated conflict, because intergroup competition intensified with this integration. In addition, Olzak's data suggest that African Americans have disproportionately been the object of racial attacks.

Measures of Traditional Prejudice

This section now examines ways in which types of traditional prejudice have been measured. In the past, prejudice was measured by items assessing overtly prejudiced responses. Individuals were asked to state their attitudes toward members of a particular group in a straightforward manner (e.g., Woodmansee & Cook, 1967), disclose the stereotypes that they associated with various outgroups (Katz & Braly, 1933), or answer questions about the amount of social distance people desired from outgroup members (e.g., Would you admit Chinese people to citizenship in your country? . . . to employment in your occupation? . . . to your street as neighbors? . . . to close kinship by marriage?) (Bogardus, 1925).

Since World War II traditional measures of White prejudice, such as attitude surveys based on negative beliefs regarding African Americans (e.g., Blacks are inferior to Whites; Blacks breed crime) and racial stereotypes assessed by adjective checklists (e.g., the belief that African Americans are lazy, unintelligent), indicate that African Americans are being assessed in an increasingly positive manner (Dovidio & Gaertner, 1986). In addition, survey data show a strong linear increase in support for the principles of equality and integration. For example, table 2.4 shows significant decreases in agreement with prejudiced responses to questionnaire items regarding intermarriage and segregated housing between 1977 and 1988–89.

	Year	All Ages	18–28	29–39	40–50	51–61	62–73	73+
Laws against inter-marriage	1977	28.3	12.7	16.0	25.5	36.5	53.0	59.8
	1988–1989	24.0	14.7	11.5	19.2	30.0	40.5	50.0
Right to segregated housing	1977	42.4	30.4	36.6	40.2	48.3	57.6	63.7
	1988–1989	23.4	16.6	15.4	19.0	32.0	34.2	39.2

Source: Kluegel, 1990. Data are from the General Social Survey. The wording of the first question is: "White people have the right to keep blacks out of their neighborhoods if they want to, and blacks should respect that right." Percentages are those responding "Agree Strongly" or "Agree Slightly." The wording of the second question is: "Do you think there should be laws against marriages between blacks and whites?" Percentages reported are those responding "Yes."

Explanations of Covert Racism

A number of theorists have noted this decline of overt prejudice, but they have also recognized the emergence of a paradox in many White Americans' racial attitudes. Whites' attitudes regarding racial and ethnic minorities and general principles of racial equality have become more favorable during the last 30 years, yet there is considerable opposition to specific policies designed to implement these general principles (Bobo, 1988). Thus the current White American attitude seems to be one supporting only limited racial change: Equal *rights* are accepted, but policies designed to ensure equal *opportunities* are not (Bobo, 1988). Stated differently, the area of controversy has shifted from whether racial and ethnic minorities should be overtly discriminated against due to biological deficiencies, to whether specific policies such as busing and affirmative action render an unfair advantage to these minorities.

In this section a variety of theories explaining the current racial attitudes of White Americans are described. These theories have been formulated as accounts of Whites' changed attitudes toward racial and ethnic minorities, particularly African Americans, since the 1950s. The initial focus of many of these theories was on attitudes toward African Americans, because prejudice and discrimination have been directed more strongly by Whites against African Americans than against other U.S. minorities. However, all of the newer theories of prejudice apply to other types of prejudice (e.g., that directed against other ethnic groups, females, homosexuals, the disabled).

Several theories are examined that explain these changes by positing a new type of prejudice and discrimination on the part of White Americans. This new racism is thought to be different from traditional racism, which was based on beliefs regarding the innate inferiority of racial and ethnic minorities. Specifically it is said to be less overt and direct than traditional prejudice and to be created by fundamental contradictions in White Americans' values, feelings, and beliefs. The notion of value contradiction was first posited by Myrdal (1944), who argued that the incongruity between American racism and the egalitarianism of the American creed created strain:

> Our problem is the moral dilemma of the American—the conflict between his moral valuations on various levels of consciousness and generality. The "American Dilemma" . . . is the ever-raging conflict between, on the one hand, the valuations preserved on the general plane which we shall call the "American Creed," where the American thinks, talks, and acts under the influence of high national and Christian precepts, and, on the other hand, the valuations on specific planes of individual and group living, where personal and local interests; economic, social, and sexual jealousies; considerations of community prestige and conformity; group prejudice against particular persons or types of people; and all sorts of miscellaneous wants, impulses, and habits dominate his outlook. (p. lxxi)

As this quote indicates, the culture of a society—its values, beliefs, rules, and basic concepts—is an important determinant of a variety of both individual-level and societal-level attitudes, behaviors, and policies. Thus, a society's values are reflected in its treatment of minority group members in the institutions of the society as well as in individuals' behaviors. The theories of covert racism all focus on this interconnection between the social and the individual.

This section examines four such theories and argues that the current racial paradox is created, at least in part, by value contradictions experienced by White Americans. These covert racism theories are: response amplification theory, aversive racism theory, symbolic racism theory, and compunction theory. Initially these theories are discussed in terms of Whites' prejudice directed against African Americans, and then their applicability to other types of prejudice is discussed. Finally, the covert racism theories and realistic group conflict theory are briefly compared and critiqued.

BOX 2.2
Covert Racism on White College Campuses

In a recent study, African American students attending predominantly White universities reported actions and comments from Whites that reflect little overt but considerable covert racism (Feagin, 1992). For instance, Blacks report being seen as "all alike." According to one student:

> Here in my dorm, there are four Black girls. Me and my roommate look nothing alike. And the other two are short, and I'm tall. They [White students] called me by my roommate's name the whole semester.

African Americans also report being viewed as representatives of their race. One student told the following story:

> This one professor . . . was trying to explain something to me about the church, and he said, "Because you're Black you'll understand this." . . . Well, I didn't understand, primarily because I'm not Baptist. I'm Episcopalian. And he didn't think for a moment that maybe I wasn't Baptist. I had to be Baptist, I was Black.

Other students reported feeling less commitment to them than to White students. One reported:

> A member of the alumni association . . . talked to us about job opportunities for graduates, saying that there are so many of our graduates all one needs to do in a particular town is say, "I'm a graduate of your university, can you help me get a job?" My response was, "That's wonderful. [What] if a Black student should do this?" . . . This person who made the presentation said, "I think the person might be insulted."

(continued on next page)

Another common complaint among African Americans was general student opposition to their subculture. One student recounted:

> If you're seen in an all-White group laughing and talking, you're seen as respectable, and probably taking care of something important. . . . You are all right. But if you're in an all-Black group, regardless if they can even hear your conversation, White people think you're trying to, you're congregated, to take over the world. . . . You're just punished for expressing your Black culture.

Situations such as these are not as dramatic as incidents of overt racism. Yet they have a cumulative impact and ultimately contribute to African American student attrition and attenuated achievement.

Response Amplification Theory

Irwin Katz and his colleagues (Katz, Glass, & Cohen, 1973; Katz, Glass, Lucido, & Farber, 1979; Katz, Hass, & Wackenhut, 1986; Katz, Wackenhut, & Glass, 1986) argue that racial ambivalence is created by a contradiction between positive and negative feelings that are held simultaneously by Whites about racial minorities. According to Katz and his colleagues:

> To follow the course of race relations in the United States in the 1950s is to be struck by a fundamental duality in White America's reactions to blacks and the civil rights movement. On one hand, there is ample documentation of almost unanimous public support for a national policy against racial discrimination. . . . Nonetheless, certain antiblack stereotypes and an aversion to close interracial contacts are still prevalent in the majority (Katz, Hass, & Wackenhut, 1986, p. 35).

Response amplification theorists argue that minorities are seen as disadvantaged in U.S. society but at the same time are seen as having psychological qualities that contradict the society's overall values. When confronted with an African American, Whites are said to feel both friendliness and sympathy, as well as disdain and aversion. This attitude duality stems from a value duality: the belief in two contrary but important American values—egalitarianism and individualism. Holding the core value of egalitarianism predisposes individuals to feel sympathy for African Americans and to support their struggle for equality. But holding the core value of individualism predisposes individuals to be intolerant of African American behavior patterns that Whites perceive to deviate from the individualistic values of self-reliance, individual achievement, and devotion to work.

Katz and his colleagues argue that holding these ambivalent feelings leads Whites to experience tension when they are in contact with African Americans. This tension stems from having both positive and negative feelings, and it produces attempts to reduce the tension. Situational factors can create feelings that especially challenge one or the other feeling, resulting in response amplification—unusually positive or negative behaviors directed toward the African American. In a situation evoking positive affect, positive response amplification will occur, and the African American will be favored over Whites; in a situation evoking negative affect, negative response amplification will occur, and Whites will be favored over African Americans. The most extreme responses are likely to occur when an African American displays traits or behaviors that are either beneficial or detrimental to the actor.

Initially the response amplification theorists used two measures to identify racially ambivalent people. The racially ambivalent were defined by their simultaneously high scores on a traditional measure of racial prejudice (taken from Woodmansee & Cook, 1967) and a measure of sympathy toward minorities (adapted from Schuman & Harding, 1963). Recently response amplification theorists have constructed Pro-Black, Anti-Black, Humanitarian-Egalitarianism, and Protestant Ethic (Individualism) Scales, and have created two relatively independent dimensions of attitudes toward African Americans, one based on pro-Black/humanitarian-egalitarian attitudes, and the other based on anti-Black/Protestant ethic values (Katz & Hass, 1988). Those with high scores on both dimensions are identified as racially ambivalent.

A number of studies have demonstrated both positive and negative response amplification. For example, in a learning experiment, subjects were led to believe they had given strong or weak shocks as feedback for errors to either an African American or White confederate (Katz et al., 1973). Although there were no differences in pretest ratings of the confederate, subjects gave more negative posttest ratings in the African American confederate/strong shock condition than in any of the other conditions. The authors attribute the amplified negative ratings of African Americans, but not Whites, to a combination of ambivalence toward African Americans plus negative affect caused by justifying the shock administration. Katz and his colleagues argue that ambivalent subjects wondered whether they enjoyed shocking an African American; subsequently they denigrated the person to justify the harm they were doing and absolve themselves from any guilt they were experiencing. The authors attempted to demonstrate the validity of their interpretation by examining ambivalence scores for a second group of subjects run in the high shock/African American condition. The results supported their interpretation of ambivalence as a causal factor in derogation: Subjects with the highest ambivalence scores (those high in both prejudice and sympathy toward African Americans) showed the greatest tendency to derogate the victim.

In another study subjects were induced to make either negative or neutral remarks to either an African American or White male stranger, under the belief that the stranger would be told during debriefing that the remarks did not reflect the subjects' true feelings (Katz et al., 1979). The subjects in the negative remarks condition were then led to think that the stranger was upset by the negative remarks, and all subjects were told that he had to leave the experiment before being debriefed. After the subjects thought the experiment was over, they received a note left by the stranger asking for help on a research project. Subjects in the negative remarks/African American confederate condition gave more help than subjects in any other condition. These results were interpreted as showing a positive amplified response to African Americans created by racial ambivalence and guilt felt over the unintentional harm to the person. These two studies thus show alternative means of reducing moral discomfort: exaggerated denigration and helping.

In summary, response amplification theorists argue that many individuals hold ambivalent feelings toward stigmatized others that stem from two contradictory values: beliefs in egalitarianism and individualism. The resulting tension is reduced by the individual directing unusually positive or negative behaviors toward the stigmatized, dependent upon whether the situation evokes positive or negative affect. This theory is thought to apply to feelings regarding any stigmatized group. Response amplification has been shown in response to a variety of groups, including other racial minorities, homosexuals, and the disabled.

BOX 2.3
The Stigmatized: Amplified Responses
and Attributional Ambiguity

Individuals who are perceived as socially or physically defective are said to be stigmatized. A primary result of stigmatization is prejudice and discrimination directed toward the stigmatized by the nonstigmatized or "normals" (Archer, 1985; Crocker & Major, 1989; Goffman, 1963). The stigmatization of racial minorities, the physically handicapped and disfigured, substance abusers, homosexuals, and ex-convicts is well documented.

Phrasing the racial ambivalence findings in stigmatization terms, one can state that "normals" may respond to the stigmatized with amplified affective, cognitive, and behavioral responses. These amplified responses pose interesting attributional problems for the stigmatized that do not exist for normals. For the stigmatized, virtually all personal feedback is attributionally ambiguous. When normals respond in any way to stigmatized people, the stigmatized must decide why they are being treated in this manner. If treated negatively, the stigmatized must decide whether this response is based on genuine views of them as individuals or is based on stigma-induced discrimination. If they believe the latter, the stigmatized can buffer and protect their self-esteems from negative feedback. If the stigmatized are treated positively, they must also decide whether they are genuinely viewed positively, or whether they are only being treated positively due to response amplification. If they believe the latter, the stigmatized may well discount positive feedback (Crocker, Voelkl, Testa, & Major, 1991).

In one study of African Americans and Whites, subjects received either positive or negative feedback from a White confederate of the experimenter, whom the subjects believed was another subject in the study. This feedback was based on a self-description completed by subjects who either were or were not visible to the partner. The results showed that African Americans were more likely to attribute feedback to prejudice when it was negative rather than positive, and when they were visible rather than not visible. These subjects thus used the attribution of prejudice in a protective manner when feedback was negative.

(continued on next page)

When their race was known to the evaluator, African Americans also tended to discount positive feedback. Viewing positive feedback as potentially due to race serves a parallel self-protective function, protecting the subjects from naive acceptance of positive evaluations that might be stated but not felt. Unfortunately, when all feedback is attributionally ambiguous, self-protective defenses can lead to the denial of positive as well as negative feedback.

Aversive Racism Theory

Like response amplification theory, Samuel Gaertner and John Dovidio's aversive racism theory (Dovidio & Gaertner, 1981; Gaertner & Dovidio, 1986) regards White Americans' racial views as being internally inconsistent. From the perspective of aversive racism theory, however, the contradiction is not between two types of feelings but between an individual's values and feelings. According to aversive racism theorists, the individual accepts the American egalitarian value system but has unacknowledged negative feelings and beliefs about African Americans. Gaertner and Dovidio believe that aversive racists are unaware that they have negative feelings about African Americans. Aversive racists see themselves as liberals who disavow racism. Nonetheless, they experience discomfort and perhaps fear around African Americans. These feelings lead to anxiety and avoidance of African Americans.

Aversive racists are believed to be concerned with avoiding recognizable discrimination to maintain a nonprejudiced self-image. Paradoxically these efforts at self-image maintenance can themselves lead to increased expressions of prejudice:

> The attempt to maintain a nonprejudiced self-image can, in itself, also increase disaffection for African Americans because interracial interactions become characterized by anxiety or uneasiness. Rather than being relaxed and spontaneous, aversive racists may have to guard vigilantly against even an unwitting transgression that could be attributed by themselves or by others to racial antipathy. Thus interracial interactions may arouse negative affect that can become associated directly with African Americans. (Gaertner & Dovidio, 1986, p. 64)

Amplified negative behavior (e.g., discrimination) may thus result from the conflict between values and feelings, but only in situations with conflicting or ambiguous norms. In structured norm-governed situations, aversive racists hide their feelings and act on the basis of their egalitarian values. Amplified positive behavior may occur as well, when the situation threatens these liberals' nonprejudiced views of themselves (Dovidio & Gaertner, 1983a).

Gaertner and Dovidio believe that overt measures of racism have become increasingly subject to social desirability effects. That is, many racists know they are not supposed to feel prejudice, so they respond to questions with socially desirable nonprejudiced responses rather than with their actual prejudiced feelings. For this reason these authors presume that aversive racism is virtually impossible to measure in questionnaire form. In some studies members of liberal political parties have been defined as aversive racists, and members of conservative political parties have been defined as dominative or old-fashioned racists (Gaertner, 1973). Studies employing college students as subjects have presumed that most are aversive racists.

Gaertner and Dovidio have tested aversive racism theory in several interracial helping experiments. In one study of help seeking (Dovidio & Gaertner, 1981), high- and low-prejudiced White male college students were paired at a task with either an African American or a White confederate. During the task the confederate either offered help or could be asked for help by the White student. Regardless of level of prejudice, subjects accepted the offer of help more often from an African American than a White partner but asked for help less often from an African American than from a White partner.

The authors believe that aversive racism led the subjects to assess what was socially appropriate in the situation and to amplify that response when the partner was African American. Pretesting suggested that refusing help when it is offered is seen as unusual, or nonnormative. Thus, they believe that aversive racism led to amplified positive behavior (acceptance of proffered help) in the African American/help-offered condition. Pretesting also showed that the norms for soliciting help are unclear. The authors therefore argue that aversive racism led to amplified negative behavior (not soliciting help) in the African American/help-available condition, because the refusal to solicit help could be viewed as usual, or normative.

In another study of helping (Frey & Gaertner, 1986), either an African American or White confederate/fellow student was portrayed as needing help to avoid failing at a task, either because he failed to work hard or the task was very difficult. White subjects were asked to help the student, either by the student or by a third party observer.

The authors hypothesized that both being deserving of help and having a third party make the request would increase the salience of the norm of helping. When either of these factors was present, Whites should thus feel obligated to help in order to avoid appearing prejudiced. Without the presence of these factors, aversive racists should respond to an African American partner with amplified negative responses, or lesser helping. As predicted, subjects helped African Americans less than Whites only in the condition in which helping norms were not salient: where the failure was the student's fault and the student himself made the request for help. In all other conditions, no significant racial differences occurred in helping.

In a study of bystander intervention, high- and low-prejudiced subjects were led to believe they were either the only bystander or were one of three bystanders to an emergency (Gaertner & Dovidio, 1977). It was presumed that subjects would believe that their failure to help could not be attributed to prejudice in the condition in which they were one of several bystanders. Thus aversive racists should only show amplified negative behavior (not helping) in the condition in which there were other bystanders. As predicted, African American victims were helped much less than White victims only in the condition in which there were three bystanders. When the subject was the only bystander, slight positive amplification occurred: The African American victim was helped somewhat more than the White victim.

In summary, aversive racism theory argues that for self-labeled liberals, a tension exists between their egalitarian values and their unacknowledged negative feelings and beliefs regarding African Americans. Aversive racists are said to maintain a nonprejudiced self-image by avoiding recognizable discrimination. Thus they should exhibit amplified positive behavior when it can be taken as evidence of lack of racial prejudice. Aversive racists are predicted to engage in amplified negative behavior only when it cannot be attributed to racism, that is, when conflicting or ambiguous situational norms exist.

Symbolic Racism Theory

David Sears and his colleague, Donald Kinder, also make the assumption that old-fashioned racism is being replaced with a new racism of a qualitatively different type, which they call symbolic racism (Sears, 1986; Sears & Kinder, 1971, 1985). Like aversive racism, symbolic racism is thought to consist of a blend of anti–African American attitudes and the values embodied in the Protestant ethic, such as individualism, obedience, and self-reliance.

Anti–African American attitudes and traditional values are thought to exert independent effects on interracial behavior and may also interact with each other (Sniderman & Tetlock, 1986a). Symbolic racists are defined as well-educated people who hold conservative political ideologies. It is argued that symbolic racists feel that African Americans are pushing too hard for change and are moving too fast toward equality. In addition, because symbolic racists think that discrimination is a thing of the past, they feel resentment because they believe that African Americans are receiving special favors (e.g., the perception of reverse discrimination).

Symbolic racism is measured by these three types of items: those designed to tap antagonism toward African Americans' demands (e.g., Blacks shouldn't push themselves where they're not wanted), resentment about special favors for African Americans (e.g., Over the past few years, Blacks have got more economically than they deserve), and denial of continuing discrimination (e.g., Blacks have it better than they ever had it before).

The focus of symbolic racism theory is on the political behaviors of Whites. According to Sears:

> the symbolic racism model involves a two-step process . . . the conjunction of traditional values and antiblack affect produces symbolic racism, which in turn produces opposition to problack policies and black candidates. (1986, p. 57)

Public opinion survey data have typically been used in studies of symbolic racism. The dependent measures employed have included racial policy preferences, evaluations of political leaders, and voting in racially relevant elections. For example, measures of symbolic racism have been associated with voting in the 1969 Los Angeles mayoral election, in which the candidates were an African American liberal councilman, Thomas Bradley, and a White conservative incumbent, Samuel Yorty (Sears & Kinder, 1971); opposition to busing (Sears & Allen, 1984); and support for the California movement to repeal taxes (Sears & Citrin, 1985).

Sears argues that the level of symbolic racism does not depend on personal racial threats (e.g., level of neighborhood crime) but stems from symbolic racial predispositions learned in childhood socialization. For this reason symbolic racism items are intended to measure abstract issues with no personal relevance to the individual. In support of this idea, in many studies direct personal racial threat has been a nonsignificant predictor of Whites' political attitudes (Sears & Funk, 1991).

Sears has employed many dependent variables to test his model of symbolic threat, including unemployment (Sears & Lau, 1983), women's issues (Sears & Huddy, 1990), support for law and order policies (Sears, Lau, Tyler, & Allen, 1980), support for national health insurance (Sears et al., 1980), and presidential performance (Sears & Lau, 1983). In these studies symbolic predispositions have been contrasted with individual self-interest as an explanation for political behaviors, with the symbolic predispositions accounting for a greater proportion of the variance in political behavior than individual self-interest (Sears & Funk, 1991).

In summary, unlike the other covert racism theories, symbolic racism theory was developed to predict a specific set of responses: the political behaviors and evaluations of elite Whites. Symbolic racism is said to be a result of symbolic predispositions that have persisted over time due to conditioned feelings learned in childhood. Because of their symbolic nature, these predispositions powerfully influence other attitudes. Symbolic racism is defined as a combination of both anti–African American attitudes and values embodied in the Protestant ethic, with symbolic racists being conservative White elites. Symbolic racists' political behaviors and evaluations are thought to be unrelated to self-interest.

Compunction Theory

Patricia Devine's theory of prejudice (Devine, 1989; Devine, Monteith, Zuwerink, & Elliot, 1991) addresses the issue of contradiction differently than the above theories. Her purpose is to examine the different cognitive processes involved in prejudice among high-prejudiced and low-prejudiced individuals.

Along with Allport (1954), Devine believes that (1) lifelong socialization in a racially divided society results in automatic activation of stereotypes in the presence of minority group members, and (2) prejudice is not the inevitable result of this socialization. Devine argues that low-prejudiced individuals have decided that prejudicial behavior is inappropriate, and they have consciously created a cognitive structure representing these nonprejudiced beliefs. Since stereotypes are automatically activated, the low-prejudiced person must intentionally inhibit the stereotype and initiate the activation of the newer belief structure.

Also like Allport (1954), Devine believes that many people who have rejected prejudicial beliefs still sometimes respond to outgroup members in a discriminatory manner. Allport felt that this contradiction between attitude and behavior would result in compunction, or feelings of guilt and self-criticism. Devine also argues that when the behaviors of low-prejudiced individuals do not meet their nonprejudiced standards, they experience compunction.

In empirical tests of these ideas, Devine first showed that cultural stereotypes of African Americans are well learned by all individuals, regardless of level of prejudice. She then demonstrated that the stereotype is automatically activated in the presence of an African American (Devine, 1989).

In a study in which homosexuals were used as the targets of prejudice, Devine et al. (1991) asked high- and low-prejudiced subjects to assess how they should and would respond to people on the basis of their sexual orientation. Both groups experienced a discrepancy between how they should and would behave and had affective reactions to this discrepancy. Low-prejudiced subjects responded with feelings of guilt and self-dissatisfaction when they violated their personal standards. High-prejudiced subjects also responded emotionally but with global discomfort and negative affect directed toward homosexuals. These findings are inconsistent with aversive racism theory, which assumes that people attempt to ensure that their feelings of discomfort are not consciously experienced.

A second study examined high- and low-prejudiced subjects' discrepancies in thoughts and anticipated behaviors regarding homosexuals (Monteith, Devine, & Zuwerink, 1993). As anticipated, low-prejudiced subjects experienced compunction, or guilt and self-criticism, when they violated their internal standards. High-prejudiced subjects did not experience compunction but, rather, discomfort associated with others' reactions to their violation of nonprejudiced societal standards. This type of discomfort produced anger directed toward the targets of their prejudice (e.g., I feel angry because these gay people cause others to think poorly of me). The authors argue that low-prejudiced subjects responded from the point of view of the group experiencing prejudice, whereas high-prejudiced subjects responded from their own points of view.

Monteith (1993) has argued that low- but not high-prejudiced individuals who experience discrepancies between their ideal and actual behavior will initiate a series of responses to help bring the discrepant behavior under control. Low-prejudiced individuals are said to (1) feel negative affect directed toward the self; (2) focus on the self, which heightens regulatory attempts; (3) focus on the stimuli present when the discrepancy occurred; and (4) link these stimuli to the discrepant response and feelings of guilt. Monteith (1993) found support for this self-regulation model (e.g., feelings of guilt and a focus on the self and on the situation in an effort to understand how the discrepancy occurred) using subjects' rejection of a law school applicant due to his sexual orientation. She also found decreased prejudice following the discrepant response that triggered the regulatory attempts.

In summary, all four of these covert racism theories attempt to explain a type of new or covert racism, believed to be based on some contradiction between racist and egalitarian views or behaviors. These theories differ with regard to the nature of the contradiction, the type of behavior created by the contradiction, whether negative affect created by the contradiction is consciously experienced, and the types of individuals who experience this racism. Table 2.5 summarizes the major differences among these theories.

Covert Racism and Realistic Group Conflict: A Critique

The covert racism and realistic group conflict explanations of the changing nature of Whites' racial attitudes are not necessarily inconsistent. In fact, the covert racism and realistic group conflict theorists each admit the validity of most of the others' arguments, differing only in the amount of racism they believe is accounted for by each theory.

Each of these views both has been supported by considerable data and has been subject to a variety of criticisms. The theories positing a new type of racism have been criticized on the grounds that the measures of this new type of racism include items that may not be associated with racism but with other values and beliefs (e.g., Is opposition to busing an automatic sign of racism?) (Jacobson, 1985; Sniderman & Tetlock, 1986a, 1986b). In addition, the existence of a different and new type of racism has been questioned; covert racism is highly correlated with traditional racism, and some scales of covert racism even include traditional prejudice items. The correlations of .60 to .70 between covert racism and traditional racism have been used both as evidence that these are and are not different types of racism (Jacobson, 1985; Sniderman & Tetlock, 1986a, 1986b; Weigel & Howes, 1985).

Moreover, some critics have argued that the assumption made by aversive racism theory that overt discrimination is largely nonexistent is unfortunately untrue (Jacobson, 1985; Sniderman & Tetlock, 1986a, 1986b). In fact, covert racism may only be a thinly disguised version of traditional racism. If so, the only new aspect of covert racism may be its current rationale (e.g., ''I don't object to school

TABLE 2.5 A Comparison of Response Amplification, Aversive Racism, Symbolic Racism, and Compunction

	Response Amplification	Aversive Racism	Symbolic Racism	Compunction
What is the contradiction?	Simultaneous positive and negative affect	Traditional American values and negative affect	Traditional American values and negative affect	Nonprejudiced beliefs and prejudicial behavior
What behavior is created?	Positive and negative response amplification	Positive and negative response amplification	Negative evaluations, nonminority votes	Guilt, regulatory mechanisms to prevent racism
To whom does the theory apply?	Most Americans	Liberals	Well-educated conservatives	Only low-prejudiced people feel compunction
Is negative affect consciously experienced?	Yes	Yes	Unclear; Sears says yes, Kinder says no	Yes; guilt for low-prejudiced, anger against target for high-prejudiced

desegregation, I just support neighborhood schools''). Further, questions have been raised regarding the possible confounding of independent and dependent variables in theories positing a contradiction between affect and values. For example, does opposition to busing stem from symbolic racism or is it the same thing as symbolic racism (Sniderman & Tetlock, 1986a, 1986b)? Finally, symbolic racism theorists' claims that these types of racism apply to more educated individuals, whereas old-fashioned racism applies to the less educated, have been shown to be inaccurate (Sniderman & Tetlock, 1986a).

Lawrence Bobo (1988) interprets the data showing more favorable beliefs concerning African Americans and increased commitment to racial equality and integration, along with opposition to specific policies aimed at improving African Americans' social and economic positions, differently from the covert racism theorists. Rather than seeing a new type of prejudice, Bobo perceives more of the same old-fashioned prejudice of the past: support for racial justice that is real but limited. Bobo argues that Americans have always combined anti–African American feelings with a commitment to traditional moral values. In his view, only the issues have changed with time; as basic civil rights were obtained by African Americans, struggles over redistribution of resources simply became more salient.

Bobo (1985) analyzed changes between 1964 and 1980 in attitudes toward the African American political movement and found support for realistic group conflict theory. His data show an association of attitudes toward the African American political movement with perceived threats to the respondents' own groups. Furthermore, perceived threats were largely independent of liking for African Americans, political conservatism, and demographic variables, a finding that contradicts symbolic racism theory. In a reanalysis of the Kinder and Sears (1981) data on opposition to busing, Bobo defined group interest more broadly than the original authors and found perceived threats to group interest to be strongly associated with opposition to busing (Bobo, 1983). In addition, Bobo interpreted the strong association of opposition to busing with political conservatism as evidence for traditional racism.

The realistic group conflict theorists believe their explanation for Whites' racial attitudes is more parsimonious than that of the covert racism theories. A new type of prejudice is not required, only the usual responses to changing social and political conditions. In this view, as opportunities have opened for African Americans the privileged position of Whites has became increasingly threatened, bringing to the surface new facets of prejudice and new avenues for discrimination.

On the other hand, the theory of realistic group conflict has been criticized for ignoring the difference between personal racial threat and threats to the group as a whole (Sears & Kinder, 1985). Although realistic group conflict theory presumes that group conflict only arises in situations involving self-interest, Sears and his colleagues (Sears & Funk, 1991) report studies involving more than 26 racial and other political issues, finding support for the self-interest hypothesis only under extremely limited, specifiable circumstances (taxpayers' views of tax cuts, politicized self-interest in the Reagan administration, public employees' defense of their jobs, busing, and restrictions on smokers).

One difficulty in summarizing and comparing these theories is that several of the covert racism theories have evolved over time, and different theorists within each school have somewhat different views. A clear restatement of the current thinking of the theorists would allow for a better understanding of the differences among them. Increased attempts to define key variables in a standard form would also contribute to the identification of testable theoretical differences among the theories (see, e.g., Katz & Taylor, 1988; Kinder, 1986; Sniderman & Tetlock, 1986a, 1986b). The difference in opinion between symbolic racism and realistic group conflict theorists regarding the appropriate definition of self-interest makes direct comparisons of data particularly difficult.

We would argue that both realistic group conflict and the covert racism theories explain different types of prejudice. It is demonstrably true that group conflicts foster prejudice and that many people are torn by contradictions in their views regarding race.

Race Relations: Future Prospects?

What do the covert racism theories and the realistic conflict theory imply about the future of race relations in the United States? Several aspects of these theories have positive implications for the future. If many White Americans are consciously aware of their egalitarian values, as response amplification and aversive racism theories suggest, and if even high-prejudiced individuals now feel pressure to change their behaviors as a consequence of the nonprejudiced standards of others, as compunction theory suggests, prejudice should ultimately decline. Further, if people can learn to inhibit prejudiced reactions and learn to practice nondiscrimination, and if nonprejudiced people experience guilt when they do behave in a discriminatory manner, as compunction theory also suggests, then the racial atmosphere should improve.

If, however, covert racism is just traditional prejudice and discrimination accompanied by a new set of excuses for inequality, as realistic group conflict theorists believe, the outlook is not as positive. In addition, if realistic group conflict is a more accurate explanation for racial prejudice, any gains by minorities will increase intergroup competition and thus increase racial prejudice and discrimination. At the same time some positive consequences should occur: The life chances of minorities should improve as opportunities heighten.

As we have seen, current quality of life indicators by race as well as measures of race relations both show mixed effects. The decline in overtly racist attitudes suggests some improvement, but the increase in inequality in U.S. society and in overt racial incidents suggests regression. It may be important to view intergroup relations in historical terms. The process of creating racial equality is clearly not quick, easy, or linear, but if judged in generations, the clear direction of change is toward more racial acceptance and harmony.

Summary

Prejudice is a negative attitude toward members of socially defined groups, whereas discrimination is negative behavior directed toward members of socially defined groups as a result of their group membership. Racism is prejudice and discrimination directed at racial or minority groups.

This chapter examined traditional explanations of prejudice and theories positing a new type of prejudice. In the 1930s and 1940s psychodynamic explanations for prejudice were popular, followed in the 1960s and 1970s by sociocultural explanations of prejudice, which argued that prejudice is rooted in the social structure of the society and passed on through socialization. Currently, realistic group conflict theory is one important theory of prejudice. Realistic group conflict theorists see continued traditional prejudice in the United States as well as support for racial justice that is real but limited. According to this theory, competition for scarce resources and inequality in the distribution of scarce resources create conflicting group interests. The majority group is in a position to define the prevailing resource inequalities as just and to engage in discriminatory behavior to protect its privileged position.

Many theorists have argued that a new type of prejudice has become prominent in the United States. Thought to be less overt and direct than traditional prejudice, covert racism is said to be created by a fundamental contradiction in White Americans' values, feelings, and beliefs. Response amplification theory posits a contradiction between positive and negative feelings held toward members of stigmatized groups. These ambivalent feelings lead to response amplification, or extremely positive reactions to minorities if the situation evokes positive affect or extremely negative reactions to minorities if the situation evokes negative affect.

Aversive racism theory assumes a contradiction between values and feelings: The individual accepts the American egalitarian value system but has unacknowledged negative feelings and beliefs about African Americans that lead to amplified negative behavior in situations with conflicting or ambiguous norms and amplified positive behavior in situations that threaten the individuals' views of themselves as liberal and nonprejudiced.

Symbolic racism theory focuses on the political behavior of White American elites. It is thought to be a blend of anti–African American attitudes and values embodied in the Protestant ethic. It is said to be created by racial predispositions formed during childhood socialization and conservative political ideologies and is not thought to be a response to self-interest. The result is amplified negative political behavior, such as negative evaluations of minority politicians or not voting for a minority candidate.

By contrast, compunction theory examines the different cognitive processes involved in prejudice among high-prejudiced and low-prejudiced individuals. In American society low-prejudiced individuals are thought to experience compunction, guilt, and self-blame when their behaviors do not live up to their consciously constructed nonprejudiced beliefs. On the other hand, high-prejudiced individuals are said to experience negative affect directed toward the outgroup as a consequence of their violations of society's nonprejudiced standards with respect to the treatment of outgroups.

The covert racism and realistic group conflict explanations are not necessarily inconsistent, and it is likely that each of them accounts for some types of prejudice and discrimination. Both the covert racism theories and the realistic conflict theory suggest that the future of race relations has both positive and negative aspects.

3

The Contact Hypothesis in Intergroup Relations

The Contact Hypothesis

Under certain circumstances desegregation . . . has been observed to lead to the emergence of more favorable attitudes and friendlier relations between the races. . . . There is less likelihood of unfriendly relations when change is simultaneously introduced into all units of a social institution. . . . The available evidence also suggests the importance of consistent and firm enforcement of the new policy by those in authority. It indicates also the importance of such factors as: the absence of competition . . . the possibility of contacts which permit individuals to learn about one another as individuals; and the possibility of equivalence of positions and functions among all the participants. (F. Allport et al., 1953, pp. 437–438)

Prejudice (unless deeply rooted in the character structure of the individual) may be reduced by equal status contact between majority and minority groups in the pursuit of common goals. The effect is greatly enhanced if this contact is sanctioned by institutional supports (i.e., by law, custom or local atmosphere), and if it is of the sort that leads to the perception of common interests and common humanity between the members of the two groups. (G. Allport, 1954, p. 267)

When World War II ended, Americans returned home from all over the globe full of hope. Their country had proved itself to be the most powerful nation on earth. America lost many lives to the conflict but otherwise was unscathed. Anything seemed possible. These world-wise men and women could look afresh at the strengths of their country and reappraise its weaknesses. Social scientists were particularly hopeful that age-old problems such as prejudice, crime, and poverty could be eliminated. During the period after the war, new solutions were proposed to deal with these problems.

One of these solutions, which came to be known as the contact hypothesis, dealt with improving intergroup relations. The various versions of the contact hypothesis were full of optimism, but this optimism was tempered by a clear acknowledgment of the complexity of the issues involved (Pettigrew, 1986). The social scientists writing about intergroup contact did not think eliminating prejudice was a simple problem that could be solved by merely bringing people from different groups together, and they did not expect to solve this problem quickly. With a hope born of victory, however, they thought this battle too could be won.

The study of relations between the races had moral overtones. Not only was knowledge of this domain of human behavior important, there was a moral imperative to improve race relations—to eliminate the scourge of prejudice and racism root and branch from the American way of life. The study of intergroup relations often deals with the marriage of objective social science and subjective social activism. Nowhere is this union more obvious than in the literature on the contact hypothesis. For instance, one of the solutions proposed to deal with the race relations problem in the United States displayed this union very clearly—the idea that desegregating the schools would help to improve race relations. Social scientists testified against segregated schools in the trials leading up to the *Brown v. Board of Education* decision in 1954, and they wrote the amicus curiae (friend of the Court) brief for the Supreme Court cited in the first quotation at the beginning of the chapter. They were presenting the best information on segregation that social science had to offer at the time, but they also were testifying because they deeply believed that segregation was wrong. Now a half century later, we can look back on this crusade to improve intergroup relations and reflect on the progress that has been made.

The first half of this chapter traces the growth of the contact hypothesis during the last half century. As you will see, the contact hypothesis is like a living organism that has evolved and developed over time. The underlying conceptual models that have guided the contact hypothesis over the years are presented, and the many factors that affect the outcomes of intergroup contact are reviewed. The second half of this chapter discusses a major experiment in intergroup contact in American society—school desegregation. Both its short-term and long-term effects are considered. Finally, a particular contact technique—the use of racially mixed cooperative groups—that has been used to improve intergroup relations in desegregated schools is examined.

Evidence Concerning the Original Contact Hypothesis

The initial versions of the contact hypothesis focused primarily on the effects of factors within the contact situation on subsequent prejudice (F. Allport et al., 1953; G. Allport, 1954; Harding, Kutner, Proshansky, & Chein, 1954; Watson, 1947; Williams, 1947). The contact hypothesis was oriented toward the present. It was less concerned with the historical causes of negative intergroup relations than with improving current relations. The problem-solving orientation of the researchers led them to be interested primarily in variables that could be controlled in actual intergroup encounters. They were less concerned with factors not subject to situational control, such as personality traits and the wider social context in which contact occurred. Also, the contact hypothesis was more oriented toward changing the prejudices of individuals than in improving relations between groups as entities.

Four factors were central to the early formulations of the contact hypothesis:

- Cooperative interaction
- Equal status among the participants
- Individualized contact
- Institutional support for the contact

The early contact theorists believed that if people could be brought together in work, school, recreational, or other settings under these conditions, improvements in intergroup relations would ensue. The discussion of the contact hypothesis begins by reviewing the evidence on these four key factors (cf. Harrington & Miller, 1992). This is followed by a discussion of societal and individual factors that have been shown to affect the outcomes of contact.

Cooperation

No factor associated with contact has received more attention than cooperation (Johnson & Johnson, 1992a; Johnson, Johnson, & Maruyama, 1984; Miller & Harrington, 1992; Slavin, 1985, 1992b; Worchel, 1986). These studies provide strong support for the proposition that intergroup cooperation improves intergroup relations. The bulk of the research has been concerned with the conditions under which cooperative contact is most likely to improve intergroup relations. The research suggests that cooperation is most effective when: it leads to successful outcomes (Blanchard, Adelman, & Cook, 1975); measures are taken to avoid the negative effects of different levels of task ability (Cohen, 1980, 1984; Slavin, 1978); the ingroup and the outgroup are similar in attitudes (Brown & Abrams, 1986); and assignment to groups does not make social categories salient (Miller, Brewer, & Edwards, 1985; Miller & Harrington, 1990). In small group settings balanced ratios of ingroup and outgroup members have been found to be most beneficial (Gonzales, 1979; Miller & Davidson-Podgorny, 1987). However, in large group settings balanced ratios may threaten the majority group and can have negative effects on intergroup relations (Hallinan & Smith, 1985; Hoffman, 1985; Longshore, 1982).

An important caveat is in order. Even under the best of conditions, the changes in attitudes toward individual outgroup members brought about by cooperation may not generalize to the outgroup as a whole (Blaney, Stephan, Rosenfield, Aronson, & Sikes 1977; Brewer & Miller, 1988; Longshore, 1982; Weigel, Wiser, & Cook,

1975). One recent study suggests that structuring intergroup cooperative learning tasks so that they produce positive interactions with
outgroup members facilitates generalization to the group as a whole
(Desforges et al., 1991). It also appears that encouraging the members
of cooperative groups to maintain an interpersonal focus during their
interaction leads to a generalization of less-biased treatment of outgroup members, whereas encouraging a task focus does not (Rogers,
1982, cited in Brewer & Miller, 1988; see also Miller & Harrington,
1990).

In Rogers's study subjects were divided into two groups on the
basis of their performance on a preliminary task. After an interaction
designed to create ingroup cohesion, members of the two original
groups were reassigned to mixed groups made up of equal numbers
of members from the original two groups. The new groups were then
asked to develop a list of the personality traits most important to space
travel. The new groups either cooperated or competed with one another. It was found that there was less bias toward outgroup members
with whom the subjects were unfamiliar when the subjects had experienced interteam cooperation than when they had experienced interteam competition.

Although cooperation between teams was found to create the
least bias in Rogers's study, other studies have found that competition
between mixed groups can have beneficial effects on intergroup relations (Slavin, 1985, 1990, 1992b). Interteam competition is often
employed as a technique to enhance task motivation among the members of mixed groups (Slavin, 1992b). However, the beneficial effects
of interteam competition may be restricted to situations in which the
outcomes are successful. When mixed groups fail, there is a danger
that the outgroup members within the mixed groups will be blamed
for the failure (Blanchard, Weigel, & Cook, 1975; Burnstein & Mc-
Crae, 1962; Rosenfield, Stephan, & Lucker, 1981). Also, it has been
found that competition increases motivation primarily for individuals
with high levels of achievement, which limits its utility as a generalized motivator (Epstein & Harackiewicz, 1992).

Equal Status

Considerable controversy exists in the literature concerning whether
there should be equal status on demographic factors external to the
contact situation (socioeconomic status, age, education) or equal
status within the contact situation (Cohen & Roper, 1972; Norvell &
Worchel, 1980; Pettigrew, 1969; Preston & Robinson, 1976; Riordan,

1978). Equal status on factors external to the contact situation is difficult to achieve in societies that are highly stratified into different status groups (Riordan, 1978). When such equal status contacts do occur, however, they have positive effects on intergroup perceptions, apparently because they increase the chances that similarities between individuals from different groups will exist and be noticed (McClendon, 1974). A study by Jackman and Crane (1986) indicated that if Whites had friendships with minority group members who were of equal or higher social status than themselves, they had more favorable attitudes toward African Americans. Friendships with lower-status African Americans produced attitudes that were no more favorable than no contact at all.

Given the overall differences in socioeconomic status between African Americans and Whites, the majority of contacts Whites have with African Americans are likely to be with lower-status African Americans, and this may explain the fact that even friendly contacts between African Americans and Whites often do not change Whites' attitudes. For instance, in many American universities there are differences between the social class backgrounds of African American and White students. Such differences may limit the chances for improved relations between groups.

If equal status on factors external to the situation cannot be arranged, it appears that creating equal status roles within some types of contact situations can still improve intergroup relations. For instance, cooperation between members of different groups has been found to have positive effects on intergroup perceptions, even when the participants differed in status on factors external to the situation (Aronson, Blaney, Stephan, Sikes, & Snapp, 1978; Weigel, Wiser, & Cook, 1975).

The ideal arrangement for intergroup contacts would be to have equal status both on demographic factors external to the situation and on relevant dimensions (e.g., role assignments) within the situation. If equal status on external factors cannot be achieved, at least an attempt should be made to create equal status within the contact situation. When status inequalities do occur, it would appear to be better for the minority group members to have higher status than the majority group members (cf. Cohen, 1980).

Individualized Contact

Traditional contact theory suggests that intergroup contact should be nonsuperficial and offer people the opportunity to get to know one another as individuals (Amir, 1976). Considerable research indicates that providing people with information about the behavior of individual group members influences judgments of those individuals and that social categories are de-emphasized in this process (Locksley, Borgida, Brekke, & Hepburn, 1980; Locksley, Hepburn, & Ortiz, 1982). Information about the behavior of individual group members is less likely to have these potentially beneficial effects, however, if the behaviors are not displayed consistently or if strong stereotypes are associated with the social group to which the individuals belong (Grant & Holmes, 1981; Krueger & Rothbart, 1988). For example, in the Grant and Holmes study (1981), it was found that categorical information on ethnicity had a greater impact on later judgments of stereotype-relevant traits than did individuating information, apparently because the ethnic stereotypes were quite strong.

When creating small-group contact opportunities in school, work, or other settings, investigators have been confronted by an interesting and complex problem. Should they encourage *interpersonal* interactions or *intergroup* interactions (Hewstone & Brown, 1986b). Interpersonal interactions occur when group participants treat one another as individuals rather than as members of distinct social groups. Intergroup interaction is the reverse: Participants are seen primarily as group members rather than as individuals. Which type of interaction do you think would be more effective in improving intergroup relations?

Norman Miller and Marilynn Brewer favor an emphasis on interpersonal interaction among individual group members (Brewer & Miller, 1984; Brewer & Miller, 1988; Miller & Harrington, 1990, 1992). They argue that only when group factors are de-emphasized are members of outgroups likely to be differentiated and treated as individuals. According to Brewer and Miller, "Differentiated and personalized interactions are necessary before intergroup contact can lead to group acceptance and reduction of social competition" (1984, p. 288).

In contrast, Miles Hewstone and Rupert Brown (1986b) argue that treating outgroup members as individuals rather than as group members is not likely to lead to changes in attitudes toward the group as a whole. The problem is that, by placing social groups in the background, interpersonal interactions are less likely to change intergroup relations because the individual outgroup members will not be viewed as members of social groups. In addition, it may be difficult to modify stereotypes unless social groups are made salient so that disconfirmations of category-based expectancies will be noted (Rothbart & John, 1985). Hewstone and Brown argue that group identities should be made salient during intergroup contact to maximize the possibilities that any positive changes that are brought about by the contact situation will generalize to the outgroup as a whole (Vivian, Hewstone, & Brown, 1994).

In an experimental study of these issues, it was found that assignment to small cooperative work groups on the basis of unique personal attributes produced more favorable treatment of members of the other group than assignment according to category membership (Miller, Brewer, & Edwards, 1985; Bettencourt, Brewer, Rogers-Croak, & Miller, 1992). Random assignment to the working groups produced similar effects (Miller & Harrington, 1990). Thus, creating the conditions under which individualized contact was likely to occur did promote favorable intergroup relations in these studies. Does this mean that only interpersonal interactions improve intergroup relations? This seems unlikely, but it will require additional research to determine the conditions under which each type of interaction (interpersonal and intergroup) is most effective.

Support by Authority Figures

Support by respected authority figures appears to enhance the effects of intergroup contact (Adlerfer, 1982; Aronson et al., 1978; Cohen, 1980; Slavin, 1985; Williams, 1977). However, there are limiting conditions to these beneficial effects. Cohen (1980) has argued that it may be difficult to create equal-status interactions between African American and White students when the authority figures in the situation are not themselves from both groups. Improving intergroup relations may also be difficult when the contact is imposed by authorities, because people often react negatively to this loss of control over their freedom of association. For example, because affirmative action plans are often imposed under the force of law, their potential to improve relations between the affected groups may be limited, although such plans can reduce the economic inequalities between the groups.

In addition, positive intergroup relations can occur without the explicit support of authority figures, as often happens in intergroup friendships (Blumberg & Roye, 1980). Studies that have examined voluntary informal contact typically find that such contact leads to favorable outgroup attitudes (Carter, Detine, Spero, & Benson, 1975; Masson & Verkuyten, 1993; Stephan & Rosenfield, 1978a; Stephan & Stephan, 1984; Webster, 1961). In combining these two threads of thought, it might be reasonable to suggest that the greatest improvements in intergroup relations are likely when ingroup and outgroup authority figures promote voluntary intergroup relationships.

The Conceptual Model Underlying the Contact Hypothesis

The early versions of the contact hypothesis were not intended to be a formal theory but, rather, were pragmatic guidelines for optimizing the conditions of contact. Nonetheless, an implicit conceptual model underlies the early statements of the contact hypothesis. Those statements were based on the premise that racial attitudes (A) are a function (f) of aspects of the social situation (S). Thus it was expected that by controlling aspects of the social environment it would be possible to create positive changes in attitudes. This early conceptual model can be represented with the following formula.

$$A = f(S)$$

We shall see as we trace the historical development of the contact hypothesis in the ensuing sections that this simple model has become increasingly complex over time.

Extensions of the Contact Hypothesis

In the decades since the contact hypothesis was originally proposed, many variables in addition to those initially proposed have been studied in intergroup contact situations. These variables will be discussed in two broad domains, societal factors and person factors. Then the consequences of contact and variables that mediate the effects of contact will be examined.

Societal Factors

In the 1960s Stuart Cook (1962; 1969), one of the original framers of the amicus curiae brief filed in the *Brown v. Board of Education* (1954) school desegregation case, emphasized the value of having minority group members behave in ways that disconfirm prevailing societal stereotypes (see also Rothbart & John, 1985). He also suggested that favorable norms and attitudes held by other ingroup members toward intergroup contact should be highlighted (Cook, 1962). Also in the 1960s Secord and Backman (1964) discussed the social roles of the participants in intergroup interactions. They cited studies indicating that prejudice decreased when minority group members occupied roles that created expectancies and behavior incompatible with their minority status (e.g., Harding & Hogrefe, 1952; Minard, 1952). Consistent with Cook's suggestion regarding the importance of the norms and attitudes of ingroup members, Secord and Backman argued that positive intergroup relations tended to prevail when the central values of the society favored intergroup contact (see also Williams, 1964). Other societal variables that were investigated during this period included the prior relations between the participating groups (Brislin & Pedersen, 1976; Tajfel, 1981; Williams, 1977) and the degree of acculturation of minority groups, such as the Sephardic Jews in Israel (Eshel & Peres, 1973). Schofield (1991) has called for greater attention to cultural differences among the groups that come together in contact situations. Thus in addition to factors within the contact situation, over the years researchers have begun to pay more attention to the broader social context in which intergroup contact occurs.

Person Factors

During the 1960s and 1970s, considerable research was also undertaken on factors associated with the characteristics of the individual participants. These person factors included demographic variables (positive change was considered most likely with younger, better-educated, higher-social-class individuals) (Williams, 1964); personality traits such as high self-esteem, adherence to egalitarian values, low authoritarianism (Katz, Wackenhut, & Glass, 1986; Stephan & Rosenfield, 1978b; Wagner & Schonbach, 1984; Weigel & Howes, 1985); and high competence in task-relevant skills (Blanchard & Cook, 1976; Cohen & Roper, 1972; Rosenfield, Stephan, & Lucker, 1981). Although these factors are usually not under the control of people arranging intergroup contact situations, they do suggest that contact programs are likely to be more successful with some populations than with others.

Consequences of Contact

By the 1970s researchers showed an increasing interest in the behavioral and affective consequences of contact in addition to their original interest in prejudice. For instance, investigators examined intergroup helping and aggression (e.g., Donnerstein & Donnerstein, 1972, 1973), participation in future interactions (Rokeach, 1971), participation in group decisions (Cohen & Roper, 1972), and the anxiety elicited in intergroup interactions (Hendricks & Bootzin, 1976; Randolph, Landis, & Tzeng, 1977).

With the addition of both societal and individual factors to the contact hypothesis, and an expanded consideration of the behavioral and affective consequences of contact, the conceptual model underlying the contact hypothesis began to resemble an extension of the classic social psychological model developed by Lewin (1951). Lewin's model considered behavior to be a function of the person and the environment. The model for the contact hypothesis considers the intergroup consequences (C) of intergroup contact to be a function (f) of the person (P), the situation (S), and the societal context (SC).

$$C = f(P + S + SC)$$

Mediators of Contact

Over the last several decades there has been a growing interest in the processes underlying the changes in cognitions, affect, and behavior that occur during intergroup contact. Ashmore (1970) discussed a variety of mediating processes that might account for the effects of contact, including stereotype destruction, unlearning assumed dissimilarities, pressures toward consistency among cognitions, and generalizing positive attitudes from individual group members to the group as a whole (stimulus generalization). To this list other investigators contributed discussions of the mediating effects of knowledge of the subjective culture of the other group (Brislin, Cushner, Cherrie, & Yong, 1986; Triandis, 1972); reinforcement of positive attitudes and behaviors (instrumental conditioning) (Hauserman, Walen, & Behling, 1973); the association of positive affect with outgroup members and the extinction of negative affect (classical conditioning) (Parrish & Fleetwood, 1975; Sappington, 1976); dependence on other group members (Erber & Fiske, 1984; Johnson & Johnson, 1992a; Ruscher & Fiske, 1990); and imitation of nonprejudiced attitudes and behavior (Williams, 1977).

A Reconceptualized Contact Model

At this stage in its development, the contact hypothesis has become so complicated that it is losing its usefulness. The complexity of the foregoing discussion makes it readily apparent that the contact hypothesis needs some streamlining if it is to survive into the twenty-first century. In an effort to move in this direction, we will reformulate the earlier conceptual models into one that more adequately integrates our knowledge about intergroup contact. This model uses some of the same categories of factors alluded to in earlier models, but it incorporates several additional factors and makes some causal assumptions.

As figure 3.1 shows, this model indicates that societal factors influence situation and person factors (Stephan, 1987). The situation

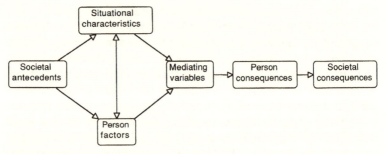

FIGURE 3.1
Causal model of the contact hypothesis.

and person factors are postulated to interact with one another. The model explicitly notes that there are factors that mediate the effects of the person and situation variables on subsequent behavior, cognitions, and affect. Finally, the model indicates that changes in people can ultimately bring about changes in society (Bochner, 1982). The model presented in figure 3.1 will be used as a basis for categorizing all of the variables that have been previously discussed, and some new variables will be added as well (see table 3.1).

Among the categories of *societal context* variables that appear to be important are: (1) the structure of the society, especially its stratification system (the emphasis a society places on distinctions in status, age, gender, religion, etc.); (2) the historical relations between the groups that are in contact with one another; (3) the current relations between these groups; and (4) the groups' socialization practices.

The variables that comprise the *situational context* in which the contact takes place can be categorized as follows: (1) the setting in which the contact occurs; (2) the nature of the interaction; (3) the composition of the groups; and (4) the task in which the participants are involved.

The *person factors* are comprised of: (1) demographic characteristics; (2) personality traits; and (3) prejudices, stereotypes, and other beliefs.

The proposed *mediators* of the effects of contact are: (1) behavioral, (2) cognitive, and (3) affective processes.

The principal *personal consequences* include: (1) behaviors, (2) cognitions (particularly prejudice and stereotypes), and (3) affective reactions.

TABLE 3.1 Variables Influencing the Outcomes of Contact

Societal Context	Situational Context	Person Factors	Mediators	Personal Consequences	Societal Consequences
Social structure	Setting	Demographic	Behavioral	Behavior	Public attitudes
Social stratification	social and physical	characterisitics	modeling	positive/negative	Social norms
Historical relations	Nature of interaction	Personality traits	rewards/	short/long-term	Group status
prior contact	purpose	Prejudice and	punishments	Cognitions	
degree of conflict	superficial/intimate	stereotypes	Cognitive	prejudice	
social norms and	voluntary/coerced	Expectancies	attention	stereotypes	
roles	individualized/impersonal		encoding	expectancies	
group size	stereotyped/		retrieval	Affective states	
Current relations	nonstereotyped		Affective		
Socialization	authority support		classical		
practices	means interdependence		conditioning		
	duration				
	frequency				
	Group composition				
	ingroup/outgroup ratio				
	relative statuses				
	similarity of participants				
	diversity of group				
	members				
	group size				
	Task				
	goals interdependence				
	outcomes				

The *societal consequences* concern the effects of contact on future relations between the groups. These changes could include: (1) modifications in public attitudes (especially attitudes and stereotypes); (2) alterations in social norms or the legal system (e.g., laws against discrimination); (3) and modifications in the relative economic or political status of the groups.

Social psychologists have traditionally been most interested in the stream of events that runs from situational factors through the mediating variables to the personal consequences, but this model also captures social psychologists' interest in the interaction between person and situation factors and in the societal antecedents and consequences of the variables they study.

The model has implications for both empirical and applied research on intergroup contact. Empirically the model makes explicit the interrelationships among these factors, and it specifies the causal relationships between the factors. For instance, it implies that societal factors shape the kinds of situations in which contact takes place, but it also implies that the contact that takes place in those situations may change relations between those groups in society and therefore affect future contact situations. The model also suggests an array of variables within each category that may have an impact in any intergroup contact situation. From an applied perspective, the model indicates the domains of factors that should be considered in attempts to improve intergroup relations through contact.

School Desegregation

The efficacy of the model for understanding an applied setting can be illustrated by considering the effects of school desegregation in the United States. The effects of school desegregation are examined in considerable detail because it is an important natural experiment that tests many of the ideas put forth in the contact literature. Before examining these effects, a synopsis of the predicted effects of desegregation that will frame the subsequent discussion is presented.

The Social Scientists' Predictions

In the *Brown v. Board of Education* case (1954) social scientists made the arguments in the amicus curiae brief quoted at the beginning of the chapter (F. Allport et al., 1953), and they presented testimony in the trials leading up to *Brown*. Although the impact of the social scientists' testimony on the *Brown* decision is still being debated (Cook, 1979, 1984, 1985; Gerard, 1983), it did shape the thinking of the judges who decided these cases. Evidence that the social scientists' arguments had an effect may be found in the opinion of Kansas Judge Walter Huxman in the original *Brown* case before the case was appealed to the Supreme Court. In his opinion he wrote:

> Segregation of White and colored children in the public schools has a detrimental effect upon the colored children. The impact is greater when it has the sanction of law; for the policy of separating the races is usually interpreted as denoting the inferiority of the Negro group. A sense of inferiority affects the motivation of the child to learn. Segregation with the sanction of law, therefore, has the tendency to retard the educational and mental development of Negro children and to deprive them of the benefits they would receive in a racial[ly] integrated school system. (Kluger, 1976, p. 424)

Judge Huxman had accepted two of the social scientists' arguments: first, that segregation causes feelings of inferiority among African American children and, second, that it reduces their achievement levels. A third element of the social scientists' argument was that segregation fostered negative race relations because it supported Whites' beliefs in their own superiority and caused African Americans to resent the inferior treatment they received. The social scientists thought these three elements, feelings of inferiority and low self-esteem among African Americans, low achievement by African American students, and poor race relations, were interrelated in a vicious circle (see fig. 3.2) (Stephan, 1978).

The vicious circle started with the fact that White prejudice, which is a societal variable in the model, was responsible for creating segregation (fig 3.2). This segregation then led to low self-esteem and low achievement among African American students, both of which are individual variables in the model. The low self-esteem and low achievement, combined with resentment over segregation and the inadequate facilities provided to them, fed African Americans' prejudice against Whites—a third individual factor. And African American prejudice and hostility toward Whites were then used by Whites to justify their prejudices—another individual variable—and the policy of segregation (a societal variable), thus completing the circle. It was expected that intergroup contact in desegregated schools would break this vicious circle. Specifically it was expected that desegregation would lead to increases in African American achievement, increases in African American self-esteem, and more favorable relations

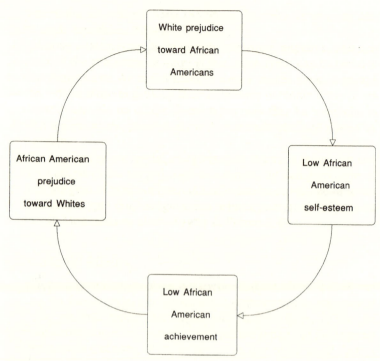

FIGURE 3.2
Causal model derived from testimony in *Brown v. Board of Education.*

between the races. All three predictions will be evaluated in the following sections using the available social science evidence, although race relations will be emphasized because that is the central topic. The discussion focuses on both the short-term effects of desegregation, where the outcomes have not been as positive as predicted, and the long-term effects of desegregation, where the outcomes have more consistently confirmed the predictions.

The Effects of Desegregation

Desegregation in the United States is first put in perspective with a brief review of the history of desegregation since the 1954 decision. Following this review the effects of desegregation are examined and an attempt is made to explain why these effects occurred.

The State of School Desegregation

After the 1954 Supreme Court decision in *Brown,* desegregation moved very slowly for the next decade. With the passage of the 1964 Civil Rights Bill, however, desegregation took place at a more rapid rate during the second decade after *Brown.* Nearly all of the desegregation that has occurred in the United States took place during the decade between 1964 and 1974. By 1972, 44 percent of African American children in the South were attending schools in which the majority of students were White, whereas in the North 29 percent of African American children were attending such schools (Pettigrew, 1975).

By 1980, 70 percent of African American students were attending school with some Whites (more than 5% White). However, a similar percentage of Whites (69%) attended schools that were *less* than 5 percent African American (U.S. Commission on Civil Rights, 1987). As in the previous decade, the South was more integrated than the North, with the West falling in between. The most recent evidence indicates a trend toward resegregation of American schools (Associated Press, 1993).

Short-Term Effects

Achievement scores, as measured by national standardized tests, furnish a crucial index of how much students have learned. These scores are used to measure the progress of individuals, to compare schools within systems, and to compare districts, states, and regions. They also have important practical implications for tracking within schools and for admission to colleges and universities. Does desegregation improve the achievement of African American students? Since many school districts routinely administer achievement tests to their students, this question has been extensively investigated. In a review of these studies done by one of the authors, it was found that desegregation improved African American achievement in about 25 percent of the cases and decreased African American achievement in less than 5 percent of the cases (Stephan, 1991). Other reviewers have reached similar conclusions (Bradley & Bradley, 1977; Crain & Mahard, 1978a; Krol, 1980; St. John, 1975; Weinberg, 1983; Wortman, King, & Bryant, 1982); that is, desegregation sometimes increases African American achievement and rarely decreases it.

Most of these achievement gains occur for verbal achievement rather than math achievement (Stephan, 1986). However, few of the studies that have been done extended beyond the first year of desegregation, so it is not known if the existing gap between African Americans and Whites in reading achievement continues to close after the first year. Younger African American children appear to experience the greatest gains (Crain & Mahard, 1978a; Stephan, 1986). No studies have found negative effects of desegregation on White achievement (St. John, 1975). Thus, whatever gains accrue to African Americans come at no cost in the achievement of White students.

Self-esteem refers to the level of positive or negative feelings regarding the self. Does desegregation increase African Americans' self-esteem? In a word—no. In reviewing these studies it has been found that during the first year of desegregation, African Americans' self-esteem increased in only 4 percent of the cases, remained the same in 71 percent of the cases, and decreased in the remaining 25 percent of the cases (Stephan, 1978, 1986, 1991).

The argument that desegregation would increase the self-esteem of African American schoolchildren was based on a false premise. It was believed that African American children in segregated schools had lower self-esteem than White children as a result of being segregated. However, research on self-esteem indicates that African Americans do not have lower self-esteem than Whites in either segregated or integrated schools (Stephan, 1986; Stephan & Rosenfield, 1979). The self-esteem of African American children, like the self-esteem of White children, appears to be a reflection of the evaluations of significant others rather than a reflection of the evaluations of their group by other groups (Rosenberg, 1986; Simmons, 1978). If segregation did not cause African Americans to have low self-esteem, then there is little reason to believe that desegregation would increase the self-esteem of African Americans. Thus, although desegregation rarely increases African Americans' self-esteem, there appears to be little reason why it should have.

The next question is, Does desegregation improve racial attitudes? In this case the answer is decidedly mixed. A review of the evidence indicates that for African Americans, desegregation reduced their prejudices toward Whites more frequently than it increased them (38% vs. 24%) (Stephan, 1986; 1991). For Whites, however, the results were just the opposite. Desegregation increased prejudice toward African Americans in three times as many cases (48%) as it decreased it (16%). Studies of parents suggest that desegregation does not lead to increases in opposition to desegregation among White parents (Rossell, 1978), and in some communities attitudes toward desegregation among parents became more positive as a result of desegregation (McConahay & Hawley, 1976; Parsons, 1986). In combination, these studies suggest that in the short run, desegregation does not produce the anticipated positive effects on race relations.

A note of caution should be sounded concerning the short-term studies of achievement, self-esteem, and prejudice. Comparing these studies with one another is often difficult because they were conducted in different regions of the country, the types of desegregation plans that were examined varied from study to study, the age of the students differed across studies, the racial composition of the communities was rarely the same, and the amount of opposition to desegregation in these communities varied considerably. In addition, many of these studies suffer from methodological problems. The sample sizes in some of the studies are quite small and the samples in other studies are not representative. Many of these studies employed measures of unknown reliability and validity. Some employed weak designs, comparing segregated and desegregated students at one point in time rather than studying changes in the same students over time.

Also these studies provide a rather narrow view of the effects of desegregation on race relations because they deal primarily with the experiences of African American and White schoolchildren and their parents during the first year or so of desegregation. The initial year of desegregation is perhaps the most atypical school year ever experienced by these students. Not only were they attending newly desegregated schools, but desegregation was often accompanied by community opposition, anxiety on the part of students and parents, and changes in curriculum and teaching staffs.

To summarize, in the short term desegregation leads to small improvements in African American reading achievement; rarely improves, and sometimes decreases, African Americans' self-esteem; and has mixed effects on race relations. School desegregation in Israel has been found to have similarly mixed effects on achievement, self-esteem, and intergroup relations (Schwarzwald & Amir, 1984). In both countries these conclusions must be regarded as tentative at best, due to the methodological and other problems with these studies.

Long-Term Effects
Until the 1980s it was impossible to begin to study the long-term effects of desegregation because so few students had graduated from desegregated schools. However, a number of studies have now been completed that examine the effects of attending desegregated schools on college attendance, occupational choice and achievement, and voluntary interracial contact.

Although the studies are not entirely in agreement, in general it has been found that desegregation increases African Americans' educational achievement and increases African Americans' willingness to interact with Whites in educational settings. African Americans who attended desegregated high schools are more likely to finish high school, attend college, earn higher GPAs while in college, and are less likely to drop out of college than African Americans who attended segregated high schools (Braddock, Crain, & McPartland, 1984; Crain, Hawes, Miller, & Peichert, 1985; Crain & Mahard, 1978b; Green, 1981; Perry, 1973; Wilson, 1979). The increase in college attendance rates appears to occur primarily in the North. In the South, African Americans who attended desegregated high schools were more likely to attend traditionally all-White universities than African Americans who attended segregated high schools (Braddock, 1987; Braddock & McPartland, 1982).

Studies on occupational achievement have obtained mixed results, but on balance they suggest that school desegregation may lead to some improvements in the earnings of African Americans (Braddock & McPartland, 1983; Crain, 1970; Crain & Straus, 1986; Crain & Weisman, 1972; U.S. Commission on Civil Rights, 1967). The results of attending desegregated colleges present a similar picture. The better-designed studies indicate that attendance at desegregated colleges enables African Americans to get better jobs than attending segregated colleges (Braddock & McPartland, 1988). African Americans are now represented in a greater variety of occupations than they were in the past (Farley, 1985; Pettigrew, 1979b), and it appears that desegregation has played a role in this process (Crain, 1970; Crain et al., 1985).

The most consistent finding in the realm of intergroup relations is that African Americans who attended desegregated schools are more likely to work in integrated environments as adults than African Americans who attended segregated schools (Astin, 1982; Braddock & McPartland, 1983). The African Americans from desegregated backgrounds also have more favorable evaluations of their White coworkers and bosses than African Americans from segregated backgrounds (Braddock & McPartland, 1983). In addition, they form more cross-racial friendships (Crain & Weisman, 1972; Green, 1981). One study found that Whites who attended desegregated schools were also more likely to work in integrated settings (Braddock, McPartland, & Trent, 1984).

Both African Americans and Whites who attended desegregated schools were more likely to live in integrated neighborhoods as adults and to send their children to desegregated schools than African Americans or Whites who attended segregated schools (Astin, 1982; Crain, 1970; U.S. Commission on Civil Rights, 1967). Desegregation is particularly likely to lead to greater integration in housing when communitywide plans are adopted because then Whites cannot easily avoid desegregation by moving to the suburbs (Braddock, Crain, & McPartland, 1984; Orfield, 1980; Pearce, 1980; Rossell, 1978).

The introduction of desegregation sometimes causes Whites to flee from newly desegregated school districts. White flight occurs primarily when desegregation plans require the reassignment of substantial numbers of White students in large, majority African American, urban school districts surrounded by suburbs (Armor, 1980, 1988; U.S. Commission on Civil Rights, 1987). However, one long-term study of nine school districts that were desegregating in response to Court orders concluded that desegregation had little effect on White flight (Smock & Wilson, 1991). When it does occur, White flight typically tapers off after the first year or so of desegregation (Rossell, 1978 cited in Armor, 1980; U.S. Commission on Civil Rights, 1987; Wilson, 1985).

In evaluating these results it should be kept in mind that the size of the effects in these studies was generally relatively small, the number of studies is still not large, and the findings, though generally consistent across studies, do show some variability. Although the sample sizes in some studies were small, a number of these studies employed national samples and were considerably more comprehensive than the studies of the short-term effects of desegregation. Thus the results concerning the long-term effects of desegregation should also be regarded as tentative, but they do appear to be generally stronger and more consistent than those for the short-term effects.

Societal Consequences of Desegregation

In addition to the direct effects of desegregation on students, desegregation has had a number of less direct effects on American society. The effects of *Brown* reverberated throughout the social system. Desegregation marked the beginning of the end of an era in American race relations. *Brown* showed how the courts could be used as a mechanism to forge social change from a reluctant majority. This example was noted by many minority groups, including Hispanics and Asian Americans, as well as the handicapped and the elderly, and it was applied to areas of American life other than the schools (Greenblatt & Willie, 1980).

There have been vast changes in the racial attitudes of Whites in America in the post-*Brown* era. For instance, the principle of equal educational opportunity is now widely accepted in the United States (Armor, 1980; Schuman, Steeh, & Bobo, 1985; *Time,* March 7, p. 23, 1988). These changes in attitudes have paralleled the changes in attitudes toward desegregation (Pettigrew, 1979a). Desegregation itself almost certainly played some role in the changes in Whites' attitudes (Pettigrew, 1979a; Rossell, 1978).

In sum, the studies of the long-term effects of desegregation suggest that it has led to some increases in educational and occupational attainment among African Americans, and greater integration in colleges and universities, in the workplace, and in housing. It also has contributed to changes in broader indices of race relations in the United States. On the negative side, desegregation has led to some short-term increases in White flight.

As a postscript, it must be said that, despite its modest successes, desegregation has come to a virtual standstill in the United States. Little or no new desegregation is occurring, some older desegregation plans have been modified to make them less stringent, and many central city school districts are becoming increasingly segregated as Whites continue to move to the suburbs. It is ironic that just when the evidence has become available to indicate that desegregation has positive effects on intergroup relations, and at a time when the call for cultural diversity has been sounded at all levels of the education system, desegregation has been all but abandoned as a social policy.

Explaining the Effects of Desegregation

As the mixed results concerning the short-term effects of desegregation began to emerge in the 1970s and 1980s, controversy arose over why desegregation was not more successful (Cook, 1979, 1984; Gerard, 1983). Cook used the contact hypothesis to explain why school desegregation did not have more positive effects on intergroup relations in the short term. In Cook's view, desegregation did not have more positive effects because the conditions set forth in the original versions of the contact hypothesis rarely existed in desegregated schools. Desegregation was often introduced by reluctant authorities; in schools where competition was characteristic; where cliques, tracking, and other factors that foster within-school segregation prevented individualized contact; and where equal status contact between African Americans and Whites was the exception rather than the rule (Schofield, 1991).

The contact model proposed here suggests that additional factors should be considered in explaining the short-term effects of desegregation on intergroup relations. In particular, the societal context in which school desegregation took place, the characteristics of the participants, additional situational factors, the mediators of change, and the long-term societal effects of contact should be considered.

The historical relations between African Americans and Whites clearly affected the short-term lack of success of school desegregation in the United States, as did the fact that the two groups are unequal in socioeconomic and political status outside of the contact situation. Also the two groups are dissimilar in a number of ways due to their different experiences in America. African Americans were brought to this country as slaves, and they had a different culture and religion from immigrant groups (Pettigrew, 1986). They faced systematic, often legalized, discrimination and were not allowed to become assimilated into the mainstream culture as other immigrant groups were. With respect to person factors, some Whites and African Americans entered the school situation with negative racial attitudes and other personal characteristics unlikely to lead to favorable outcomes (e.g., ethnocentrism, low self-esteem, authoritarianism).

In addition to the situational factors already mentioned, other factors may have worked against improved intergroup relations, such as the fact that the outcomes of intergroup contact in the schools were frequently not positive, stereotype-confirming behaviors may have occurred, and the contact was nonvoluntary. A consideration of some of the mediators of the effects of contact indicates further problems. The conditions of contact may have led to categorical rather than individual processing of information and to other information-processing biases that worked against the unlearning of stereotypes. Role models of positive intergroup contact were usually absent, as were rewards for positive contacts. And, outside of the athletic field, Whites and African Americans rarely cooperated together in situations where they were interdependent.

The model also suggests that the long-term societal effects of contact should be considered. The evidence presented earlier suggests that the long-term effects of desegregation have been more positive than the short-term effects. How could desegregation have such mixed effects in the short term, yet have so many positive effects in the long run?

A complete answer to this question is not available, but the following processes probably played a role. First, desegregation may provide African Americans with knowledge of the norms, behaviors, and values of Whites that enable them to interact with Whites more effectively. Second, attending desegregated schools may foster interpersonal networks between African Americans and Whites that help create access to higher paying jobs in integrated settings (Braddock & McPartland, 1987; Crain & Weisman, 1972). Third, attending desegregated schools may lead African Americans to believe that greater occupational opportunities are available to them, which may cause them to apply for jobs that students from segregated schools do not even attempt to get.

Cooperative Learning in the Schools

Although the conditions specified by the contact hypothesis have not been met in the typical desegregated school in America, it is reasonable to ask what would happen if these conditions *were* met. As the evidence of the lack of positive short-term effects of desegregation began to accumulate, a number of researchers set themselves the task of designing techniques to improve intergroup relations in the schools. All these techniques are based on the use of small cooperative groups composed of children from different ethnic backgrounds.

The emphasis on cooperation in these techniques has its origins in the classic studies of Morton Deutsch and Muzafer Sherif. Deutsch laid the foundation for these techniques by developing a theory concerning the effects of cooperation and competition on interpersonal relations (Deutsch, 1949). Sherif and his colleagues conducted a classic study the "Robbers Cave" study, illustrating the utility of Deutsch's theory for intergroup relations (Sherif, et al., 1961). Conducted at a summer camp for boys, the study illustrated the effects of competition and cooperation (Sherif, et al., 1961). When the boys arrived at the camp, they were divided into two groups, the Eagles and the Rattlers, and placed in competition with one another in activities such as football, tug-of-war, and cabin inspections. Gradually, hostility developed between the Eagles and the Rattlers that culminated in vandalizing one another's cabins and a food fight at a picnic. Later in the camp session, the investigators used cooperative interactions to improve relations between the groups. Several "emergencies" were created, such as having a vehicle break down or finding a break in the water line, that required the cooperative efforts of the members of both groups. As a result of this cooperation, the hostility between the Eagles and the Rattlers began to subside. The boys made friends with members of the other group and they began to work together spontaneously.

Using the principles developed in these studies, in combination with the ideas contained in the contact literature, social psychologists created cooperative groups in desegregated schools that were designed to improve intergroup relations (Hertz-Lazarowitz & Miller, 1992; Johnson & Johnson, 1992b; Slavin, 1978; Weigel, Wiser, & Cook, 1975). One of these techniques is known as the *jigsaw classroom* (Aronson et al., 1978; Aronson & Thibodeau, 1992). When using this technique, the material the students have been assigned is divided into as many parts as there are students in the group. The students then learn their own parts of the material and present their pieces of the puzzle to the other members of their group. The students in each group are dependent on one another to learn all of the material effectively. Once all of the material has been presented, the students are graded individually on their performances. The groups do not compete with one another. Thus, the students are means interdependent but not goals interdependent. The groups in these studies usually meet for one class period a day for four to six weeks and then new groups are formed.

The jigsaw classroom fulfills all of the criteria specified by the original contact hypothesis (cf. Slavin, 1992b). The students in each group must cooperate with one another to do well on the assignments. The members of each group all have equal status. The small-group setting also provides the students with an opportunity to get to know one another as individuals and to learn about their similarities. In addition, the intergroup contact is supported by the school authorities.

The results of a number of studies using variations of cooperative learning teams indicate that cooperative groups improve intergroup relations. These studies have found that cross-ethnic helping and friendships increase (DeVries & Edwards, 1974; Johnson & Johnson, 1992b; Slavin, 1978, 1992b; Weigel, Wiser, & Cook, 1975, Ziegler, 1981) and that empathy and liking for other students increase (Blaney et al., 1977; Bridgeman, 1977; for a review of the effects of cooperative learning techniques, see Johnson & Johnson, 1992a, 1992b). In addition, the predictions of the social scientists concerning the effects of desegregation on self-esteem and achievement receive some support in these studies. Both the self-esteem and the achievement of minority students can be increased in cooperative groups (Blaney et al., 1977; Devries & Slavin, 1978; Johnson & Johnson, 1992a, 1992b; Lucker, Rosenfield, Aronson, & Sikes, 1977; Sharan & Shachar, 1988), although achievement gains are not always found (Slavin, 1990). All of the studies just cited were conducted in the United States, but cooperative techniques have been used with similar effects in Israel (Hertz-Lazarowitz, Sapir, & Sharan, 1982; Sharan & Shachar, 1988).

A variety of factors appear to be operating together to produce these favorable results. Working in cooperative groups tends to undercut ingroup-outgroup bias. Ingroup-outgroup bias is based on identification with the ingroup and rejection of outgroups. When students work together in mixed teams, they come to identify with and favorably evaluate their own team, which contains members of both the ingroup and the outgroup (Gaertner, Mann, Dovidio, Murrell, & Pomare, 1989; Gaertner, Mann, Murrell, & Dovidio, 1989). The teams thus become superordinate groups in which initial distinctions between ethnic groups are submerged.

Interaction with outgroup members in cooperative groups also provides the students with an opportunity to acquire information that is inconsistent with their stereotypes. This stereotype-disconfirming information can change stereotypes because it occurs frequently, for a variety of outgroup members, and across a variety of situations (cf. Rothbart & John, 1985). The students also learn that outgroup members vary considerably, which can lead to differentiated perceptions of the outgroup. In addition, in this context the students are dependent on one another and dependence leads to an increased focus on individuating information (Erber & Fiske, 1984). After reviewing more than 600 studies on cooperative learning groups, one set of researchers concluded that interdependence is the key to the positive effects of cooperative learning (Johnson & Johnson, 1992a). The Johnsons suggest that mutual interdependence leads people in cooperative groups to put aside their own immediate interests in favor of striving to help all members of the group achieve their joint goals. People take pride in the accomplishments of others and become bound to them by ties of mutual obligation and responsibility leading to feelings of cohesion and attraction to other group members.

One problem that often remains in cooperative classroom groups is that the White students are higher in social class and achievement than the minority students. Cohen (1980) and her coworkers have found, however, that even these status inequalities can be overcome if the minority students are highly competent on the assigned tasks. In her studies Cohen trained the minority group members to explicitly disconfirm negative stereotypes concerning minority competence. Another solution to the status inequality problem was originally developed by DeVries and Edwards (1974). In their cooperative groups, each student's performance contributes to the team's overall standing. To avoid the possibility that low-achieving students will hinder the team, the students in each team receive points on the basis of comparisons with other students at their own achievement level. In this way, low-achieving students help or hinder their team as much as high-achieving students (Slavin, 1992a). These solutions to the status inequality problem have the added benefit of making it unlikely that blame will be attributed to low-achieving students when the team performs poorly (cf. Rosenfield & Lucker, 1981).

Summary

The contact hypothesis was originally proposed after World War II as a solution to the problem of race relations in the United States. The early versions of the contact hypothesis included four variables: cooperation, equal status, individualized contact, and support by authority figures. Cooperation is most effective when it is successful, when the groups are numerically balanced, when the interaction is socially oriented, and when efforts are made to counteract differences in ability. When used to enhance motivation, competition between mixed groups may not have the harmful effects of competition within mixed groups, provided that the outcomes are positive. Equal status on factors external to the contact situation and on factors within the situation is desirable. Individualized information about outgroup members can play a more important role in judgments of outgroup members than category information but may not change views of the outgroup as a whole. Support by authority figures can facilitate contact, especially if the authority figures come from all the groups that are represented, but favorable outcomes of intergroup contact can occur in the absence of support by authority figures.

Subsequent research added a host of societal and person factors to the situational factors emphasized in the original versions of the contact hypothesis. Among the societal factors examined were: disconfirming societal stereotypes, norms that favor contact, favorable prior relations among the groups, and a high degree of acculturation among minority group members. Contact is more likely to have positive outcomes if the participants are young, well educated, and come from the higher social classes. High self-esteem, low authoritarianism, and adherence to egalitarian values all promote positive outcomes of intergroup contact.

As research continued to accumulate, there was an increased interest in the behavior and affective outcomes of contact, as well as the attitudinal outcomes stressed in the early research. This research focused on such behaviors as helping, participation in group decisions, and participation in future intergroup interactions. Anxiety as a reaction to contact was also examined.

The research on societal and person factors and the interest in behavioral and affective consequences broadened the model implicit in the original contact hypothesis. This conceptual model was broadened further by research on the mediators of the outcomes of contact. A consideration of societal antecedents and consequences, as well as the mediators of the effects of contact, results in a causal model that incorporates most of the research done to date and can be used to understand and design contact programs. This model suggests that the prior relations between the groups influence the contact situation and the people participating in them. Situational and person factors interact to determine the outcomes of contact that are mediated by a variety of cognitive, affective, and behavioral processes. These outcomes have consequences for both individuals and society.

This causal model was used to understand the outcomes of school desegregation. Studies of the short-term effects of desegregation indicate that it leads to small improvements in the math achievement of African American students, rarely increases and sometimes decreases the self-esteem of African American students, and has mixed effects on the racial attitudes of African American and White students. The long-term studies indicate that desegregation leads to modest increases in the educational and economic achievements of African Americans, and it increases the willingness of African Americans and Whites to live and work together, although it also leads to White flight under some conditions. The factors included in the updated causal model help to understand why desegregation did not have the anticipated positive effects in the short term but did have generally positive effects in the long term.

Studies using mixed, cooperative groups in the schools to improve race relations indicate that they can create more favorable attitudes toward outgroup members, increase cross-ethnic friendships and empathy for other students, and raise the achievement and self-esteem of minority students.

Social Identity, Self-Categorization, and Intergroup Attitudes

Take a minute to examine the following categorizations:

African American/White/Asian/Latino

Old/young

Heterosexual/homosexual

Disabled/able-bodied

Male/female

Americans/foreigners

Upper class/middle class/lower class

Christian/Jew/Hindu/Buddhist/Muslim/atheist

These categorizations are easily recognizable as important social distinctions that divide people into ingroups and outgroups. What are the consequences of making these distinctions? One consequence is the tendency to emphasize the differences between groups. Your group (your ingroup), whether it be race, age, sexual preference, physical status, sex, nationality, class, religion, or some other distinction, is perceived to be different from other groups (the outgroups).

A second consequence is the assumption that, within each group, people are alike. The ingroup thinks that its members share certain usually positive characteristics and that members of the outgroup share other often negative characteristics. For example, Somalians who backed clan leader Mohamed Farrah Aidid perceived themselves as an ingroup with shared positive characteristics and perceived the backers of previous dictator Mohamed Siad Barre as an outgroup with shared negative characteristics. These two common consequences of social categorization mark the beginning of the process by which mere categorization is transformed into negative stereotyping.

This chapter discusses two related theories, social identity and self-categorization, that explore the causes and consequences of categorization into groups. The major assumptions of social identity theory are first discussed, and then recent models concerning the perception of outgroup homogeneity deriving from social identity theory are examined. Next, a related theory, self-categorization theory, is described. Finally, two proposals to mitigate the negative aspects of the categorization of individuals into ingroups and outgroups, both of which use concepts derived from social identity and self-categorization theories, are described.

Social Identity Theory

Henri Tajfel and his colleagues (Tajfel, 1978, 1982; Tajfel & Turner, 1979, 1986) believe that the self is composed of multiple identities. For Tajfel, *personal identity* consists of those aspects of the self that are based on individual characteristics, such as personality traits; *social identity* consists of those aspects of the self that are based on group memberships (Turner, Hogg, Oakes, Reicher, & Wetherell, 1987). Personal and social identity are inversely related; when one's focus is on oneself as a unique individual, the focus is not on oneself as a member of a group or groups, and vice versa.

Any interpersonal interaction can be placed on a continuum ranging from purely interpersonal, dependent solely on individuals' personal relationships and characteristics (personal identity), to purely intergroup, dependent completely on individuals' membership in social groups (social identity). At the social identity extreme, an interaction leads one to think of himself or herself as a member of an ingroup and to conceive of others as members of some outgroup. The nearer the interaction to the intergroup extreme of the continuum, the more social identity is evoked.

Tajfel's social identity theory expanded perceptual work on the salience of physical stimuli (e.g., Bruner, 1958) to social stimuli. A major premise of Tajfel's social identity theory is that social identity creates and maintains attitudinal and behavioral discriminations favoring the ingroup (Tajfel, 1978, 1982; Tajfel & Turner, 1986). In addition, the more important the identification of oneself as a member of an ingroup, the more uniform will members of both the ingroup and the outgroup appear to be, and the stronger will be the tendency to treat outgroup members as undifferentiated members of a social category. At the same time, these processes cause ingroup members to perceive themselves as dissimilar from the outgroup.

These overgeneralized views regarding the ingroup and outgroup that derive from social identity provide the basis for stereotyping, with negative value judgments and affect attached to stereotypic traits of the outgroup. For example, in a desegregated neighborhood, a White resident who knows her African American neighbors and interacts with them is likely to think of herself and her neighbors as individuals, with some of the neighbors being brighter, more interesting, and more pleasant than others. However, a White resident who does not know her African American neighbors may view them simply as members of the outgroup—highly similar to one another and possessing the stereotypic characteristics of their group. Simultaneously, she will think of herself as a member of a White ingroup.

A second major premise of social identity theory posits a linkage between individuals' attempts to maintain or enhance their levels of self-esteem and ingroup favoritism, the more favorable judgments of ingroups than outgroups. Tajfel assumes that important aspects of an individual's self-image are derived from his or her memberships in social groups. He further assumes that a primary way of maintaining or enhancing self-esteem is by making positive comparisons between the groups with which one identifies and relevant outgroups. For this biased intergroup judgment process to have the desired effect on self-esteem, the individual must identify with the ingroup. Moreover, the comparison must be relevant to the distinction between the groups. So, for example, the relevant distinctions between Palestinians and

Israelis are ethnicity and religion, while the relevant distinction between the Palestine Liberation Organization and the (Palestinian) Fatah Hawks involves a degree of political radicalism. Finally, the social situation must provide for comparisons on variables that favor the ingroup over relevant outgroups. Thus, if my group were higher in prestige but lower in wealth than another group, the comparison I would deem important and that I would wish to make would be based on prestige.

Self-esteem maintenance provides a motivational explanation for an otherwise puzzling intergroup phenomenon: The mere fact of belonging to one group rather than another is sufficient to trigger discrimination favoring the ingroup (e.g., Allen & Wilder, 1975; Billing & Tajfel, 1973; Tajfel, Billing, Bundy, & Flament, 1971). The effects of mere self-categorization have been tested in minimal categorization settings, those in which no face-to-face interaction occurs among subjects, group membership is anonymous, and the individuals make reward decisions (e.g., dividing money) between an ingroup and an outgroup member that have no bearing on the individual's own rewards.

In one study demonstrating discrimination in a minimal categorization setting, subjects were divided into two groups on the basis of alleged preferences for the paintings of Klee or Kandinsky (Tajfel et al., 1971). Subjects did not interact with or even know the composition of members of their group or the other group. Despite this fact, when subjects were given an opportunity to allocate money to two other subjects identified only by code number and group membership, subjects allocated more money to ingroup than to outgroup members. Furthermore, the pattern of the monetary allocations suggested that creating a difference between groups was more important than ingroup profit. This pattern of results suggests that the subjects' purpose was not to benefit the ingroup, but to compete with the outgroup.

Similar results have been found even when the basis for intergroup differentiation is a random coin toss (Billing & Tajfel, 1973; Turner, Brown, & Tajfel, 1979; but see also Rabbie & Horowitz, 1969). Parallel findings showing ingroup favoritism have been documented for trait ratings of group members, ratings of group cohesiveness, and the distribution of other resources (Brewer, 1979; Wilder, 1986). Consistent with the concept of self-esteem maintenance, research findings have also shown that group differences are exaggerated when the ingroup performs well relative to the outgroup and that these differences are reduced when ingroup performance does not exceed that of the outgroup (Brewer, 1979; Wilder, 1986).

It should also be noted that none of these studies shows 100% ingroup preference; though ingroup members are favored, the data also show evidence of a motive to be fair or equitable. Thus, outgroup members are given a substantial minority of the rewards to be distributed. In fact, in a study in which outcomes were negative (exposure to noxious noise) instead of positive, no ingroup favoritism occurred at all (Mummendey et al., 1992).

Early theorizing on prejudice and discrimination assumed that ingroup favoritism and the perceptions of ingroup similarity and outgroup dissimilarity were based on realistic group conflict: the actual conflict of group interests in a zero-sum world in which limited status, wealth, and power exist. For example, Sumner (1906) argued that the categorization of individuals into distinct ethnic groups originated in the first humans' struggles for existence. Ingroup loyalty and outgroup hatred and contempt were hypothesized both to reflect and sustain these categorizations. Consistent with these ideas, competition with an outgroup and hostility directed toward the outgroup have been shown to be associated (LeVine & Campbell, 1972). For example, Sherif's studies on intergroup competition at a children's camp show that opposed group interests generate competition, dislike, and discriminatory acts (Sherif, Harvey, White, Hood, & Sherif, 1961). In addition, they found that intergroup competition enhanced *intragroup* cohesiveness and cooperation.

However, social identity theorists argue that the data showing discrimination in minimal categorization situations demonstrate that realistic group conflict cannot be the sole reason for prejudice and discrimination, although doubtless much prejudice and discrimination is based on such factors. Although incompatible group goals are necessary for realistic group conflict, the mere creation of groups is sufficient for prejudice and discrimination to occur. Interestingly, the tendency toward intergroup bias is found even when it conflicts with obvious self-interest (Turner, 1978)! In a minimal categorization paradigm in which subjects divided money between themselves and an anonymous ingroup or outgroup member, subjects gave less money to themselves when the other was an ingroup member rather than an outgroup member. In this situation, competition with the outgroup appears to be a more salient motive than individual profit. The tendency of intergroup bias to take precedence over self-interest can explain a variety of seemingly dysfunctional political behaviors, such as the past willingness of the White governments of South Africa to endure economic sanctions from a variety of countries to maintain its system of apartheid.

But what of negative intergroup comparisons? It is not possible for every ingroup to perceive itself as superior to every relevant outgroup on every appropriate comparison. According to social identity theory, potentially negative social identities can be addressed through a variety of strategies, including leaving or dissociating from the group if possible. However, dissociation from the group is often impossible, and where possible, it is likely to have dysfunctional effects for the group, since weakened group identity lowers concern with the group's interests. Other strategies are to seek some new avenue of comparison and to change the value associated with the group attribute so the comparison is now positive rather than negative (e.g., black is beautiful). Alternatively, one can change the comparison group. An additional strategy is to attempt to reverse the relative positions of the groups by engaging in direct competition. Finally, if outcomes favoring the ingroup (e.g., winning a game, having higher status) are not available, differences between the ingroup and outgroup will be minimized (Brewer, 1979).

Outgroup Homogeneity

Previously we stated that categorization creates the perception of dissimilarity between ingroup and outgroup and similarity within each group. However, it has also been shown that individuals are more aware of the variety that exists within their group, whereas members of the outgroup are more likely to be perceived as undifferentiated (Brewer, 1979; Quattrone, 1986). The social identity theory explanation for outgroup homogeneity involves using groups in the search for positive self-esteem (Tajfel & Turner, 1986; Turner et al., 1987).

As we have seen, social identity theorists believe that we evaluate groups with reference to the self. Since we define our ingroups positively, and we are more familiar with the diversity of the ingroup than the outgroup, our ingroups are viewed as being positive, differentiated categories of people. The existence of our unique selves as the most salient example of an ingroup member further increases our sense of ingroup differentiation. Another factor that promotes the perception of homogeneity of the outgroup is that comparisons between groups are likely to be made between the ingroup and the outgroup as a whole, whereas comparisons within the ingroup are made among individuals (Tajfel & Turner, 1979).

BOX 4.1
Addressing Negative Identities

Every individual is sometimes faced with negative comparisons between an ingroup and an outgroup. A variety of strategies can be used to change the negative comparison to a positive one, thus changing the negative identity to a positive one.

However, at times the identity is strong enough and the disadvantage so obvious that the negative identity is difficult to dispel. Imagine you are a member of a college sports team that is currently trailing the league. You can hardly attach your loyalties to a team other than your own, nor can you successfully deny the win-loss record.

In a clever study of college hockey players, one researcher studied the ways in which the members of a losing team managed to perceive their team favorably in comparison with opposing teams, even after losses to them (Lalonde, 1992). While the team members acknowledged the winning teams' skills and motivation, they also found a consistent positive comparison that provided at least a partial explanation for losses: The opposing team was always viewed as playing dirtier than the ingroup!

A variety of competing models have been proposed to explain the perception of the greater variability of ingroup than outgroup members. Each of these models begins with concepts derived from social identity theory but then diverges in some way. They differ in their explanations of (1) the cause of the outgroup homogeneity effect; (2) how variability information is processed; and (3) how variability information is encoded in memory. Three models of outgroup homogeneity are discussed, the current findings are summarized, and exceptions to the outgroup homogeneity effect are discussed.

This issue has been chosen for a detailed scrutiny because of the importance of the implications of outgroup homogeneity. First, members of outgroups are typically viewed as similar to each other, as dissimilar from the ingroup, and as having generally negative attributes. These perceptions decrease the probability that outgroup members will be treated as individuals rather than as generic group members. Here we have the very foundation for negative stereotyping and for discriminatory actions based on these negative stereotypes, such as dehumanization of the outgroup and increased aggressive responses toward them. Thus these processes lie at the heart of negative intergroup relations. In addition, understanding the ways in which information regarding groups is stored and retrieved should be useful in mitigating the negative effects of this process.

Linville's PDIST

Patricia Linville and her colleagues believe that greater familiarity with the ingroup results in greater perceived differentiation and variability (Linville, 1982; Linville, Fischer, & Salovey, 1989; Linville, Salovey, & Fischer, 1986). Second, they believe that information about the ingroup is encoded differently than information about the outgroup, with individual information emphasized more for ingroup than outgroup members. Third, they feel that people have greater incentives to make distinctions among ingroup members because they interact more with ingroup than outgroup members.

Linville proposes that knowledge of a social category is represented in long-term memory by a list of specific exemplars (instances) of the category or generalizations regarding subtypes of category members. Each item in the list is assumed to be represented by a group of elementary properties (e.g., category labels, physical traits, personality characteristics, behaviors, attitudes). Linville further assumes that people generate perceived distributions of the characteristics of category members through a memory probe of the category, based on the set of exemplars and generalizations activated from long-term memory. For example, the characteristics attached to the category of teenagers includes one's perception of the distribution of individual teenagers on a variety of attributes associated with the category (e.g., high in energy, like loud music, know about popular culture).

Because of the hypothesized greater familiarity with the ingroup, more exemplars and generalizations are thought to be stored for the ingroup than the outgroup. In particular, the self is a likely exemplar for all ingroups. Since the self is viewed as both similar to one's ingroup in some respects but as different in a number of other respects (Tajfel & Turner, 1986), using the self as an ingroup exemplar may further enhance perceptions of ingroup variability.

Using age as the independent variable (young people vs. older people), Linville and her colleagues (Linville et al., 1989; see also Linville, 1982) found that ingroup members perceived the ingroup to be more differentiated than the outgroup. That is, people perceive members of their age group to be more dissimilar from one another than people from the other age group. The authors attribute this finding to greater familiarity with one's own age group than other age groups. In another study, no evidence of greater ingroup differentiation was found when gender groups were used. This finding was predicted, based on equal familiarity with members of both genders. In a final study, greater familiarity with the members of a college class over time was shown to increase differentiation.

However, in a test of the familiarity hypothesis, Charles Judd and Bernadette Park (1988) held constant the size of the ingroup and outgroup so that greater familiarity of the ingroup than the outgroup could not account for the outgroup homogeneity effect. Their data did not support a familiarity explanation for differences in perceived variability. Their data did support the idea that, when familiarity is held constant, the outgroup homogeneity effect only occurs when group distinctions are salient. In their study, subjects who were placed in one of two groups based on their alleged perceptual styles rated the outgroup as more homogeneous only when the groups were competing (high group salience) rather than cooperating (low group salience) at a task.

Park and Rothbart's Dual Storage Model

Bernadette Park and Myron Rothbart (1982) agree that both individual exemplars and broader information are stored in memory and that different types of variability information are retrieved for the ingroup and the outgroup. Park and Rothbart believe that group level information is retrieved for both the ingroup and the outgroup but that exemplars—particularly the self—also come to mind when thinking about the ingroup. Because less information exists about the outgroup, and the information about the outgroup is coded in a less-differentiated manner than information about the ingroup, the outgroup is perceived as more homogeneous than the ingroup. Thus different levels of categorization are thought to be used in encoding ingroup and outgroup members' behaviors. Greater contact with ingroup members creates specific, differentiated cognitive structures consisting of subordinate categories (e.g., young White cashier), whereas lower levels of contact with outgroup members create relatively broad, undifferentiated cognitive structures consisting of superordinate categories (e.g., African American).

In support of their ideas, Park and Rothbart (1982) found an outgroup homogeneity effect using gender and sorority groups: Members of subjects' own gender and sorority were viewed as more variable than others' gender and sorority. The data regarding gender are inconsistent with those of Linville et al. (1989). However, the two sets of investigators used different operationalizations of the independent as well as the dependent variables.

Unlike Linville et al. (1989, 1986), in this model it is not presumed that more ingroup than outgroup examples are stored in memory. Park and Rothbart also believe that the cognitive structures for ingroups and outgroups become self-fulfilling: The failure to differentiate outgroup members perpetuates the view of outgroups as relatively homogeneous.

Park and Judd's Abstraction Model

Bernadette Park and Charles Judd (1990; Park, Judd, & Ryan, 1991) argue that differentiation takes place for important and relevant groups on the basis of whatever information presents itself, whether by encountering exemplars of categories, subcategories, or whole groups. Unlike Linville and Park and Rothbart, they believe that outgroup homogeneity effects are not due to familiarity differences but to the fact that the initial process of encoding information differs for ingroups and outgroups. According to this model, initial estimates of an ingroup's variability are made tentatively and are subject to frequent revision when new exemplars are encountered. For outgroups, the initial estimates of variability are revised less frequently, because the individual is less motivated to view the outgroup accurately. Perceived ingroup variability is also based on larger samples and is thus more heterogeneous. Retrieval biases may also facilitate this effect: The motive to be accurate causes a greater search for extreme exemplars of ingroup than outgroup members.

To test these ideas, Park and Judd examined outgroup homogeneity using gender as the independent variable. The data showed outgroup homogeneity, measured by judgments of variability within the group and extent to which the group fit the group's stereotype. This finding is consistent with Park and Rothbart's speculations regarding more-differentiated encoding of ingroup characteristics relative to outgroup characteristics and suggests the existence of a more complex knowledge structure for ingroups than for outgroups.

Their data also suggest that the discrepancy of the self from the group and the discrepancy of a set of exemplars from the group mean are related to judgments of variability for the ingroup but not the outgroup. Although Park and Judd hypothesize that information about both categories and individual exemplars is used to form stereotypes, the level of information used depends on whether expectations regarding the category already exist (Hastie & Park, 1986). If a previous category exists within which an instance can be expected to fit (e.g.,

Latinos), the existing category information will be used. Where previous category information does not exist, relevant exemplars will be used to create a new category (e.g., music teachers who race cars). Even where category information does exist, individual instances can be retrieved and used to update the category information. For example, meeting a new Latino can cause individuals to change their category information to include new information derived from this new Latino exemplar.

In earlier work (Park & Hastie, 1987) it was found that stereotypes formed on the basis of specific instances of group members' behavior differed from those formed from category-based information describing the whole group. Subjects perceived greater variability in the group when they were first given the information regarding the individual members' behaviors and later given information regarding the category, rather than vice versa. The explanation for this finding may be that, once a general stereotype exists, discrepant individual information may be assimilated into the group stereotype.

One difference between this and the models detailed previously is that the variability information is thought to be computed from exemplars on-line, as information describing the group is received. This variability information is then stored as part of the mental representation of the group.

The Storage of Variability Information: A Summary
Current variability models suggest variability information is encoded and retrieved at a variety of cognitive levels (Park et al., 1991; Smith, 1990; Smith & Zarate, 1990). Thus, your stereotype of college professors is probably based on a combination of individual exemplars (e.g., examples of individual college professors you have encountered), subcategory information (e.g., psychology professors), and category information (e.g., generalizations regarding professors as a whole). It is unclear whether variability assessments are computed on-line or from information stored in memory. It is possible that information about the ingroup is coded differently from information about the outgroup and that initial estimates of the variability of the ingroup are made more tentatively than initial estimates of the variability of the outgroup. The role of mediators of these variability judgments has only begun to be explored. It appears that the salience of group boundaries, discrepancy of the self from the group, the variability of the exemplars, actual variability among group members, the type of dependent measure employed, familiarity, memory biases, the order in which category-based information and exemplars

BOX 4.2
The Existence of Ingroup Homogeneity

Although outgroup homogeneity is the typical finding, a small number of studies have found the reverse, the ingroup being judged as more homogeneous than the outgroup. Interestingly, just as social identity theory has provided the impetus for the study of outgroup homogeneity, so too has it been used to explain the reverse effect.

According to social identity theory, the presence of an outgroup promotes intergroup comparisons. One way of increasing self-esteem is to exaggerate between-group differences and minimize within-group differences on positively evaluated dimensions (Tajfel & Turner, 1986; Turner et al., 1987). Thus, the search for a positive social identity may also lead group members to perceive ingroup similarity on positive characteristics associated with the group, particularly when identity with the group is salient.

Several studies have predicted and found ingroup homogeneity within a small minority on positive traits strongly associated with the group (Simon & Brown, 1987; Simon & Pettigrew, 1990; see also Kelly, 1989; Mullen & Hu, 1989). These results have been interpreted as being motivated by the need for consensus and cohesion among smaller groups. However, the differences in group size itself may have caused differences in the variability estimates; it is reasonable to presume that a smaller group has lower variability than a larger one. Further, Stephan (1977) found ingroup homogeneity for the racial majority as well as for two minority racial groups. In the absence of convincing theoretical tests that distinguish these sets of results concerning ingroup homogeneity, the explanation of perceived ingroup homogeneity will remain unclear.

are encountered, and affect may influence inferences regarding variability (Park et al., 1991; Stroessner, Hamilton, & Mackie, 1992).

Social Identity Theory: An Assessment

We have seen that social identity theory differentiates between personal (interpersonal identity) and social (intergroup) selves. The theory has demonstrated that mere categorization of oneself as a member of a group can result in the view of outgroup members as homogeneous as well as discrimination against outgroup members. (For a summary of social identity theoretical accomplishments, see chapter 10 in Hogg & Abrams, 1988.)

According to social identity theory, these outcomes occur because part of one's self-esteem is derived from the groups to which one belongs, and making comparisons that favor the ingroup over the outgroup results in the creation and maintenance of high self-esteem. Although much of the social identity data presented here has been interpreted as confirming the self-esteem maintenance hypothesis, more direct tests of this hypothesis have often not been supportive (Hogg & Sutherland, 1991; Messick & Mackie, 1989; Wilder, 1986). For example, some studies have not found elevated self-esteem to be a result of intergroup discrimination (Hogg & Turner, 1985a, 1985b, 1987). Further, low self-esteem does not always motivate intergroup discrimination (Hogg & Abrams, 1988, 1990; Ng, 1985). In fact, some studies have found dominant and high-status groups to be more discriminatory than subordinate and low-status groups (Sachdev & Bourhis, 1987, 1991). Since self-esteem hypotheses have also been supported or partially supported in many other studies (e.g., Hewstone, Islam, & Judd, 1993; Hogg, Turner, Nascimento-Schulze, & Spriggs, 1986; Islam & Hewstone, 1993; Lemyre & Smith, 1985; Oakes & Turner, 1980; Mummendey et al., 1992; Vanbeselaere, 1991), clearly a more complex understanding of the role of self-esteem is needed. One clue is provided by the fact that the self-esteem maintenance hypothesis has been supported more often in minimal group situations, where groups are equal in status and power and where response options are limited, than in other situations (Hogg & Abrams, 1990). Studies showing an interaction of category salience and discrimination on self-esteem (Hogg & Abrams, 1990; Hogg et al., 1986; Lemyre & Smith, 1985) provide another clue. In these studies neither category salience nor discrimination alone were sufficient to elicit increased self-esteem. It also appears that self-esteem is only one of several motives directing intergroup behavior. Others include self-knowledge, meaningful interpretation of the world, power and control, self-efficacy, and self-evaluation (rather than self-enhancement) (Hogg & Abrams, 1990).

Another problem with social identity theory is that it is stated so broadly that often its predictions are not precise, and in some cases competing predictions can be derived from the theory. For example, the theory has been used to explain perceived similarity within the ingroup and within the outgroup, outgroup homogeneity, and ingroup homogeneity. Occasionally, nonsupportive findings seem to be interpreted as supporting social identity theory (see, for example, Simon et al., 1990). Clearly, to have greater predictive power, the theory needs more precise specification.

Finally, a number of alternative interpretations of the findings from social identity studies have been proposed, including rational behaviorism (Rabbie, Schot, & Visser, 1989), equity (Diehl, 1989), social value (McClintock, 1972), fate control/equity (Ng, 1981), and self-denying perceptions (Crosby, Pufall, Snyder, O'Connell, & Whalen, 1989).

We turn now to a discussion of a theory derived from social identity theory, self-categorization theory. Self-categorization theory differs from social identity theory in two major respects: (1) It is a much broader theory, encompassing more aspects of human behavior, and (2) it is strictly a cognitive theory, without reference to motivations such as self-esteem maintenance. In addition, an attempt has been made to state clearly the tenets of self-categorization theory so they can be subjected to rigorous testing.

Self-Categorization Theory

In self-categorization theory, John Turner and his colleagues attempt to specify the cognitive mechanisms underlying social identity and other group processes (Abrams & Hogg, 1990; Hogg & McGarty, 1990; Turner, 1985; Turner et al., 1987). They use Tajfel's interpersonal/intergroup continuum as a point of departure for an analysis of the self. According to Turner, the self is composed of three levels of self-categorization: the self as a human being, as a member of a variety of social groups, and as a unique individual. Unlike Tajfel, who saw a continuum from self to group behavior, Turner views all three levels of behavior as levels of the self. Turner perceives self-categorization as a theory that explains human behavior at all three levels of analysis, thereby encompassing social identity theory, which he views as a theory of individual behavior.

According to self-categorization theory, which of these three components of the self is activated depends on the specific situation. Turner argues that factors enhancing the salience of ingroup-outgroup categorizations and increasing the perceived identification of the self with the ingroup evoke the group self. Factors that personalize self-perception and increase the salience of distinctions made on the basis of an individual's unique characteristics, such as personality traits, evoke the individual self. Thus, if you were the only person from France in a room filled with Canadians, your national group identity would probably be evoked, causing you to think of yourself as French. However, if you were an American working out in a gym in the United States, situationally relevant individual-level distinctions would be likely to shape your identity, causing you to think of yourself as an individual who is in very good or not so good shape. Further, there is an inverse relationship between the salience of the individual and group levels of self-categorization; focusing on one level necessarily diminishes the relevance of the other. The process of evoking the group self, called *depersonalization,* is the basic process underlying all group phenomena.

According to self-categorization theory, individuals think of themselves as members of a group when they perceive similarities between themselves and a set of other individuals. They also think of themselves as group members when they perceive differences between themselves (and those similar to them) and other individuals who are perceived to be unlike them. For example, if you attend a football game without favoring one team over another, you are more likely to perceive yourself as an individual than if you are a fan of one team, in which case you are likely to perceive yourself as a member of one group (e.g., Chicago Bears fans) and not as a member of the other group (e.g., Minnesota Vikings fans).

The perception of similarity depends on the context. In two studies, when an individual with an attitude somewhat different from the subject's own was viewed as more similar to the self, the greater were the differences in attitudes within the subject's own group (Haslam & Turner, 1992). Similarly, in another study in this series, an individual was seen as an ingroup member when the differences in attitudes within the subject's own group were moderate or large but perceived as an outgroup member when the range of attitudes within the ingroup were thought to be extremely restricted (see also Haslam, Turner, Oakes, McGarty, & Hayes, 1992).

The fewer differences there are between the person being categorized and the individual making the judgment, the more likely it is that the other person will be perceived as an ingroup member. In addition, individuals are perceived as similar if they have the same group label and are perceived as dissimilar if they carry a different group label. These hypotheses have been generally supported.

Like social identity theory, self-categorization theory assumes that the very act of categorization causes the tendency to evaluate oneself and one's group positively. The more positively the ingroup is evaluated, the more one will perceive similarity between oneself and members of the ingroup and the more cohesive the ingroup will be. Ingroup and outgroup evaluations tend to be inversely related: The more positive the ingroup evaluation, the more negative the outgroup evaluation.

Although we are members of many different groups, two factors determine which specific group is likely to be salient in a given situation: the relative accessibility of a category and the fit between the stimulus input of the current situation and the features that define the category. Thus, given two equally fitting categories, the one that better fits the environment and the person's current motives will become salient. For example, if one of the authors finds herself the only woman in a room crowded with men, the situation highlights categorization on the basis of gender. If two individuals happen to become acquainted at a political rally, the situation is likely to cause their primary identification to be as supporters of a specific candidate or political party.

Since accessibility and fit vary, group categorization and evaluation also change. For example, in a study of Australian students' views of Americans conducted during the Persian Gulf War, the authors hypothesized that stereotypes would change as the war progressed (and behavior was increasingly more or less consistent with stereotypes) and as comparison groups varied (and a single group thus became more or less like the ingroup, relative to other groups). These hypotheses were supported. The stereotype of Americans held by these antiwar subjects was quite negative at the beginning of the Persian Gulf War. As the war progressed, stereotypes became even more negative (Haslam et al., 1992). Second, the characteristics attributed to Americans changed when the comparison countries changed. The difference in judgments of Australians and Americans increased when comparisons included more groups perceived to be similar to Americans on dimensions relevant to the war. For example, Americans were viewed as more aggressive and ignorant when comparison countries included the USSR than when they did not.

Ingroup favoritism, or *accentuation,* should occur only when the comparison dimension is relevant to the group categorization. Let's make the assumption that most people think that men and women are equally intelligent but also think that men are more competitive than women. If individuals find themselves in a situation that is likely to lead to categorization on the basis of gender (e.g., in a competitive game, an all-male team playing an all-female team), accentuation should not occur on the trait of intelligence, because it is irrelevant to the categorization. However, accentuation should occur on the trait of competitiveness, particularly since the situation itself makes this perceived difference relevant. In two recent tests of these ideas, sex and college major were used as group identities. The results confirmed the hypothesis that group identity was perceived to be the explanation for individuals' attitudes only when group identity was salient and when the expressed attitudes were consistent with those of the group in general. Attitudes were most likely to be attributed to the group rather than to the situation or to aspects of the individual when the members of a group (males or art students) agreed with each other and disagreed with the members of the other group (females or science students) and the expressed attitudes were consistent with the stereotype of the group (Oakes, Turner, & Haslam, 1991).

Although there is a tendency to evaluate the ingroup more favorably than the outgroup, group members do not ignore reality. If an outgroup is clearly superior to an ingroup on one characteristic, this superiority is likely to be acknowledged. However, the overall comparison of the ingroup to the outgroup is still likely to be positive. Further, the more important the dimension to the group categorization, the more extreme should be the tendency to accentuate a positive comparison. Thus, Americans are not likely to view Americans as better skiers than Austrians, but they are likely to view Americans in more positive terms overall than Austrians, and they may believe that international political power is a particularly important dimension for comparison between these two groups.

These predictions have been supported overall. In one study, students from two British universities agreed that students from the higher-status school (Exeter University) had better job prospects than students from the lower-status school (Manchester University), although Exeter students agreed more strongly with this assessment (Spears & Manstead, 1988). However, students from each school found traits on which they could positively compare themselves with the other school; students from Manchester rated themselves as more easygoing and aware of trends in music and fashion, whereas Exeter students rated themselves as more self-assured and articulate. In a second study, Manchester University students who first were faced with comparing themselves with Oxford University and Exeter University students later responded by enhancing their evaluation of themselves on relevant dimensions when comparing themselves to students from a lower-status school (Manchester Polytechnic) (Spears & Manstead, 1988).

Other studies generally support these findings and, in addition, suggest that smaller groups may be more likely to discriminate in favor of the ingroup than larger groups. In a laboratory study in which students were categorized by type of cognitive style, for both large and small groups, it was found that (1) favoritism was highest on dimensions important to the ingroup but unimportant to the outgroup, (2) ingroup favoritism was lowest on dimensions unimportant to the ingroup but important to the outgroup, and (3) ingroup favoritism was mitigated for both groups on dimensions that were important to both groups. However, ingroup favoritism on dimensions highly important to the outgroup but unimportant to the ingroup was found only in the relatively smaller (minority) group (Mummendey & Simon, 1989; see also Mummendey & Schreiber, 1983, 1984; Schaller, 1991).

Self-categorization theorists argue that this theory has broad applicability in social psychology. They believe that many social psychological topics can be explained more parsimoniously by self-categorization theory than by the diverse explanations to be found in the current literature. Described next is the self-categorization explanation for social influence as an example of the broad application of this theory.

Self-Categorization and Social Influence

There are two typical explanations for social influence in the social psychological literature (for discussions, see Hogg & Abrams, 1988; Turner et al., 1987). First, informational social influence is used to decrease situational ambiguity. Where ambiguity exists, others can exert influence to the extent that their views appear to provide evidence regarding correctness or objective reality. Attraction to others and dependence on others (e.g., experts) lead people to rely on them to help define what is correct or real. Second, normative social influence is based on the need for approval. In this case, we accept social influence so we will not be rejected as deviant by members of our group (Festinger, 1954; Kelley, 1952). In an intergroup setting we will be influenced by others' views of an outgroup when we are not sure what the outgroup is like and when we fear rejection by our ingroup because we differ from its view of the outgroup.

Self-categorization theorists believe that these arguments are flawed. First, the explanations for this group phenomenon are individualistic; from the perspective of social influence theory it is the individual who seeks information regarding reality or seeks acceptance. In addition, social influence theorists seem to assume that social influence is a poor relation to primary, individual perception. Thus they think of social influence as "secondary, unreliable, indirect, abnormal, and coercive and . . . useful only in default and in so far as it functions as an extension of individual perception'' (Turner et al., 1987, p. 70). Finally, self-categorization theorists claim that current social influence theory cannot account for a variety of social influence findings (see Turner et al., 1987, for an extended discussion of this point).

In contrast, self-categorization theory argues that social influence is a group phenomenon, one that follows directly from self-categorization into ingroups and outgroups. According to self-categorization theory, the perception of shared consensus within groups leads group members to make the attribution that members of their group are objective and correct in their views. If members of one's group are correct, then one should be influenced by their views. Thus self-categorization leads directly to social influence. For example, we are usually influenced more on domestic policy by individuals from political parties holding domestic views similar to ours than by individuals from political parties holding domestic views divergent from ours because parties with similar views seem more objective and more knowledgeable than those with divergent views.

Several testable hypotheses can be derived from these assumptions, such as: (1) Confidence in one's opinions is a function of the extent to which similar others are perceived to share one's opinions; and (2) social influence will be successful to the extent that it is perceived to reflect the responses of the ingroup. For example, if you perceive that your ingroup shares your negative opinions about an outgroup, you should have more confidence in these opinions than if you perceive that members of your ingroup do not share this opinion. In addition, others' opinions of the outgroup should influence your opinion the more that you view these opinions as those typical of your ingroup. One current focus of self-categorization research is the testing of these and other applications of the theory.

Self-Categorization Theory: An Assessment

Although self-categorization theory is a more testable theory than social identity theory, many of its major hypotheses have yet to be thoroughly tested. Further, much of the research reports unanticipated interactions (e.g., Mummendey & Schreiber, 1984, on legitimacy and stability of status; Mummendey & Simon, 1989, on importance of comparison dimension; Spears & Manstead, 1988, on the devaluation of the outgroup). In other cases, conceptual clarity is lacking. For example, at least three views of the consequences of cross-cutting

BOX 4.3
Nationalism and Social Identity

Many of the former second world countries divided into nationalist states in the early 1990s. The ex-republics of the USSR, already fairly well geographically divided along ethnic lines, became ethnic-dominated nations. Czechoslovakia also divided into ethnic nations, with the result that some older Slovaks who have lived in the same small village all of their lives have been the citizens of four nations. Most dramatically, the degree of violence and the explicit policy of "ethnic cleansing" directed against Muslims in the countries that once comprised Yugoslavia caught the attention and the concern of the world community.

Even where nations have been created nonviolently along ethnic lines, problems associated with ethnonationalism have not disappeared. In the modern world it is almost impossible to create a nation with members from only a single group within its boundaries, so ethnic minorities remain everywhere. Further, many partitioned nations have guaranteed themselves hostile neighbors composed of former citizens.

Ethnonationalism is of course not a new phenomenon. The nationalistic concerns in the Middle East and Quebec, for example, have been apparent for decades. What is new is the sudden nationalistic resurgence worldwide at a single point in time, a movement not predicted by politicians or academic specialists in these countries.

Although social psychologists studying intergroup relations can claim no better powers of prediction, certainly social categorization theorists understand how nationalism can become an important element of identity, and they are able to predict its consequences. Large-scale political changes create an environment in which ethnic similarities and differences can be acted upon. The loss of a superordinate group label for all people in a given territory (e.g., those living in the former USSR or Yugoslavia) makes it more likely that ethnic labels will become highly accessible.

categorizations (group identities in which those similar on one dimension are dissimilar on another) exist (Doise, 1978; Tajfel & Turner, 1979; Turner, 1981; Vanbeselaere, 1991). It seems clear that self-categorization theory does not mirror the complexity of intergroup relations.

Remedies for the Consequences of Social Categorization

As those who attempt to mitigate prejudice and discrimination know, once categorizations have been made they are difficult to change. A variety of mechanisms are used to maintain our group stereotypes, including the principle of least effort, the tendency for individuals to persist in believing their early simple generalizations as long as they possibly can (G. Allport, 1954). For example, it has been shown that once categories have been distinguished, new information is incorporated in a way that enhances category differences, rather than reduces them (Krueger, Rothbart, & Sriram, 1989). Furthermore, it appears that judgments about the attributes of categories are based predominantly on the exemplars that best fit the category, effectively allowing the individual to discard information about variability in the group (Rothbart & Lewis, 1988).

Social categorization theorists are just beginning to research the consequences of social categorization, such as stereotyping and prejudice. The tendency to categorize appears to be a cognitive fact of life; individuals use categorization to make sense of complex stimuli. Some social identity theorists argue that prejudgments and social stereotyping are an inseparable part of the process of categorization and are thus inevitable. However, they believe prejudice and negative stereotyping are subject to elimination, but only as power differences between groups are eliminated and thus differences between the behaviors of group members are reduced (Hogg & Abrams, 1988). Other theorists believe that prejudice and stereotyping are more readily changed. The discussion turns next to research from this latter persuasion designed to reduce or eliminate the negative intergroup relations produced by categorization through changing the categorization process itself.

Changing Categorization

In this last section two techniques are explored that use social identity theory and self-categorization theory as a conceptual base for their attempts to decategorize people: Brewer and Miller's personalization technique, and Gaertner and Dovidio's common intergroup identity technique.

Personalization
Marilynn Brewer and Norman Miller (Brewer & Miller, 1984; Miller & Brewer, 1984, 1986; Miller & Davidson-Podgorny, 1987) have argued that intergroup relations can be improved by structuring

intergroup interactions on an interpersonal rather than an intergroup basis, causing information about members of outgroups to be organized on personal rather than group dimensions. Their argument stems from Tajfel's continuum of interactions from those that are purely interpersonal, dependent on individuals' characteristics and relationships, to those that are purely intergroup, dependent on individuals' membership in social groups. If the basis for the assignment of roles, statuses, and social functions in a particular situation is perceived to be independent of intergroup categories, and if the nature of the interaction promotes an interpersonal orientation, individuals from different groups should be less likely to perceive themselves in terms of ''us'' and ''them'' and merely perceive each other as individuals. Brewer and Miller argue that this type of personalization should lead to acceptance of the individual, as well as generalization of positive attitudes to the outgroup as a whole. Positive outcomes from interactions that reduce the importance and salience of group membership should also promote greater acceptance and positive generalization.

In a study of Hong Kong schoolchildren, social identities (gender and ethnicity) were either cross-cutting or nonoverlapping (Brewer, Ho, Lee, & Miller, 1987). The results showed that desired interaction and perceived similarity was greater for students with cross-cutting rather than nonoverlapping social identities. Nonoverlapping social identities only allowed for treatment on the basis of intergroup categorization, resulting in lowered feelings of similarity and less desire to interact with outgroup members. By contrast, cross-cutting social identities paved the way for interpersonal categorization, leading to higher perceived similarity and desire for interaction.

In another study, students were first divided into two groups, then assigned to two new groups cross-cutting the original group categorization. One of these cross-cutting groups worked under cooperative conditions and one worked under competitive conditions. Half of the students in each of the two conditions were given an interpersonal orientation and half were given a task orientation. Cooperation and an interpersonal orientation were hypothesized to increase interpersonal categorization. As predicted, the findings show that ingroup favoritism decreased under cooperative relative to competitive interaction, and in interpersonal relative to task orientation (Miller, Brewer, & Edwards, 1985).

A third study was conducted to determine if conditions of ingroup salience, when personalization should be low, would increase stereotyping of an outgroup member. In this study, subjects were given an opportunity to stereotype an outgroup member when alone, in the presence of an audience, or in the presence of ingroup members (Wilder & Shapiro, 1991). The authors anticipated that stereotyping would be increased in the presence of ingroup members, where categorization would make the ingroup distinction salient and would thus reduce the possibility of personalization. As predicted, stereotyping of the outgroup and identification with the ingroup were increased in the presence of the ingroup, relative to the other two conditions. This finding suggests that, as would be expected by personalization theory, identification with the ingroup is positively associated with stereotyping.

Unfortunately, cross-cutting categories may yield negative as well as positive effects. Although cross-cutting categories decrease negative evaluations of groups that are ingroups on one dimension and outgroups on the other (e.g., people from one's own sex but another race), the judgments made about the double outgroups (e.g., people of the other sex and another race) are the most negative (Hewstone, et al., 1993; Islam & Hewstone, 1993; Vanbeselaere, 1991). In some studies, derogation directed toward outgroup/outgroup members has been even more pronounced than single-category outgroup derogation (Islam & Hewstone, 1993; Vanbeselaere, 1991).

Recategorization

Samuel Gaertner and John Dovidio believe that intergroup bias can be mitigated by transforming the cognitive representations of ingroup and outgroup members from the perception of two groups to perceptions of a single superordinate group (Gaertner, Mann, Dovidio, Murrell, & Pomare, 1990; Gaertner, Mann, Murrell, & Dovidio, 1989). If group members can recategorize themselves as belonging to a superordinate group, then attitudes should become more positive toward members of the former outgroup. This effect is predicted on the basis of the social identity theory tenet that ingroup favoritism is one way of using groups to maintain or enhance the individual's self-esteem (Tajfel, 1978, 1982), and on Sherif's findings regarding the reduction of negative intergroup relations through identification with a superordinate goal (Sherif et al., 1961).

In a study demonstrating the benefits of recategorization, subjects from previously formed pairs of three-person groups were induced to view themselves as one 6-person group, as two 3-person groups, or as six individuals by treatments such as segregation of seating, color coding of groups or individuals, naming of groups or individuals, and the nature of the interdependence among the individuals (Gaertner et al., 1989). Reduced bias toward the individuals who initially comprised the outgroup occurred in both the one group and six individuals conditions, as compared to a control condition in which the two 3-person groups were not recategorized. Greater reduction occurred in the single group than in the six individuals condition. Intergroup cooperation has been shown to further decrease intergroup bias and strengthen single-group feelings (Gaertner et al., 1990). However, in another test of decategorization, superordinate identification decreased rather than increased intergroup friendliness (Brown & Wade, 1987).

Changing Categorization: A Summary

It thus appears that, despite potential problems (Rothbart & John, 1985), both personalization, changing individuals' cognitive representations from an intergroup to an interpersonal orientation, and recategorization, changing individuals' cognitive representations from ingroup and outgroup to one superordinate group, show potential for eliminating intergroup bias in small-group interaction contexts. Cooperation appears to be an important precondition for decreased prejudice through both personalization and recategorization.

Summary

According to social identity theory, the process of categorizing oneself as a member of an ingroup and others as members of an outgroup (social identity) creates and maintains discrimination favoring the ingroup. Social identity theory posits a link between ingroup favoritism and individuals' attempts to maintain or enhance their levels of self-esteem. Unlike ingroups, which are perceived as being composed of diverse individuals, the members of the outgroup are generally perceived to be highly similar. Because viewing our ingroups more positively than outgroups increases self-esteem, we are predisposed to view outgroups as similar and as possessing negative characteristics.

Three theories explaining this outgroup homogeneity effect were presented—those of Linville, Park and Rothbart, and Park and Judd—all of which derive from social identity theory. It is clear that information about group variability is encoded and retrieved at a variety of cognitive levels. It seems likely that information about the ingroup is coded differently from information about the outgroup, but the processes by which encoding and retrieval occur are not fully understood.

Self-categorization theory is a theory derived from social identity theory. Unlike social identity theory, it does not posit self-esteem maintenance and enhancement as a motivational factor. According to self-categorization theory, the process of evoking the group self underlies all group phenomena. Self-categorization theory has been used to explain a broad range of group behavior, including social influence.

Two techniques of prejudice reduction use social identity theory and self-categorization theory as a conceptual framework. Both theories attempt to mitigate negative intergroup relations by changing ingroup-outgroup categorization. Brewer and Miller argue that intergroup relations can be improved by structuring intergroup interactions on interpersonal rather than intergroup bases. They use cross-cutting categories (e.g., overlapping gender and ethnicity categories) to promote an interpersonal rather than an intergroup orientation toward others.

Gaertner and Dovidio use a reverse strategy, that of transforming the cognitive representations of group members from perceptions of ingroup-outgroup membership to the perception of membership in a single superordinate group. In their research, group members are induced to view themselves as members of a single superordinate group. Preliminary research findings suggest that both strategies hold promise of reducing the tendency to categorize groups into mutually antagonistic ingroups and outgroups.

Intercultural Relations

In England, Americans are often perceived as being loud and insincere. In the United States, Americans often find the British to be passive and cold. Americans characterize themselves as being outgoing and friendly, while the British characterize themselves as being reserved and polite.

Islamic nations believe that segregating the sexes protects women and honors the special roles they perceive that women play in life. Many individuals from non-Islamic nations believe that women under Islam are powerless and devalued.

European tourists to Japan, experiencing the pushing and shoving that can accompany boarding public transportation, sometimes complain that the Japanese are rude. The Japanese, however, feel they uphold basic principles of respect and honor for others much more than Europeans.

115

People commonly misinterpret the values and behaviors of individuals from other cultures by interpreting them through the values and behaviors of their own culture. These misinterpretations arise because the ways in which members of one culture categorize the world are often different from the ways in which members of other cultures make these categorizations (Brislin et al., 1986). Even basic concepts such as time and space vary cross-culturally, as do more specialized but still important categorizations, such as food and property. The U.S. concept of "animals that can be eaten" includes animals that are viewed as sacred in some cultures (e.g., cows in India) and some that are perceived as unclean in others (e.g., shellfish and pigs in Israel). Further, Americans' view of this concept excludes animals that are delicacies in other cultures (e.g., dogs in China, grubs in some parts of Africa). In the United States, land constitutes property but brides do not, whereas among the Abipon people of South America and the Rwala Arabs, the reverse is true (Rudmin, 1994).

Concern with such intergroup misunderstandings lies at the heart of this chapter on intercultural relations, the interaction of individuals from different societies. Cultural differences can lead to almost complete misunderstanding of the thoughts, values, actions, and intentions of others, thereby turning attempts at intercultural communication into serious miscommunications.

The topic of intercultural relations is one of increasing importance in intergroup relations. Social, political, economic, and technological changes in the late twentieth century have yielded greater face-to-face intercultural contact. The interdependency of the peoples of the world has made the outcomes of this contact ever more important (Brislin, 1981; Landis & Brislin, 1983). Increases in communication networks, travel, and international migration have revealed that individuals frequently know next to nothing about the culture and social norms of individuals from other countries. Lack of information often leads to misunderstandings, resulting in uncertainty, ambiguity, difficulty, and failure in intercultural communication.

Many of the problems that plague intercultural interaction are the same problems that bedevil intergroup interaction within a single culture. Intergroup and intercultural communication problems are often based on the same mechanisms and have the same types of effects. White Americans often experience problems and confusion in interaction with East Indians just as they would in interaction with American Indians. Throughout the chapter an attempt is made to note such parallels between intercultural and intracultural relations problems.

This chapter first defines culture and explores the many cultural differences that can lead to problems in intercultural interactions. It then examines cognitive and affective factors in perception and interpretation that can lead to intercultural interaction problems. These factors include stereotyping, attributional biases, ethnocentrism, intergroup anxiety, and culture shock. Finally, the chapter explores cross-cultural training programs designed to increase effective intercultural communication.

Culture

Culture can be defined as the sum of all learned behavior in a society. Aspects of culture include basic values, beliefs, attitudes, language, nonverbal communication, norms and rules, activities, time orientation, spatial relations, worldview, social organization (e.g., economic, kinship, political, educational, religious, health management, social control), history, personality, material culture, and art (Dodd, 1982; Samovar, Porter, & Jain, 1981).

Culture can also be more simply defined as communication (Lofland, 1973). In Dean Barnlund's words:

> In the sounds and syntax of language, the norms of social interaction, and the hierarchy of occasions one confronts a culture in its most tangible form. What the members of a culture share above all else is a way of conducting their affairs, a commitment to similar ways of managing meaning. Mastery of these communicative norms equips each new generation with a way of forming friendships, validating their experience, and contributing to the life of their times. *It is through communication that we acquire a culture; it is in our manner of communicating that we display our cultural uniqueness.* (1989, pp. xiii–xiv)

A culture provides the context from which the meaning of a physical act is derived. Similarly culture provides the context for the derivation of the meaning of language acts. According to one group of researchers:

> "Behaving as a native behaves" does not constitute "acting like a native" . . . knowing all the "rules" a native knows cannot enable one to act as a native acts, because every rule that tells you to act in a certain way has exceptions, there are other rules that countermand it, and people often act in ways that violate the rules but are still perceived as acting as a native. Rather, "acting like a native" consists of *being perceived by natives as using the cultural resources* that

contain the "moral order" or "language games" that are "intended" by particular acts. (Pearce & Kang, 1988, p. 27)

Language is the essence of culture. Language provides the basis for each culture's system of meanings, and without shared meanings elementary solutions to problems of survival would have to be re-created with every generation. At the same time that language allows us to create culture, language can be said to create us. It structures our perceptions of reality so that from an infinite variety of possibilities a finite number of cultural concepts come into being.

Cultural Differences

If we consider the central feature of culture to be language, then the task of intercultural communication is the construction of common shared meanings or a common reality. Intercultural communication is problematic because cultures vary in the meanings and motives underlying actions. Many dimensions of cultural variation have been studied, such as:

1. individualism versus collectivism, the degree of support for individual goals versus common goals;
2. tolerance for deviation, the degree of tolerance for deviation from cultural norms;
3. tolerance for uncertainty, the degree to which indetermination and ambiguity are tolerated;
4. masculinity versus femininity, the degree of emphasis on stereotypically masculine qualities or stereotypically feminine qualities;
5. orientation toward human nature, the extent to which humans are seen as innately good, evil, or mixed;
6. cultural complexity, the degree of differentiation in the cultural environment;
7. emotional control, the degree of emotional expressiveness allowed in the culture;
8. high versus low contact, the extent to which the culture allows touching of others and close distances among interactants;
9. power distance, the degree of acceptance of unequal power relations;
10. low context versus high context, the degree to which communication is found in the physical context and internalized in the person (high context) or is contained explicitly

in the message or resides in the explicit language (low context); and
11. person-nature orientation, the extent to which nature is seen as something to be mastered, to be lived with in harmony, or to be subjugated (Gudykunst & Kim, 1992; Hall, 1976; Hofstede, 1984; Hofstede & Bond, 1984; Kluckhohn & Strodtbeck, 1961; Triandis, 1990).

Cultures vary simultaneously on all of these dimensions. For example, the United States is considered to be an individualistic, high tolerance for deviation, high tolerance for uncertainty, and low power-distance culture, while Japan is considered to be a collectivist, low tolerance for deviation, low tolerance for uncertainty, and high power-distance culture. The United States is also a low-context culture; communication lies clearly in the meaning of the words used. By contrast, Japan is a high-context culture; communication may not reside in the spoken word but in the body language of the speaker, the setting in which the communication is made, or in some other contextual aspect.

As an example of the importance of these aspects of cultural variation, we will examine the influence of a single dimension of cultural variation, individualism-collectivism, on behavior. Collectivist cultures such as Japan differ from individualistic cultures such as the United States in the extent to which they hold different views regarding the importance of values on at least four dimensions: family integrity (the relative importance of the family unit), interdependence (degree of interrelatedness with others), hedonistic self-reliance (the relative importance of one's own wishes and happiness), and separation from ingroups (degree of concern for extended family members).

Collectivist cultures emphasize group over individual goals and regulate behavior through ingroup rather than individual norms. Collectivists are more likely than individualists to behave differently to ingroup than to outgroup members, regulate the behavior of ingroup members, define the self in terms of the ingroup, and emphasize obedience and duty in childrearing practices (Triandis, 1990). Collectivistic cultures also are more concerned with hierarchical relationships than egalitarian relationships and emphasize social skills associated with harmony and dignity over those associated with self-expression and independence (Triandis, 1990; Triandis, Brislin, & Hui, 1988).

The collectivistic concern with the group over the individual can be seen in the Japanese desire to conform to group norms rather than asserting individual views or needs. This group concern can also be seen in Japanese idioms, such as "A nail that sticks up will be hammered down." The collectivistic concern with the ingroup over the outgroup partially accounts for the Japanese pushing and shoving on public transportation about which European tourists complain; concern for strangers' feelings is not a cultural priority. These differences between individualistic and collectivistic cultures have been demonstrated in a number of studies. In one study, in which students in Hong Kong and the United States evaluated insults allegedly given by a manager to another worker, the Chinese students evaluated the insults and the manager much more negatively if the insults were given to an ingroup rather than an outgroup member (Bond, Wan, Leung, & Giacalone, 1985). By comparison, the North American students judged insults to ingroup and outgroup members more similarly. In a study of communication, intimacy of self-disclosure, perceived similarity, information seeking, attributional certainty (feelings that the partner understands the individual), and shared time together were examined. Greater differences on all these measures were found between ingroup and outgroup members in three collectivistic cultures (Hong Kong, Taiwan, and Japan), as compared to two individualistic cultures (the United States and Australia) (Gudykunst et al., 1992). Thus, when strangers from individualistic and collectivistic cultures meet, the differing norms regarding outgroup members are likely sources of intercultural miscommunication.

In addition, individualistic and collectivistic cultures are thought to produce different conceptions of the self (Kitayama & Markus, 1992; Kitayama, Markus, & Kurokawa, 1991; Markus & Kitayama, 1991). In individualistic cultures the self is seen as an entity independent of other people. Collectivistic cultures stress an interdependent conception of the self in which the self is viewed in terms of relationships with other people. The independent self is thought to contain a unique set of inner attributes that are independent of the social context, whereas the interdependent self is thought to emerge in relationships with others occurring in specific social contexts. People with independent selves strive to assert their inner attributes; people with interdependent selves strive to maintain a harmonious equilibrium in interpersonal transactions (Markus & Kitayama, 1991).

Emotional expression has also been shown to differ in individualistic and collectivistic cultures (Matsumoto, Kudoh, Scherer, & Wallbott, 1988). Kitayama et al. (1991) found that in Japan, subjects reported experiencing considerably more socially engaged emotions (e.g., friendly feelings, feelings of indebtedness) than socially disengaged emotions (e.g., pride, anger). The difference in the extent to which these types of emotions were experienced was smaller in the United States, a more individualistic culture. Degree of comfort experienced in emotional expression has also been shown to differ in individualistic and collectivistic cultures. In a comparison of Costa Rica, a collectivistic culture, and the United States, Costa Ricans expected to feel much less comfortable expressing negative emotions than did subjects from the individualistic United States (Stephan, Stephan, & Cabezas de Vargas, in press). Because emotional expression differs in individualistic and collectivistic cultures, it is likely that members of these cultures will find each others' emotional expressions strange and inappropriate.

Since Japan is a collectivistic culture while the United States is an individualistic culture, a U.S. citizen wishing to interact effectively with the Japanese would need to pay attention to group membership and status relationships, emphasize harmony in interpersonal relationships, anticipate relationships to be long term, cultivate an air of modesty, and interact closely with the group, foregoing a degree of privacy and independence (Triandis, 1990). A Japanese citizen wishing to interact effectively with Americans would need to pay attention to individual accomplishments, be tolerant of competition, anticipate a preference for peer and short-term relationships, and anticipate a de-emphasis on the extended family.

Think about how the collectivist-individualist distinction might influence management styles in Japan and the United States and how Americans might react to Japanese management styles. Studies of American managers in Japanese-run businesses have shown that the American managers have mixed views of the Japanese management style. The Americans voiced concerns regarding the Japanese emphasis on consensus decision making, which runs counter to their cultural expectations of having their own decision-making authority and making decisions quickly. At the same time, the Americans were surprised and pleased that their input was sought and acted on by upper management, and they felt they were learning much more about the overall operation of the business than in a comparable American firm (Kume, 1985).

In a study of 40 cultures, individualism-collectivism was one of four values found to be important in all cultures (Hofstede, 1980, 1984). The other dimensions found in each culture were masculinity-femininity, the relative cultural emphasis on achievement versus interpersonal harmony; power distance, amount of respect and deference subordinates should show to superiors; and uncertainty avoidance, degree to which planning and stability are thought necessary to avoid life's uncertainties. For example, the United States is an individualistic, masculine, low power-distant, low uncertainty-avoidant culture; Peru is a collectivistic, masculine, high power-distant, high uncertainty-avoidant culture. These dimensions have also been found to be important in two other large samples of cultures (Chinese Cultural Connection, 1987; Schwartz & Bilsky, 1987, 1990).

Parallel Processes in Intergroup and Intercultural Relations

It has been discussed that in our society a variety of cognitive and affective factors, such as stereotyping, attributional biases, ethnocentrism, and intergroup anxiety negatively influence our judgments of outgroup members. Not surprisingly, many of these same factors also influence judgments of outgroup members in intercultural contexts. The next section examines the effect of some of these factors on intercultural relations.

Stereotyping

We have previously argued that categorizing others as outgroup members is based on perceived dissimilarities between the ingroup and the outgroup. This categorization and perception of dissimilarities may form the basis of stereotypes of outgroup members. In a parallel manner, categorizing cultural groups into ingroups and outgroups occurs. Categorization and perception of differences often lead to cultural stereotypes.

For example, categorization of individuals into Western cultures and Eastern cultures tends to bring to mind differences between the two cultural groups. People focus on the differences between Western values, such as pragmatism and mastery over nature, and Eastern values, such as spirituality and oneness with nature. Focusing on these differences increases the likelihood that people will think of both groups as being homogeneous and that they will exaggerate the differences between the groups. Further, these perceived differences form the basis of stereotypes.

Ample empirical evidence of cultural stereotypes exists. The first studies of national characteristics, conducted in the 1930s, clearly showed that North American college students held shared stereotypes of many cultures (Katz & Braly, 1933). More recent data demonstrate that shared stereotypes of cultural groups continue to exist across cultures (Inkeles & Levinson, 1969; Peabody, 1985). For example, in a study of stereotypes of the English, Germans, French, Italians, Austrians, and Finns by members of these groups, the cultural groups were perceived to be quite different from each other. However, all six groups agreed on the characteristics of each cultural group, with correlations of the judgments of a single group ranging from .63 to .82 (Peabody, 1985).

Stereotypes held by outgroups, called heterostereotypes, are often similar to the perceptions held by the ingroup, termed autostereotypes (Peabody, 1985). Convergence has been shown between auto- and heterostereotypes of Americans and Greeks (Triandis & Vassiliou, 1967), French- and German-Swiss (Fischer & Trier, 1962), and Hispanics and Anglos (Triandis et al., 1982). In a study of autostereotypes and heterostereotypes of Japanese and North American students, scenarios of interactions between individuals with conflicting views were employed (Iwao & Triandis, 1993). Subjects were asked to state how they, a typical North American, and a typical Japanese would respond. Considerable overlap in auto- and heterostereotypes was found. As predicted, consistency of stereotypes was stronger after reading scenarios that the subjects from the different countries perceived similarly. When a scenario was perceived differently by Japanese and North American subjects, their auto- and heterostereotypes differed somewhat.

Heterostereotypes can also be extremely divergent from autostereotypes. For example, researchers have found that North Americans' and Europeans' stereotypes of Russians are quite dissimilar from Russians' self-descriptions (Peabody, 1985; Stephan, Ageyev, Stephan, Abalakina, Stefanenko, & Coates-Shrider, 1993). In one study Americans viewed Russians as being more disciplined and hardworking than Americans, while Russians viewed Russians as being more wasteful and irresponsible than Americans (Stephan et al., 1993). These researchers attribute the Americans' responses to lack of information regarding Russia, as well as to information gleaned largely from American political policies.

In addition, stereotypes of cultural groups are weakly associated with attitudes toward groups. These associations are stronger when stereotypes are weighted by the affect associated with the stereotypic trait. For example, in a study of American students' stereotypes of and attitudes toward six cultural groups, the correlation between the stereotype/affect measure and the attitude measure ranged from .26 to .54 (Stephan & Stephan, 1993). In a study of Russian and American students' attitudes toward Americans, Russians, and Iraqis, the stereotype/affect measure was a significant predictor of attitudes in four of the six comparisons (Stephan, Ageyev, Coates-Shrider, Stephan, & Abalakina, 1994).

Although stereotypes of outgroups are often negative, one implication of the preceding findings is that stereotypes can be positive as well as negative. As social identity theory makes clear, ingroups can be judged more negatively than outgroups on some dimensions and more positively on others. Stereotypes may thus be beneficial to intercultural relations, particularly if they are accurate and shared by both groups.

Social identity and social categorization theorists argue that stereotypes are part of a normal cognitive process of categorization. If so, then the goal of positive intercultural relations should be to foster positive stereotypes that recognize but respect intergroup differences (Taylor & Moghaddam, 1987; Taylor & Porter, 1994).

Attributional Biases

Intergroup interaction involves a variety of attributional biases, including the fundamental attribution error, attributing the behavior of others to personal rather than situational factors (Ross, 1977); the ultimate attribution error, viewing the positive actions of the ingroup and the negative actions of the outgroup as due to personal factors but the negative actions of the ingroup and the positive actions of the outgroup as due to situational factors (Gilbert & Jones, 1986; Snyder, Stephan, & Rosenfield, 1978); and the principle of least effort, the tendency to retain generalizations about others as long as possible (G. Allport, 1954).

Intercultural interaction falls prey to these same biases. Because so much of the behavior of people from other cultures is surprising, we tend to judge the behavior as unwelcome, and attribute it to negative personal characteristics of the members of other cultures (Brislin, Cushner, Cherrie, & Yong, 1986). Particularly when the interaction has positive or negative consequences for the self, people are likely to perceive others' actions as due to personal factors when the action is inappropriate in their culture. For example, if a Greek neighbor asks an American visitor how much money she makes, the American is apt to interpret the Greek's behavior in terms of American cultural norms. The American may then falsely infer that the Greek is nosy, rather than correctly inferring that in Greece personal questions regarding money are appropriate questions among acquaintances. Or Americans may falsely interpret the Japanese avoidance of shaking hands with them as an indication of personal dislike of Americans, not understanding that Japan is a low-contact society, where bowing rather than handshaking is normative. Further, even knowledge of the cultural rule does not always change our attributions. It is very difficult to learn to view behaviors that we have been socialized to view as rude, hostile, or uncaring as merely expressions of different cultural rules; the people engaging in them indeed seem "uncivilized."

Differences in attributions have also been found between individualistic and collectivistic cultures with respect to self-serving biases. Whereas North Americans consistently show self-serving biases, the Chinese and Japanese show the reverse, a pattern of self-effacing biases (Bond, 1994; Holloway, Kashiwagi, Hess, & Azuma, 1986; Kashima & Triandis, 1986). Other researchers have found that East Indians make more contextual explanations—focusing on the context of the actions and the way in which different actions fit together—while North Americans focus more on their own and others' actions (Miller, 1984; Shweder & Bourne, 1982; Smith & Bond, 1993). External attributions provide common means of resolving conflict in collectivistic cultures, particularly when others' "face" is at stake (Ting-Toomey, 1988). Among personal attributions, effort is more likely to be made in collectivistic cultures, whereas ability is more likely to be made in individualistic cultures (Bond, 1991; Stevenson et al., 1985).

Ethnocentrism

Categorization on the basis of culture and perceptions of cultural dissimilarities may set in motion a process by which we judge ingroup members more positively than outgroup members. At the intercultural level, this process is termed ethnocentrism. Ethnocentrism is "the view of things in which one's own group is at the center of everything, and all others are scaled or rated with reference to it" (Sumner, 1906, p. 13). Thus one's own group's norms, values, and behaviors are seen as good, right, and proper; other groups that differ from one's own are therefore seen as bad, wrong, and improper.

Ethnocentrism is a natural outcome of childhood socialization aimed at teaching children the basic values, norms, and roles of their society. Ethnocentrism may be functional during early socialization, since it motivates children to conform to societal norms and values. This motivation leads children to engage in behaviors that benefit the society as a whole rather than to fulfill individual selfish needs.

However, ethnocentrism can be quite dysfunctional in intercultural interactions. Ethnocentrism leads groups to see themselves as superior to other groups, which are viewed as contemptible, immoral, and inferior. It also causes them to view their own standards of value as universal, to reject outgroup values, and to see their group as strong and to see others as weak (LeVine & Campbell, 1972). Further, ethnocentrism leads people to exaggerate group differences (Sumner, 1906). Although it leads to cooperation and a sense of cohesion with other ingroup members, it induces an absence of cooperation with outgroup members. Similarly, it creates obedience to ingroup authorities and nonobedience to outgroup authorities. Ethnocentrism culminates in the maintenance of social distance, negative affect, hate, distrust, fear, and blaming the outgroup for ingroup problems.

Although ethnocentrism is taught in all cultures, it varies in strength across cultures (Bond, 1988; Ramirez, 1967). Some researchers have found people in collectivistic cultures to be more ethnocentric than those from individualistic cultures (Al-Zahrani, 1991; Smith & Bond, 1993). Others have found less ingroup bias in non-Western collectivistic cultures (Bond, Hewstone, Wan, & Chiu, 1985; Boski, 1983; Hewstone, Bond, & Wan, 1983; Taylor & Jaggi, 1974). Consistent with this argument, in a study of ingroup bias Wetherell (1982) found that Polynesians displayed less bias than Europeans. One explanation for this cultural difference is that the value placed on modesty and harmony in collectivistic societies prevails unless groups have a history of negative intergroup conflict or have very negative stereotypes about each other (Bond, Leung, & Wan, 1982; Hewstone & Ward, 1985).

Less ingroup bias in collectivistic cultures is the reverse of what would be expected on the basis of the previously discussed findings regarding treatment of ingroup and outgroup members in collectivistic and individualistic cultures. However, this inconsistency may be the result of an artifact of the relative cultural homogeneity of cultures such as Hong Kong and Japan (Lee & Ottani, 1993; Triandis, McCusker, & Hui, 1990). The studies finding low or no ingroup bias all used ingroups and outgroups from within single, homogeneous cultures. Individuals presumed to be members of the outgroup (e.g., classmates divided into different groups for the duration of the experiment) may actually have been perceived as ingroup members (Smith & Bond, 1993).

The definition of ingroup and outgroup also varies by culture (Triandis, 1994). Tribes in Africa, national and ethnic groups in the former USSR and Yugoslavia, religion in Jerusalem, age in Eastern cultures, sex in Muslim societies, and class during the French, Mexican, and Russian Revolutions provide examples of distinctions that are particularly important in determining ingroup and outgroup.

BOX 5.1
Cross-Cultural Correlates of Ethnocentrism

A survey of 30 ethnic groups in East Africa (10 groups in each of three countries) examined the effects of proximity to other groups and perceived similarity on three aspects of intergroup relations: liking, evaluative ratings of trustworthiness and moral virtue, and perceived achievement or respect (Brewer & Campbell, 1976).

On all three measures, the ingroup was rated more positively than the outgroup, demonstrating an ethnocentric effect. However, the ratings varied by measure. On the measure of achievement/respect, ingroup favoritism was considerably less strong than on the liking and trustworthiness/virtue measures. Fully one third of the groups gave a higher respect/achievement rating to at least one outgroup than to the ingroup.

In examining the liking data, the relationship between proximity to other groups and liking was positive, as was the relationship between perceived similarity and liking. The authors interpret these data to mean that opportunity for contact and ease of interaction are reflected in intergroup attraction. By contrast, the trustworthiness/virtue measure showed a negative relationship with proximity to other groups. The authors interpret these data to reflect the consequences of conflicts associated with proximity. The achievement/respect data exhibited only a weak association with perceived similarity and proximity.

Ethnographic studies consisting of interviews with elderly informants in 20 field sites in northern Canada, the South Pacific, and West Africa replicated each of the preceding findings (Brewer, 1986). First, ethnocentrism was found among all groups, although most rated outgroups higher on some dimensions. Second, proximity to the outgroup was associated with greater perceived similarity to and liking for the outgroup. However, proximity was also associated with greater overt conflict. Finally, proximity was not associated with measures of respect. Thus, nearby groups tend to be accepted more than distant groups, but only if the groups have no history of negative intergroup relations.

Ethnocentrism and Delegitimation

According to Daniel Bar-Tal, extreme levels of ethnocentrism can result in delegitimation, which he defines as "categorization of a group or groups into extremely negative social categories that are excluded from the realm of acceptable norms and/or values" (1990, p. 65). Delegitimation maximizes intergroup differences and implies the overwhelming superiority of the ingroup. The more dissimilar the groups, the easier delegitimation becomes. The purpose of delegitimation is to differentiate the groups completely to exclude the outgroup from humanity so it can be exploited or even annihilated. A group defined as inhuman can then be treated inhumanely.

Bar-Tal argues that ethnocentric delegitimation occurred both in the first European-Native American Indian encounters and in Nazi Germany. In the former case, the Europeans' need for land led to delegitimation and then exploitation. In the latter case, the mechanism by which Germans came to believe that Jews were inhuman was the ethnocentrism embedded in their racist ideology of Aryan superiority. In both instances, differences in physical appearance, norms, religion, language, and other aspects of culture were great enough to facilitate delegitimation.

Other researchers have noted that people tend to subscribe to ethnocentric "mirror images" of their own country and countries perceived to be one's country's enemies (Sande, Goethals, Ferrari, & Worth, 1989). One's country is viewed as moral, and its actions are attributed to altruistic motives, whereas enemy countries are viewed as diabolical, and their actions are attributed to self-serving motives. In war, for example, each party tends to see God (or Allah or another supreme being) as always on its side. Thus delegitimation creates the most negative, exploitative types of intergroup relations.

Intergroup Anxiety

Intergroup anxiety encompasses intercultural interactions, as well as some interactions with individuals from one's own culture (e.g., interactions that cross racial, ethnic group, or class lines; interactions with the stigmatized). Thus the concept of intergroup anxiety is useful in studying intergroup as well as intercultural relations.

Intergroup anxiety originates in the anticipation of negative consequences during intergroup interactions (Stephan, 1992; Stephan & Stephan, 1985, 1989a, 1989b, 1993). These negative consequences include:

1. Negative psychological consequences for the self (e.g., ingroup members may feel confused, frustrated, or

incompetent when interacting with outgroup members). To cite an example, Americans do not bow to each other and thus, without cultural training, are not prepared to respond correctly when the Japanese bow to them. The response of the Americans is usually to bow back and then to feel frustrated and confused if the Japanese bow again. Given the American reciprocity norm, an extended period of reciprocal bows can ensue before the Americans stop bowing. In the meantime, feelings of incompetence and embarrassment are common.

2. Negative behavioral consequences for the self (e.g., ingroup members may fear that the outgroup members may exploit, dominate, or harm them). For example, during the war in the former Yugoslavia, Bosnians had ample reason to fear loss of life from Croatian as well as Serbian aggression.

3. Negative evaluations by outgroup members (e.g., ingroup members may fear that outgroup members will reject or ridicule them). Thus an encounter between a Bangladeshi and a British citizen may be marked by complementary fears: The Bangladeshi may fear being treated in a patronizing manner, and the British citizen may fear being despised for perceived patronizing behavior.

4. Negative evaluations by ingroup members (e.g., ingroup members may fear rejection by other ingroup members or fear being identified with the outgroup). For instance, before the collapse of the Second World, people in the United States who had visited Communist countries were often viewed as suspect and unpatriotic.

Minimal prior contact and previous conflict with members of the outgroup, status differences between groups, low knowledge regarding the other group, high levels of prejudice and stereotyping, and large group differences are thought to increase intergroup anxiety. Structured norms for interaction, cooperative interaction, and a relatively high ratio of ingroup to outgroup members are thought to decrease intergroup anxiety.

The results of a study of the influence of intercultural contact on intergroup anxiety support a number of aspects of this theoretical formulation. In this study college students' anxiety about interacting with Moroccans decreased significantly as a result of a brief stay in Morocco (Stephan & Stephan, 1992). An examination of the predictors of change in anxiety showed that contact that was viewed as nonthreatening and provided insights into Moroccan culture (e.g., interactions with Moroccans at cultural events, at social events such as parties, and in institutions such as schools) was associated with decreased intergroup anxiety. In addition, high levels of ethnocentrism were associated with increased anxiety. In other studies, high levels of intergroup anxiety have been associated with low levels of contact, negative prior relations, few positive contacts with outgroup members, and with stereotyping, ethnocentrism, and assumed dissimilarity (Stephan & Stephan, 1985, 1989a).

Intergroup anxiety has behavioral, cognitive, and affective consequences that are usually negative. The affective consequences include amplified positive and negative emotional and evaluative responses. For example, subjects' emotional reactions to success and failure on an achievement task are amplified when the partner is an outgroup member as opposed to an ingroup member (Stephan & Stephan, 1989b). Subjects tend to like an outgroup partner more than an ingroup partner when they succeed, but an outgroup partner less than an ingroup partner when they fail at a task. In addition, high levels of intergroup anxiety are associated with lower levels of self-disclosure to outgroup than to ingroup members during initial interactions with these individuals (Stephan et al., 1991).

Culture Shock

Culture shock refers to the experience of confusion, anxiety, and disorientation experienced upon entering a new culture. Stemming from a loss of familiar symbols and signs (Furnham & Bochner, 1982; Oberg, 1960; Smalley, 1963), culture shock is a major barrier to successful intercultural interaction (Gudykunst, 1988; Gudykunst & Kim, 1984; Landis, Brislin, & Hulgus, 1985).

Virtually all individuals experience feelings of anxiety, uncertainty, and unpredictability in extended stays in unfamiliar cultures (Barna, 1983; Gudykunst, 1988). In fact, culture shock is so common as to be labeled ''mundane'' (Brislin, 1981). Businesspersons on foreign assignment experience distress and adjustment problems (Furnham & Bochner, 1986), as do military personnel (Boxer, 1969); about 60 percent of early returning Peace Corps volunteers do so because of adjustment problems (Brein & David, 1971); and a considerable literature on foreign students documents their distress and discomfort (e.g., Paige, 1983, 1990; Spaulding & Flack, 1976).

The onset of culture shock is not immediate; initially most foreign visitors experience elation and optimism as they are confronted with a new and interesting experience. Frequently, however, this elation is followed by a period of frustration, depression, and confusion, as the visitors begin to grapple with the differences between their own and the host culture. During this period people are most likely to experience culture shock. When they begin to adapt successfully to these cultural differences, the symptoms of culture shock slowly turn into experiences of confidence and satisfaction (Du Bois, 1956; Selltiz & Cook, 1962; Smalley, 1963).

Culture shock is clearly associated with disconfirmed expectancies (Brislin et al., 1986). Expectations regarding intercultural interaction are based on group members' own culture's rules regarding social interaction. When their culture's guides fail them, they experience interpersonal difficulties and emotional turmoil. Consistent with this argument, empirical studies have shown the magnitude of problems of cultural adaptation to be directly related to the disparity between the cultures of the interacting individuals (Babiker, Cox, & Miller, 1980; Furnham & Bochner, 1982). For example, Germany, Scandinavia, Switzerland, and the United States are all low-context cultures; people communicate what they mean directly. By contrast, China, Japan, Korea, and Vietnam are high-context cultures; their communication systems involve preprogrammed information in the receiver and the setting, with less information transmitted in the actual message (Hall, 1976). In a low-context culture, disagreement is expressed directly, whereas in a high-context culture, such direct expression of disagreement is inappropriate. Disagreement must be inferred from such cues as ambiguous assertions (e.g., we found your proposal very interesting) and by paying close attention to nonverbal and extraverbal cues (Ting-Toomey, 1985). Individuals from low-context cultures will experience fewer problems interacting with people from low-context cultures than from high-context cultures, and the reverse is true of individuals from high-context cultures. Members of high-context cultures may well be offended by the low-context communication style of directly stating feelings. On the other hand, individuals from low-context cultures will be likely to miss or misunderstand the major message of individuals from high-context cultures.

In a study of foreign students studying in Britain, a strong linear relationship was found between culture difference and social difficulties (Furnham & Bochner, 1982). Social difficulty was measured in 40 situations using six different factors: formal relations, intimate relations, public rituals, initiating contact, public decision making, and assertiveness. Students from countries considered culturally near to Britain (e.g., Belgium, Denmark, France, Germany, Holland, Luxembourg, Norway, Sweden, and Switzerland) experienced the lowest levels of social difficulties, whereas those from countries considered

Most of those who travel to foreign cultures eventually return home, where they may experience "reentry shock," a remarkable parallel to culture shock (Martin, 1984; Paige, 1990). This shock is likely to be unanticipated, thus adding to its unpleasantness (Brislin & Pedersen, 1976). It includes feelings of not fitting in, having acquired different values and patterns of behavior; perceiving negative aspects of one's own culture that were not previously noticed; and poor adaptation to changes in one's own culture. In particular, both verbal and nonverbal communication patterns may remain those of the foreign rather than the home culture (Brislin & Pedersen, 1976; Martin, 1984).

Similar to culture shock, the degree of reentry shock varies with the degree of cultural difference (Martin, 1984). Ironically, the individuals who have made the best intercultural adjustment are likely to experience the most intense reentry shock, because they have changed the most during their intercultural sojourn (Brislin & Pedersen, 1976).

Based on the assumption that acknowledging and thinking through likely reentry problems will lessen them, reentry programs have been designed to encourage thought and discussion regarding common problems such as reestablishing relations with family and close friends and returning to school or work (Brislin & Pedersen, 1976). Participants are encouraged to think about the specific short-term and long-term adjustment problems they will encounter in their particular situations, and experiential learning techniques are used to help participants rehearse solutions.

culturally far from Britain (e.g., Algeria, Egypt, India, Iraq, Iran, Indonesia, Japan, Korea, Libya, Saudi Arabia, and Thailand) experienced the highest levels of social difficulties.

Just as some cultures are more similar to one's own than others and are thus less likely to induce culture shock, some individuals are more prone to culture shock than others. High levels of empathy (E. Rogers, 1983; Samovar et al., 1981) and behavioral flexibility (Kim, 1977, 1979; Triandis, 1983) and low levels of ethnocentrism have been associated with ease of adaptation to another culture (Brewer, 1986; Brewer & Campbell, 1976; Stephan & Stephan, 1992).

We have seen that the processes producing negative intergroup interactions also produce negative intercultural interactions. The next section examines the intercultural training programs designed to counteract these processes and create more positive intercultural interactions.

Intercultural Communication Training

A number of training programs have been successful in making intercultural interactions more successful (Black & Mendenhall, 1990; Brislin & Pedersen, 1976; Landis & Brislin, 1983; Stephan & Stephan, 1984). Success has been defined as both the ingroup and the outgroup having positive feelings regarding the interactions, accomplishing the goals of the interaction, and the absence of stress-related problems among returning ingroup members (Abe & Wiseman, 1983; Gudykunst & Hammer, 1984; Hammer, Gudykunst, & Wiseman, 1977). The goal of these programs is to reduce levels of the previously discussed factors that promote negative intercultural interactions (e.g., stereotyping, attributional biases, ethnocentrism, intergroup anxiety, culture shock).

Types of Training

The current methods employed in cross-cultural training include fact-based, attribution, and experiential programs. Each is examined in turn. Then two general intercultural training issues are considered: Should training be general or specific to the culture? Should training focus on differences among cultures or on the similarities among cultures?

Fact-Based Training

The goal of fact-based programs is to provide an intellectual understanding of a foreign culture. The majority of fact-based programs provide information regarding a specific culture in some combination of lecture, written, and filmed materials. This material typically contains facts about a specific country, information about social attitudes, and information regarding known problems the trainee will face in the culture (Gudykunst & Hammer, 1983). These training programs may also include language training.

Like fact-based programs designed to promote intergroup understanding within a single culture, fact-based intercultural training is not highly effective (Bhawuk, 1990; Furnham & Bochner, 1986; Stephan & Stephan, 1984). One problem with fact-based programs is that they typically introduce expert information regarding well-defined problems and ask the respondents to look at issues rationally and make written responses. By contrast, actual cross-cultural interaction usually involves collecting one's own information about the culture and improvising responses to problematic situations in contexts that are emotionally challenging and stressful and that require good verbal skills (Bhawuk, 1990). In addition, these programs have been criticized for being too general and for emphasizing the exotic rather than the mundane. They have also been criticized for implying that cultures are easily mastered by learning a few simple facts, thus neglecting the role of experience in learning (Furnham & Bochner, 1986).

Attributional Training

Attributional training programs also focus on ignorance of a foreign culture. The principal goal of attributional training is isomorphic attributions: teaching the trainee to make the same attribution for a cultural outgroup member's behavior as do members of that culture. This type of attribution is achieved by giving trainees information regarding the culturally based reasons for the behaviors exhibited by the cultural ingroup. The most commonly used attributional training device, the cultural assimilator, is designed to provide information regarding the subjective culture of a group, the often unrecognized and implicit values, roles, norms, and attitudes of a group (Albert & Adamopoulos, 1980; Triandis, 1975, 1976, 1977). For example, differences between two cultures in use of personal space, gift-giving, and helping norms might be the topics of items in a cultural assimilator.

In intercultural interaction, it is assumed that the interpretations of behaviors are more important than the actual behaviors themselves (Albert & Triandis, 1979). Correct interpretations or attributions can only be made from knowledge of the subjective culture of the outgroup. Ignorance of the subjective culture of another country often leads individuals to wrongly interpret a situation in terms of the subjective culture of their own country. The goal of attributional training is to remedy these misattributions. By teaching the subjective culture of the foreign culture, one also teaches the appropriate attributions for the cultural host's behaviors.

The typical assimilator consists of a programmed learning workbook of 75 to 100 incidents in which members of one culture are likely to misunderstand members of another culture because the incident has different meanings in the two cultures. The learner is asked to read each incident and choose among several attributions explaining the outgroup member's behavior. Correct answers are followed by explanations regarding aspects of the host subjective culture that make the attribution correct. Incorrect answers are followed by explanations as to why the attribution is incorrect and then asks the learner to select another answer. The learner continues to make attributions until the correct one has been selected.

Most assimilators have been devised for pairs of cultures (e.g., to teach Americans about Arab culture). In addition, a general cultural assimilator has been devised, using 18 themes of cultural misunderstanding found in a variety of cultures (Brislin et al., 1986).

Attributional training has met with more success than strict information-based orientation or training programs (Albert, 1983; Brislin & Pedersen, 1976; Stephan & Stephan, 1984; Triandis, 1983). However, attributional training has been criticized for its lack of experiential learning and its emphasis on the most dramatic misunderstandings that are likely to occur (Furnham & Bochner, 1986).

Experiential Training
Experiential training programs are designed to give an individual experience with the culture. Experiential programs range from low to high involvement and can include laboratory and field simulations, role playing and critiques of performance, exercises to increase general or country-specific cultural sensitivity, case studies, sensitivity training, interactions with ''old hands'' from the trainee's culture who have had extensive experience in the culture in question, field trips, cultural immersion, and interactions with individuals from the other culture (Bhawuk, 1990; Brislin, Landis, & Brandt, 1983; Gudykunst & Hammer, 1983).

Role-playing simulations such as the Contrast American, the Albatross, and BAFA-BAFA provide examples of experiential training exercises. In the Contrast American exercise, an American trainee interacts with a Contrast-American trainer, who portrays an individual whose values and assumptions contrast with those of the typical American (Stewart, 1966; Stewart, Danielian, & Foster, 1969). The latter techniques are simulation games. In the Albatross, trainers use a ceremonial greeting that leads to incorrect inferences if interpreted with North American values and assumptions (Gochenour, 1977). In BAFA-BAFA, North American trainees interact with each other in a structured situation as if they were from cultures with values and assumptions different from the North Americans' (Shirts, 1973). One is a patriarchal culture that values developing friendships through

BOX 5.3
An Item from the Thai-American Cultural Assimilator

One day a Thai administrator of middle academic rank kept two of his assistants waiting about an hour for an appointment. The assistants, although very angry, did not show it while they waited. When the administrator walked in at last, he acted as if he were not late. He made no apology or explanation. After he was settled in his office, he called his assistants in and they all began working on the business for which the administrator had set the meeting.

If you had happened to observe the incident exactly as it is reported in this passage, which one of the following would you say describes the chief significance of the behavior of the people involved?

1. The Thai assistants were extremely skillful at concealing their true feelings.
2. The Thai administrator obviously was unaware of the fact that he was an hour late for the appointment.
3. In Thailand, subordinates are required to be polite to their superiors, no matter what happens, nor what their rank may be.
4. Clearly, since no one commented on it, the behavior indicated nothing of any unusual significance to any of the Thais.

You selected 1: The Thai assistants were extremely skillful at concealing their true feelings. This is not entirely correct.

It is quite characteristic of Thais to try to appear reserved under any circumstances. If the assistants were extremely skillful at concealing their true feelings, would you know that you weren't seeing their true feelings? Also does the reference to the chief significance of the behavior of "the people involved" limit it to the assistant?

You selected 2: The Thai administrator obviously was unaware of the fact that he was an hour late for the appointment. A very poor choice.

While the administrator acted as if he were unaware of his tardiness after observing the hour's wait, don't you suspect that perhaps he was acting?

(continued on next page)

You selected 3: In Thailand, subordinates are required to be polite to their superiors, no matter what happens, nor what their rank may be. Very good. You are utilizing the information in the episodes to the fullest extent. Continue. This is the correct response.

To some extent their "deference to the boss" may be observed almost anywhere in the world, but you are far more likely to find it carried to a higher degree in Thailand than in the United States.

There were certain clues to help you select 3: the assistants' concealed feelings, the administrator's failure to apologize, the fact that no one mentioned the tardiness, and the subsequent keeping of the appointment that the administrator had set.

Did you use them all?

What you've already learned from earlier sections of the culture assimilator can help you. What did you learn about respect for older and higher-status persons in Thailand? And about the attitude of students toward an American professor?

You selected 4: Clearly, since no one commented on it, the behavior indicated nothing of any unusual significance to any of the Thais. This is completely wrong.

While the behavior reported in the passage does not seem so significant for the Thais in this relationship as it might be to Americans, why was nothing said about the tardiness? And why were the assistants "very angry" although they "did not show it"?

Isn't there a more significant level of meaning for this behavior? (Brislin & Pedersen, 1976)

established ritual, and the other is an egalitarian culture that values accumulating points through bargaining.

Some Peace Corps training provides an example of field simulation. In one such simulation, volunteers destined for small Pacific Islands were taken to a rural Pacific Island, living for two weeks as they would in their new locations (Trifonovich, 1977). They were responsible for finding their own food and fresh water; they had to improvise waste disposal systems; and their sole transportation consisted of walking.

Because experiential programs have been shown to have some advantages over other training techniques, they have been recommended as additions to fact-based and attribution-based programs (Bhawuk, 1990; Brislin et al., 1983; Gudykunst & Hammer, 1983). The primary advantage of these programs is that active training is more involving and realistic than passive training. In addition, trainees receive experience in problem solving, and they have the opportunity to test their capabilities. As a result, they have the opportunity to drop out if they feel they cannot handle the intercultural context. Not surprisingly, high-involvement programs tend to provide more valuable and realistic training than low-involvement programs. Because high-involvement programs are also labor, cost, and time intensive, it is not always feasible to use them. However, experts in intercultural training recommend that experiential involvement be as high as possible.

Culture-General Versus Culture-Specific Training

Training programs can be either culture general, designed to promote adaptation and effective functioning in any culture, or culture specific, designed to help individuals adapt to a specific culture (Brislin & Pedersen, 1976). The fact-based training programs described earlier and almost all the cultural assimilators are culture specific; most of the experiential exercises described earlier are culture general. Cultural self-awareness training provides another example of culture-general training (Kraemer, 1974). The goal of self-awareness training is to make individuals more aware of their own culture and thus their culturally learned assumptions. It is assumed that individuals' cultural judgments are nonconscious; they cannot be suspended until individuals have been made aware of their judgments. This awareness is accomplished by identifying one's own culture's values and assumptions, which are displayed in videotaped sequences showing an American engaged in conversation with an individual from a non-Western culture.

Which type of training results in the most effective intercultural interactions? Not surprisingly, each type of program has advantages and disadvantages. Culture-general training programs are superior in making individuals more aware of their own cultural assumptions, but they do not necessarily increase the individuals' ability to respond effectively in another culture. Culture-specific programs are better at teaching effective communication within a specific culture, but the learning may not point up trainee's ethnocentric tendencies (Rhuly,

1976). Also, culture-specific training may not enable trainees to interact effectively in cultures about which they have not received training.

Training in Similarities Versus Training in Differences

Training programs can either emphasize the similarities among all peoples, the differences between cultures, or provide some combination of the two. The fact-based training and cultural assimilators emphasize differences; experiential programs tend to stress both similarities and differences.

Programs that emphasize similarity and those that focus attention on differences have complementary strengths. The focus on people's shared needs and goals undercuts the tendency to see outgroup members as different from and less valuable than ingroup members. However, intercultural effectiveness training emphasizes cultural differences because it is the differences, not the similarities, between people that create problems. These differences are real and thus need to be understood, not denied. Not surprisingly, the empirical data suggest that the most effective intercultural training programs stress both similarities and differences (Hewstone & Brown, 1986; Stephan & Stephan, 1984).

Lessons for Intergroup Interaction

This chapter began with the argument that intercultural interaction can teach us about intracultural interaction. The chapter has shown that individuals are often unaware of the many cultural differences that separate them and, as a result, misunderstand the behaviors of outgroup members, particularly those whose cultures are quite different from their own. Negative stereotyping flows from people's tendency to categorize and can be associated with negative attitudes toward the stereotyped group; attributional biases are commonplace in interaction with outgroups; ethnocentrism is dysfunctional in interaction with outgroups; and working with others can produce intergroup anxiety and culture shock. These statements are as true of intracultural as intercultural interactions.

Summary

Differences among cultures can readily turn attempts at intercultural communication into cultural miscommunication. Greater face-to-face contact among peoples of the world as well as the interdependency among these peoples has made the outcome of intercultural contact increasingly important.

Culture can be defined as the sum of all learned behavior in a society. Culture can also be viewed as communication. The task of intercultural communication is the construction of a common reality. This task is complicated by the many cultural variations in meanings and motives. For example, cultures vary in individualism-collectivism and in masculinity-femininity, power distance, and uncertainty avoidance.

Many factors associated with problems of intracultural interaction are also associated with intercultural interaction problems. Stereotypes of cultural outgroups are associated with negative attitudes toward them. Outgroup behaviors are often attributed to negative characteristics of the cultural outgroup, and groups tend to make differing causal attributions for events. Although auto- and heterostereotypes are often dissimilar, they can also be quite similar. All cultures teach their members to be ethnocentric, even though ethnocentrism can be dysfunctional in intergroup interactions.

Intergroup anxiety originates in the anticipation of negative consequences during intergroup interactions. It usually has negative behavioral, cognitive, and affective consequences. Culture shock is the experience of confusion, anxiety, and disorientation experienced upon entering a new culture due to a loss of familiar symbols and signs. Virtually all individuals experience some culture shock in extended stays in another culture. Culture distance is associated with the degree of culture shock experienced.

A variety of training programs have successfully increased intercultural effectiveness. Among these are fact-based programs that provide an intellectual understanding of a foreign culture; attributional training, such as the cultural assimilator, designed to create isomorphic attributions regarding an outgroup member's behaviors by outgroup and ingroup alike; and experiential programs that may include simulations, role playing, case studies, sensitivity training, interactions with acculturated individuals from one's own culture or with individuals from the foreign culture, field trips, and cultural immersion.

Training programs can be either culture general, designed to promote adaptation and effective functioning in any culture, or culture specific, designed to help individuals adapt to a specific culture. Training programs can also emphasize the similarities among all people, the differences between cultures, or provide some combination of the two.

Intergroup Conflict and Its Resolution

One of the most intransigent political problems of the twentieth century has been the conflict between the Palestinians and Israelis. The two sides have engaged in countless terrorist and counterterrorist attacks over the last half century. Hatred and mistrust run deep. The dispute involves real differences over territory, religion, politics, economics, and culture. The Palestinians feel greatly deprived in comparison to the Israelis, and these feelings of deprivation have bred deep resentment and anger. The Israelis have been reluctant to make the concessions demanded by the Palestinians, particularly those that might threaten their own security and identity. The full range of conflict resolution strategies have been used by both sides, including open conflict, the use of threats as deterrents, direct negotiations, mediated negotiations, and unilateral concession making. Over the years progress has been made, but the conflict seemed to defy resolution until 1993, when a major breakthrough was achieved.

In 1993 the Israelis and the Palestinians signed a peace accord, and in 1994 they began the difficult process of implementing it. This accord came about in a most unusual way. It was not initiated by top officials of either group, nor was it brokered by the superpowers or the UN. Instead an obscure Israeli academic, a well-connected Palestinian, and a Norwegian academic married to a Norwegian diplomat informally created a peace plan in comfortable surroundings in the Norwegian woods (Elon, 1993).

The process started when Yair Hirschfield, an Israeli historian, was in London for a university seminar. While there Hirschfield met with Abu Alaa, a prominent Palestinian, at a breakfast arranged by Terje Larson, a Norwegian sociologist. After this first meeting, Larson and his wife Mona Juul, a Norwegian diplomat, used their connections with the Norwegian government to arrange a set of subsequent meetings between Hirschfield and Alaa in Norway. At their initial meetings they simply brainstormed. Abu Alaa said they should agree not to discuss the past, not to compete over who could be more clever in the present, and instead should focus on the future. The Palestinians were prepared to make concessions, Alaa said. Hirschfield suggested they create a joint declaration of principles. Larson and Juul served as father and mother to the negotiations. They did not try to mediate, but rather they lent both parties a sympathetic ear, gave advice when asked, defused tension when needed, and apparently fed them well (Hirschfield gained 25 pounds). Both parties were tough negotiators, reported Larson: "They used every trick in the book, screaming, bluffing, taking risks."

Together they came up with a new tit-for-tat formula for peace—a staged withdrawal of Israeli forces and gradual autonomy for the Palestinians. The final sticking point was solved by an agreement that the two sides would simultaneously recognize each other. How could such a simple set of ideas be new? Because the Israelis and the Palestinians had never before been in direct contact so they could not determine where the other side could give and where the other side was firm. How could such a small country as Norway succeed where the world's great powers had failed? Because the Norwegians could not be suspected of hidden agendas nor could they threaten anyone or offer inducements to anyone.

This chapter discusses what researchers and practitioners have learned about conflict resolution. This discussion will reveal many of the facets of conflict resolution and will shed considerable light on why it is generally so difficult to resolve protracted conflicts, such as the one between the Palestinians and Israelis. Like the discussion in the preceding chapter, attention will often be turned to the international arena in this chapter. International conflict resolution has been much more extensively studied than conflicts between groups within cultures. Because experiments cannot be done on nations, the database for this chapter is decidedly less experimental than the database for most of the earlier chapters. Nonetheless, it is extremely important to discuss what is known about conflict resolution because this type of information is crucial to improving relations between groups, domestically as well as internationally.

Origins of Group Conflict

The very concept of a social group implies that there is some basis for differentiating one set of people from another. Usually this differentiation consists of some type of similarity in condition (race, handicap), location (city, state, nation), or interest (clubs, hobbies). As a consequence, when we categorize people into groups we are necessarily emphasizing the differences among sets of people—a point made by social identity theorists. These differences may be real or perceived, but regardless of their validity, they are the basis for intergroup conflict. Sometimes the differences are numerous and substantial, such as those between the nations of the East and those of the West, but perhaps more often the differences between groups are few and seemingly insubstantial, such as those between Catholics and Protestants in Northern Ireland (but of course they are not perceived to be insubstantial by the contending parties) (Rose, 1990). Nonetheless, as the studies examining minimal groups clearly indicate, identifying with any group can result in discrimination and prejudicial evaluations that can constitute the basis for conflict between groups. When you consider how many and how profound the differences in culture, history, geography, and type of economy are, it is a wonder that any nonconflictual relationships occur at all.

This chapter's purpose is to explore conflict between groups—its origins and its solutions. The chapter begins by defining intergroup conflict and its origins. It then traces the origins of intergroup conflict to realistic conflict between the groups, perceptions of relative deprivation, and unmet psychological needs. Following this the discussion focuses on techniques of resolving intergroup conflicts, starting with one of the most time-honored and least effective—deterrence. After deterrence, the discussion turns to more effective techniques, such as negotiation, mediation, and unilateral de-escalation.

A social psychological analysis of intergroup conflict focuses on the relations of groups or their members in terms of their group membership. Thus it could encompass both conflicts between representatives of nation-states and between groups within nations (e.g., relations between African Americans and Whites). Intergroup conflict can be said to exist when groups attempt to achieve incompatible goals or when one group attempts to impose its values on another.

Realistic Group Conflict Theory

The fundamental premise of realistic group conflict theory is that many intergroup conflicts have their basis in competition for power or scarce resources (land, money, natural resources) or in differences in values, beliefs, or norms (cf. Katz, 1965; Taylor & Moghaddam, 1987). Wars are often fought over territory, differences in religion, or attempts by one group to gain power over another. These same factors can create conflict within societies, but so too can social class differences, and differences in the status of racial, religious, gender, or other groups. For instance, as mentioned in chapter 2, Bobo (1988) has argued that there has been a fundamental change in relations between African Americans and Whites in the United States over the last four decades. This change involves a shift from struggles over basic civil rights to conflict over the distribution of educational, economic, political, and social resources. He suggests that despite the general improvement in Whites' attitudes toward African Americans, there is evidence of racism in Whites' opposition to policies that will improve the economic and political power of African Americans.

In the hands of Robert LeVine and Donald Campbell (1972), realistic group conflict theory has been used to predict the psychological consequences of realistic group conflicts. They predict that realistic group conflicts cause increased cohesion and ethnocentrism within the group. These changes are accompanied by increased hostility toward the outgroup. There is substantial evidence from both experiments and field studies that making category distinctions salient, which real conflict certainly does, enhances ingroup-outgroup bias (Brewer, 1986). LeVine and Campbell also suggest that under conditions of realistic group conflict, group boundaries are more carefully maintained and deviance or defection from the ingroup is punished more severely.

For instance, during the breakup of Yugoslavia in the early 1990s, the Serbs' obsession with maintaining their own ethnic purity had tragic consequences for other groups. The Serbs attempted to "cleanse" members of other groups such as Croats, Muslims, and Albanians from their territory by killing them or driving them from their homes. One province of the former Yugoslavia, Bosnia, was a microcosm of Yugoslavia containing Croats, Muslims, and Serbs. The Bosnian Muslims were distinguished from the Serbs primarily by their religion and the fact that they were more urban and affluent than the more rural Serbs. The leadership in neighboring Serbia led the Serbian minority in Bosnia to believe that they would be annihilated by the other groups if they did not protect themselves. Playing on fears that had their origins in antagonisms stemming from World War II, the Serbian leadership supported vicious attacks on the Bosnian Muslims, including the killing of civilians and systematic campaigns of rape and destruction (Laber, 1993).

Another version of realistic group conflict theory, ethnic competition theory, argues that ethnic conflict is produced when rigidly maintained inequalities between ethnic groups begin to break down due to such factors as large-scale immigration, competition for jobs, economic decline, and increased prosperity among disadvantaged groups (Olzak, 1992). For instance, increasing migration from the southern United States around the turn of the century allowed White employers to reduce their labor costs and undercut White unions by hiring African American workers at low rates of pay. The result was increased levels of violence directed at African Americans by the Whites whose jobs were threatened. Similarly, violence against European immigrant groups in the early twentieth century in the United States increased during periods of economic decline. When some of these immigrant groups did begin to succeed in the United States, increasing resentment and hostility were directed toward them by members of the assimilated majority.

Relative Deprivation Theory

In contrast to realistic group conflict theory, which emphasizes real differences between groups, relative deprivation theory emphasizes perceptions of being disadvantaged. Based on W. I. Thomas's (Thomas & Thomas, 1928) famous dictum, "If men define situations as real, they are real in their consequences," relative deprivation theory argues that perceptions of deprivation can lead to conflict, even if the perceptions are not entirely accurate. A group experiences relative deprivation when it perceives that it is deprived in comparison to some relevant outgroup. Frequently the outgroups that are selected for this social comparison possess more status, power, or wealth than the ingroup. When upward comparisons are made, it increases the chances that the ingroup will feel deprived (Crosby, 1982). For instance, one study found that professional women who compared themselves to men were less satisfied with their jobs, felt they were getting less than they were entitled to, and thought they were less well paid than professional women who compared themselves with other women (Zanna, Crosby, & Lowenstein, 1987). In a study of 84 countries, Feirabend and Feirabend (1972) found that the countries that had the highest incidence of strikes, riots, and revolts were those suffering from poor economic conditions and who simultaneously were well acquainted with the higher living standards of more-industrialized countries.

The concept of relative deprivation is closely linked with social exchange theory (Homans, 1961; Walster, Walster, & Berscheid, 1978). Relative deprivation is experienced when an ingroup regards itself as disadvantaged when comparing its inputs and outcomes to those of a relevant outgroup. Because feeling disadvantaged is distressing, the ingroup is motivated to redress its grievances. Social exchange theorists have suggested that disadvantaged parties can redress their grievances by altering the inputs and outcomes of each party or by changing their perceptions of the situation (table 6.1). For instance, members of the ingroup can attempt to decrease their own inputs or increase their own outcomes to create a more equitable situation. Alternatively they can attempt to decrease the outcomes or increase the inputs of the outgroup to make the situation more equitable. Psychologically the ingroup can devalue itself and come to believe it deserves no more than it is receiving, but this is not a very palatable option. A slightly less costly psychological approach is for the ingroup to reevaluate the outgroup and raise its opinion of this group in such a way that the outgroup appears to be justified in getting what it receives. Since only one of these solutions, increasing the outcomes of the ingroup, is very attractive, it is easy to see why inequity so frequently results in conflict.

The critical issue in social exchange theory is the perception of equity—the idea that each party's ratio of inputs to outputs is equivalent. However, it is important to note that equity is only one way of defining what is just in social relations. There are at least two other basic conceptions of justice. When justice depends on equality, the outcomes of all parties are expected to be equal, regardless of their inputs. And when justice depends on needs, each party should receive what it needs, regardless of its inputs or outputs. The latter conception of justice is what the Communists had in mind when they said, "From each according to his ability, to each according to his needs." The perception that the ingroup is not being treated justly leads to relative deprivation, regardless of the particular sense of justice being used.

BOX 6.1
Two Types of Relative Deprivation

According to Runciman (1966), people may experience two types of relative deprivation. One concerns an individual who feels deprived relative to other people in his or her own group. This type of deprivation is referred to as egoistic relative deprivation. The other type concerns groups who feel they are deprived relative to other groups. This type of deprivation is referred to as fraternal deprivation. The two may be combined as you can see in figure 6.1.

Egoistic deprivation

(personal situation compared to ingroup)

	Better	Worse
Better	Doubly gratified	Egoistically deprived
Worse	Fraternally deprived	Doubly deprived

Fraternal deprivation
(personal situation compared to outgroup)

FIGURE 6.1
Types of relative deprivation.

A study of White voters in the United States found that those who felt that they were fraternally deprived relative to African Americans were the most reluctant to vote for African American mayoral candidates (Vanneman & Pettigrew, 1972). Feeling deprived relative to their own group (egoistic deprivation) was not related to voting preferences. Thus this study indicates that with respect to intergroup relations, feelings of fraternal deprivation may be more important than feelings of egoistic deprivation.

TABLE 6.1 Inequity (Being Disadvantaged)

$\dfrac{\text{Inputs A}}{\text{Outcomes A}}$	Greater Than	$\dfrac{\text{Inputs B}}{\text{Outcomes B}}$
	A = Ingroup	
	B = Outgroup	

Actual Changes Producing Equity	**Psychological Changes Producing Equity**
Decrease A's inputs	Evaluate the ingroup less favorably
Increase A's outcomes	Evaluate the outgroup more favorably
Increase B's inputs	
Decrease B's outcomes	

Relative deprivation is more likely to occur when a group is experiencing rising expectations than when its expectations are declining (Gurr, 1970). In analyzing the French Revolution, de Tocqueville wrote, ''Revolutions are not always brought about by a decline from bad to worse. Nations that have endured patiently and almost unconsciously the most overwhelming oppression often burst into rebellion against the yoke the moment it begins to grow lighter'' (de Tocqueville, 1856, p. 214). Thus relative deprivation can lead to conflict even in a climate of positive social change. Improvements in economic circumstances create a climate of rising expectations that may not be fulfilled, causing feelings of frustration and relative deprivation in comparison to groups that are doing even better. For instance, in the period prior to the civil rights protests and riots during the 1960s, the economic and social conditions of African Americans were improving. However, the economic conditions of Whites were improving at an even faster rate than those of African Americans, leading African Americans to experience relative deprivation (Jones, 1972). One study found that the more unfairly African Americans felt their group had been treated, the more they favored protests, increased political power for African Americans, and racial separatism (Abeles, 1976).

Interestingly, lower-class Whites also experienced relative deprivation during the period of the civil rights movement. They felt deprived because civil rights programs were providing advantages to African Americans that they did not receive. A study of antide-segregation protests by Whites in Boston in 1980 found an association between a belief that Whites had experienced less economic gain than members of another race and their feelings of hostility toward African Americans (Begley & Alker, 1982). In a related vein, support for separatism in Quebec was stronger among French-speaking Canadians who felt deprived relative to English-speaking Canadians than among those who felt deprived relative to French-speaking Canadians (Guimond & Dube-Simard, 1983). In sum, people experiencing relative deprivation feel there is a discrepancy between their present status and what they are entitled to, and this perception can be a powerful source of conflict.

A contemporary example of increasing conflict during times of increasing prosperity is provided by events in China in the 1990s. In 1989 the Chinese government clamped down on political dissent by violently suppressing pro-democracy demonstrations in Tiananmen square in the heart of Beijing. Nonetheless, at the same time they continued to modernize the Chinese economy and increased their level of participation in the global economy. China experienced an unprecedented economic boom during the next few years, achieving some of the highest rates of economic growth in the world. By 1993 there were increasing signs of social unrest, even as the boom continued. Peasant uprisings occurred in 20 of 29 provinces, industrial workers staged more than 600 illegal strikes, and 200 riots were reported (Link, 1994).

Basic Psychological Needs

> Our understanding of human social relations, including international relations, will remain incomplete—if not flawed—until it is recognized that human needs are a fundamental source of political and social interaction in world society. (Rosati, Carroll, & Coate, 1990, p. 157)

Another approach to the causes of intergroup conflict stresses that the fundamental basis for one very important type of conflict, protracted conflict (intense, long-term conflict), consists of disputes over fulfilling basic psychological needs. This position is championed by John Burton (1986, 1987) and Edward Azar (1986) among others. In contrast to realistic group conflict theories, which argue that competition over scarce resources that are basic to survival, such as food,

water, or land, underlie conflict, Azar and Burton stress the importance of psychological needs as a basis of conflict. They acknowledge that protracted conflicts are often due to ethnic or communal
cleavages occurring in the context of societal disintegration, under-
development, or injustice. However, they argue that the underlying
issues in such conflicts are the denial of basic psychological needs
for security, identity, recognition, and participation. Burton (1986)
has noted that conflict can even be a reaction to lack of respect,
consideration, or an experience of humiliation. Burton also includes
differences in values as a source of conflict. Here too, he argues that
it is not competition for scarce resources that is the basis of conflict,
but more intangible psychological factors.

For example, in 1979 Azar brought together influential Egyptians
and Israelis to discuss the rights of the Palestinians (Cohen & Azar,
1981). The Israelis maintained that if a Palestinian state were created,
it would reduce their security. The Egyptians countered by arguing
that security for Israel could only come about if the Arabs accepted
Israel, and this acceptance hinged on autonomy for the Palestinians.
Thus what appeared on the surface to be a territorial conflict was in
fact a conflict involving psychological needs: the central issue for
both sides was security, rather than territory (Cohen & Azar, 1981).

Burton and Azar contend that in protracted conflicts the most
important units are the groups with which people identify to fulfill
their social identity needs. Even most nation-states are composed of
numerous subgroups, each with its own identity. When national
leaders engage in international disputes, they do so primarily to satisfy the domestic social needs of some of these subgroups. Burton
and Azar believe that identity-related conflicts now dominate the
world scene. Recent or ongoing conflicts in Israel, Lebanon, Sri
Lanka, Northern Ireland, the former Soviet Union, Ethiopia, Somalia,
Cyprus, the former Yugoslavia, and Turkey are all identity-related.
For instance, there are Kurdish people in Turkey, Iraq, and Kurdistan,
all of whom would like to be free from the sovereignty of the countries
in which they reside and form a nation-state of Kurdish peoples.
These types of nationalist movements based on shared ethnic identities pose one of the greatest threats to peace in our time.

Although most approaches to conflict resolution stress negotiation, bargaining, and compromise, Burton and Azar emphasize that
basic psychological needs cannot be negotiated, exchanged, or bar-
gained away. It follows from this position that conflict resolution
requires an examination of the basic psychological needs of the contending parties that are not currently being satisfied. War, threats,

intimidation, terrorism, imprisonment, and other types of force can be used to manage or even settle conflicts, but they cannot *resolve* conflicts that are based on psychological needs. Conflicts that are deeply rooted in psychological needs tend to endure until the needs are satisfied. However, unlike conflicts over finite material resources such as food, land, or mineral resources, conflicts involving psychological needs such as security and identity are not necessarily win-lose propositions. A cessation of hostility may increase the security of both sides to a dispute, and the identity needs of both groups may be met through mutual recognition. Thus outcomes beneficial to both sides are possible in conflicts based on psychological needs, despite the fact that such needs cannot be exchanged or compromised. For instance, in a labor-management dispute an important element of settling the dispute is to find a solution that enables each group to emerge with its honor intact.

Critics of the human needs approach to conflict argue that it is difficult, if not impossible, to specify what the basic psychological needs are (Rosati et al., 1990). Obviously there are innate biological needs for food, water, air, etc. that must be fulfilled for survival. But are there innate psychological needs that are equally necessary for survival? The answer to this question is unclear. Sociobiologists have argued that to survive in the small bands in which humans lived for much of their existence on earth, there was a need for cooperation, altruism, and attachment within the group (Ross, 1991; Shaw & Wong, 1989). In this view, the survival of the group is necessary for the survival of its members. As a result, sociobiologists argue that there may be an evolutionary basis for strong identification with the ingroup, where the ingroup can be demarcated by such features as skin color, hair texture, facial appearance, and other physical features (van den Berghe, 1981). Thus it is possible to argue that there is a biological basis for at least one of the basic psychological needs mentioned by Burton.

Even if psychological needs are not grounded in biology, it is possible to argue that a number of psychological needs, such as the need for identity, are valuable in maintaining mental health. Unfortunately we do not know if such needs are universal, and if they are not, then the failure to meet them may not be a fundamental basis of conflict between groups. Even if psychological needs were universal, they would be subject to at least as much cultural variation as customs for eating and drinking, which would complicate conflict resolution. For example, the manner in which needs for identity are satisfied may be very different in cultures with an interdependent (group-oriented) concept of self, such as Japan, and in cultures with an independent (individualistic) concept of self, such as the United States (Markus & Kitayama, 1991). Thus, even if identity needs exist in both cultures, resolving a conflict based on meeting these needs would require different solutions in different cultures. Despite these criticisms, the psychological needs approach to conflict is appealing because it fits so well with other theories, such as social identity theory, that also stress psychological factors.

Realistic group conflict, relative deprivation, and the failure to meet psychological needs all cause conflict in a way we have not yet considered. Each of these sources of conflict creates negative feelings among ingroup members that can generate negative reactions from outgroups. Real group differences frequently result in deeply felt hostility and hatred of outgroup members. Similarly, feelings of relative deprivation breed resentment and anger against outgroups. Strong identity with the group feeds feelings of ethnocentrism. Outgroup members may react to the hatred, anger, and ethnocentrism directed toward them in ways that cause or prolong conflict.

Having discussed some of the major causes of intergroup conflict, the next section turns to techniques of resolving conflict.

Conflict Resolution

Deterrence

One of the most primitive and common techniques of dealing with conflict consists of the use of threats in an attempt to deter the outgroup from acting against the ingroup. In deterrence the ingroup seeks to convince the outgroup that certain actions should not be taken because the costs of these actions will outweigh any possible gains (Jervis, Lebow, & Stein, 1985). One of the best examples of the use of this strategy for dealing with conflicts is the concept of mutually assured destruction (MAD) that evolved during the Cold War between the Soviet Union and the United States. Each side threatened the other with total annihilation if it made a nuclear first strike. The threat of total annihilation was intended to deter the other side from using its nuclear weapons. Since it would have been *mad* to use them, in this instance, deterrence worked.

Lebow and Stein (1987) argue that the use of deterrence in international relations relies on three assumptions. First, deterrence assumes that groups rationally weigh the costs and benefits of their actions. Second, deterrence assumes that the ingroup can influence the weights the outgroup gives to various factors in the cost/benefit equation. Third, deterrence assumes that the best way to influence the other side's decision is by increasing the perceived cost of certain actions. Each of these assumptions can be challenged.

As to the first assumption, groups and their leaders do not always approach intergroup relations using strictly rational analyses. Factors such as hatred, anger, fear, pride, and honor often play significant roles in group decision making. For instance, in the early days of the nuclear arms race, President Eisenhower arranged a meeting with the Soviet leader Nikita Khrushchev in Paris to discuss a nuclear test-ban agreement. Shortly thereafter, the Soviet Union shot down a U.S. spy plane over Soviet territory. In response, "an enraged Khrushchev demolished the meeting in Paris and withdrew an invitation to Eisenhower to visit the Soviet Union" (cited in Janis, 1986). Khrushchev's angry response to this incident meant that a chance to reduce nuclear proliferation was lost.

The ingroup's judgments may also be influenced by biases introduced by ethnocentrism, stereotyping, and the use of cognitive heuristics, instead of more rational information-processing strategies (Janis, 1986). Less than optimal decision-making strategies are most likely when the groups are under stress or in a state of crisis, as when they are faced by a threat from another group.

The second assumption, that the ingroup can influence the weights the outgroup assigns to various options, depends on how persuasive the ingroup is, and persuasion depends on a variety of variables. The variables associated with fear appeals are particularly relevant, since threats used in deterrence are often designed to instill fear. The literature on persuasion suggests that fear appeals are most likely to be influential when there are no effective ways of avoiding the threatened consequences, the probability of the threatened consequences is high, and the threatened individuals believe they are capable of making the required changes in their behavior (Rogers, 1983). Thus, if a threatened group is not persuaded that changing its behavior will lead to an avoidance of the threatened consequences (e.g., the outgroup will attack anyway), or if they believe the outgroup will not follow through on the threat, or if the ingroup is incapable of making the requested change, the threat is unlikely to be an effective deterrent. Fear itself can interfere with persuasion attempts because the arousal it generates may undermine rational thought processes.

The third assumption suggests that having the other group focus on the high costs of their behavior is the most effective way of getting them to change (or not engage in) some specific behavior. Although costs are weighed heavily by many decision makers (Janis & Mann, 1977), they may not weigh these costs in the rational manner required for deterrence to be effective. Janis (1986) has suggested that even capable and courageous group leaders often adopt a "can do" attitude toward deterrents that stand in the way of their policies. They concentrate their energies on ways of overcoming all of the costs. Janis argues that President Carter fell prey to this attitude when he ordered the ill-fated military strike in Iran in 1980 to rescue American diplomats being held hostage in Tehran. Carter and his advisers convinced themselves that the nearly insurmountable obstacles—an undetected desert landing, entering heavily patrolled Tehran, locating the carefully hidden hostages, freeing the hostages before they were killed, getting the hostages back through Tehran, and successfully leaving the country—could all be overcome. In the event, a desert sandstorm interfered with the strike group's attempt to land and the mission had to be aborted. In this situation any attempt by Iran to deter the Americans from their plans by pointing out the high costs involved probably would not have worked because the American leaders truly believed all of these obstacles could be overcome. As Lebow and Stein (1987) put it, "Deterrence can thus be defeated by wishful thinking" (p. 7).

Also, in some instances outgroups and their leaders may be more interested in gains than losses. In these cases it would be more effective for the ingroup to convince the outgroup that it has much to gain by taking certain courses of action, rather than focusing on increasing the perceived costs to the outgroup. For instance, farm workers seeking a pay raise might be better off talking to the farmers about the higher productivity of a contented workforce than about the costs of boycotts and demonstrations to the farmers. Carrots are sometimes more persuasive than sticks.

As if this laundry list of difficulties were not enough, the process of making a credible threat is itself quite complicated. For deterrence to have a chance of working, the behavior the ingroup wants the outgroup to change must be clearly defined, the ingroup must be committed to follow through on the threat it is making, it must possess the means and resolve to follow through on the threat, and the outgroup has to understand all of this. One impediment to making credible threats is that they require the ingroup to understand the outgroup well enough to know what the outgroup considers to be unacceptable costs. The greater the differences between the groups in culture, values, and beliefs, the less likely it is that the ingroup will possess this knowledge.

In addition, when decision makers are committed to a course of action, they may engage in the "defensive avoidance" of information that might reveal the shortcomings of their choices (Janis & Mann, 1977). Under these circumstances deterrence is unlikely to be effective because the costs involved may be ignored or minimized. Once the United States became committed to the war in Vietnam, its leaders consistently ignored or minimized information on the failure of our policies there. One of the authors recalls that his own pessimistic reports on the economic and military situation in one province of South Vietnam were rewritten by his superiors to present a more optimistic view. He recalls being told by the American ambassador in Saigon in 1965 that the war would be over within six to twelve months. The war finally ended in defeat for the United States in 1972, but not before both sides had sustained thousands upon thousands of additional casualties.

Can deterrence ever be effective? For deterrence to work, the outgroup must reevaluate its situation in such a way that it perceives that behaving in accordance with the ingroup's desires is in its interests. After a careful analysis of case studies, Lebow and Stein (1987) suggest several conditions that make such a reevaluation likely during international conflicts. When uncommitted outgroup leaders are motivated primarily by gain, have the freedom to exercise restraint, receive undistorted information early in a crisis, and are vulnerable to the ingroup's threats, deterrence can be effective in the short term. Given how difficult it is to meet these conditions, it is easy to see why Lebow and Stein conclude that deterrence is a "risky and uncertain strategy" (p. 36). There are reasons to think that Lebow and Stein's analyses of national groups would apply to other groups as well. Threats to strike, threats of boycotts, threats of economic sanctions, threats to protest, and threats of nonmilitary violence are all conceptually similar to threats of military coercion. Each entails communicating a threat that is designed to deter the actions of another group by increasing its costs. On the other hand, the two types of conflict differ in important ways. In international disputes, communication among the parties and among the constituents of the group may be more difficult than in internal conflicts, stress levels may be higher, and the antecedents, issues, and consequences of the conflict may be more complex than in most internal conflicts (Streufert & Streufert, 1986).

Negotiation

> To understand the permanent use of diplomacy and the necessity for
> continual negotiations, we must think of the states of which Europe is
> composed as being joined together by all kinds of necessary
> commerce, in such a way that they may be regarded as one Republic
> and that no considerable change can take place in any one of them
> without affecting the condition, or disturbing the peace of another.
> (de Callieares, 1716, p. 11)

As it was in Europe in 1716, so it is now in all the world. Free trade
agreements, common markets, and increasing international trade all
make negotiation imperative. But what is negotiation, and is it really
the answer? Before addressing these questions, we should point out
that negotiation is not simply a technique of resolving international
disputes. It can be used in a wide range of settings, including family
disputes, divorces, neighborhood disputes, labor-management disputes, and other disputes, many of which were formerly handled by
the judicial system (Pruitt & Kressel, 1985). Put simply, negotiation
involves discussion between disputants with the goal of resolving a
conflict (cf. Carnevale & Pruitt, 1992). The following examination of
negotiation discusses the motives of the disputants and the strategies
that result from different sets of motives. After this, a special case of
negotiation, mediation—which involves the participation of a third
party whose role is to facilitate resolution of the conflict—is
examined.

Motivation and Strategies in Negotiation

In 1993 there was a deadly outbreak of a killer virus in the south-
western United States. Most of the early victims were Navajo Indians.
The disease became known as the hantavirus, a name the Navajos
found objectionable because it suggested to many people that this was
a Native American disease and they felt it unfairly stigmatized Navajos. Investigators at the Centers for Disease Control in Atlanta who
had named the disease quickly became accustomed to the name and
did not want to change it. There are four basic strategies the scientists
could have used to approach this conflict. The scientists could have
yielded to the Navajos' requests, they could have argued for the utility
of continuing to use the name they gave the disease, they could have
tried to work together to solve the problem, or they could have
avoided the controversy and hoped it went away. After much wran-
gling, a decision was finally made to change the name. These four
approaches to conflict resolution have been combined in the *dual concern* model.

The dual concern model is a way of systematizing the strategies that people use to resolve conflicts. The dual concerns in this model are: a concern about one's own outcomes, and a concern about the other party's outcomes (Rubin, Pruitt, & Kim, 1994). Combining high and low concern for one's own outcomes with high and low concern for the other's outcomes yields the four basic strategies presented in figure 6.2. People who are high in concern for others but low in concern for themselves are most motivated to make *concessions*. People who are low in concern for others and high in concern for themselves are most motivated to engage in *contentious tactics*. People who are high in concern for both others and themselves are most motivated to engage in attempts at *problem solving*. People who are low in concern for both others and themselves are motivated to *avoid* negotiations. In the dual concern model a fifth strategy is sometimes mentioned. People who have a moderate concern for others combined with a moderate concern for themselves are motivated to *compromise*.

Experimental evidence is generally supportive of the dual concern model of motivation, except that high concern for others combined with low self-concern has not been shown to lead to high levels of concession making (Ben-Yoav & Pruitt, 1984; Carnevale & Keenan, 1990; Pruitt, 1991b; Pruitt, Carnevale, Ben-Yoav, Nochajski, & Van Slyck, 1983). Let us consider the consequences of each of the three most thoroughly researched types of negotiation strategies: conceding, contending, and problem solving.

Concessions

Negotiation is a term used to describe the demands made by each party to the dispute and the responses of the other side. With respect to the ultimate outcomes of negotiations, there appears to be a rather complex relationship between level of demands and concession making (Carnevale & Pruitt, 1992). When one party starts out with high demands and makes concessions slowly, the disputants often fail to reach an agreement, so outcomes are low. When one party starts with low demands and makes concessions quickly, agreements are easily reached, but they yield low outcomes for the party making the concessions. From the perspective of the participants, the most satisfactory outcomes are obtained when demands and concession making are both intermediate (Benton, Kelley, & Liebling, 1972; Hammer, 1974; Harnett & Vincelette, 1978).

In any negotiation one party can match the other's strategy by making demands when the other side makes demands or conceding when the other side makes a concession. Alternatively one party can

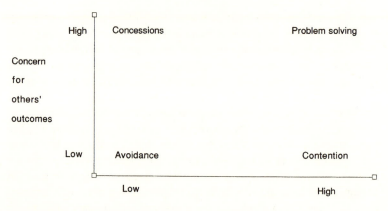

FIGURE 6.2
Dual concern model of negotiation.

mismatch the other by making large demands when faced with small demands or by making concessions slowly when the other side is making rapid concessions. One of the optimal approaches to concession making is called the ''tit-for-tat'' approach. In this approach one party makes a concession that is matched in kind by the other and this concession, in turn, tends to elicit further concessions (Axelrod, 1984; Patchen, 1988; Wall, 1977).

A fascinating example of the tit-for-tat approach occurred during the Cuban missile crisis in 1962. This crisis occurred at the height of the Cold War and brought the United States and the Soviet Union closer to war than any other event during that period. It was triggered by a Soviet attempt to introduce nuclear-tipped ballistic missiles into Cuba. This attempt was discovered on October 14, when missile launching sites were just weeks short of completion. On October 22, President Kennedy ordered a naval quarantine of Cuba's harbors and demanded that the Soviets withdraw their missiles from Cuba. For nearly a week the Soviets refused. On October 27, they shot down a U.S. spy plane that had been photographing the missile sites in Cuba and tension mounted. The two countries were poised at the brink of war. On that same day, Premier Khrushchev made a tit-for-tat offer. He said the Soviets would pull their nuclear missiles out of Cuba, if the United States would pull its nuclear missiles out of Turkey. After demanding assurances from the Soviets that the U.S. withdrawal of missiles from Turkey would never be publicly linked to the Soviet withdrawal of missiles from Cuba, Kennedy agreed and the crisis was ended on October 28 (Morganthau, 1992).

Time pressures, positive relations between the parties, and a commitment to a long-term working relationship all promote concession making (Fry, Firestone, & Williams, 1983; Smith, Pruitt, & Carnevale, 1982). Concessions are particularly unlikely when the issues involve basic physical and psychological needs such as life itself, security, honor, or identity (Pruitt, 1991b). One reason it is so difficult to negotiate with terrorist groups is that their lives and the honor of their groups are at stake. Terrorists demand concessions but are reluctant to make them. Governments who do make concessions to terrorist groups may solve the immediate crisis but often pay a heavy price in the future, because in this case concessions encourage future terrorist attacks—a contentious reaction (Hayes, 1991). For instance, paying ransom to terrorist groups for kidnapped leaders typically encourages further kidnappings.

Contending

Contentious tactics include using threats, making excessive demands, committing oneself to a position to force concessions from the other party, arguing or bullying, and putting time pressure on the other party. Threats, as discussed previously, can work when they are credible, but creating credible threats is difficult. Committing oneself to a position is most likely to lead to concessions when the commitment is public and justified by the reasons for the commitment, such as citing pressure from one's constituents (Schelling, 1960; Wall, 1977). Putting time pressure on the other side by creating deadlines can promote concession making, but it is a risky strategy because if the deadline fails, the party establishing the deadline must then follow through on its threats or risk losing credibility.

Contentious strategies often fail because they elicit contentious responses (e.g., threats elicit counterthreats) and because they reduce the chances of cooperative problem solving (Pruitt, 1991a). Interestingly, laboratory studies suggest that when both parties have equal capacities to threaten the other with contentious tactics, agreements are likely, presumably because each party is reluctant to experience the contentious responses of the other (Hornstein, 1965; Vitz & Kite, 1970). Recall that the concept of mutual reprisal capacity was the fundamental principle on which the nuclear power policy of mutually assured destruction (MAD) was founded. The policy was effective in preventing war, but at the enormous cost of having to maintain well-stocked nuclear arsenals.

Hostility between parties promotes the use of contentious tactics (Zubek, Pruitt, Peirce, & Iocolano, 1989). Consistent with this finding, one laboratory study found that contentious tactics are perceived to be more effective in intergroup negotiations than in negotiations between members of the same group (Rothbart & Hallmark, 1988).

In certain circumstances, contentious tactics can be very effective. A particularly interesting example of the successful use of contentious tactics concerns nonviolence. Its master practitioner, Mahatma Gandhi, used nonviolence against a militarily superior opponent to gain the independence of India. Gandhian nonviolence can only be used when the group using it is willing to sustain considerable suffering, because the use of strikes, boycotts, demonstrations, and other forms of civil disobedience often bring about violent counterreactions. After selecting an issue, such as the tax the British imposed on salt in India, Gandhi would select his tactics. Then he would get his followers to publicly commit themselves to the use of these tactics and to disavow violence. Next he would implement his tactics and escalate them when necessary. In the case just mentioned, Gandhi initiated a long, well-publicized march across India to defy the tax law by obtaining free salt from the sea. His followers in the salt march were beaten and many were arrested. His goal in using these tactics was to demonstrate the moral superiority of his cause. Nonviolent tactics were also used with great success by Martin Luther King during the civil rights movement in the United States in the 1960s. These tactics can only work against opponents who are susceptible to moral suasion and the force of public opinion. They are unlikely to be effective against ruthless opponents, such as a Hitler or a Saddam Hussein.

Problem Solving

Problem solving often occurs after contentious tactics have failed or when it is difficult to make concessions (Carnevale & Pruitt, 1992; Pruitt, 1991a). Problem solving involves attempts to find mutually satisfactory solutions to conflicts—to create what are known as win-win outcomes. Problem solving often entails compromising, but in some cases it may not. For instance, a solution to a dispute that enhances both sides' feelings of security may be reached with no compromises (e.g., if each side renounces the use of force against the other). When the Sandinistas, who were then in power in Nicaragua, agreed in 1988 to hold elections and renounced the use of force against the Contras (a revolutionary force), both groups experienced an increased sense of security because the chances of violent attack by the other side decreased.

Effective problem solving often requires that each party understands the goals, values, and needs of the other, a process that usually involves a substantial exchange of information (Pruitt & Rubin, 1986). Such information exchanges often rely on trust, which makes problem solving impossible in situations where the contending parties have little reason to trust one another. One reason that it was so difficult for Lebanon to re-create itself as a nation after the long civil war of the 1980s was that the level of distrust among the warring factions there was so high, due to the violence each group had committed against the other groups.

Problem-solving tactics include brainstorming, active listening (checking to see that one has understood the other side), empathy, and avoiding attacks on the other side, among others. The goals of using these tactics include: *expanding the pie,* in which both parties receive increased benefits; *cost cutting,* in which one party cuts the costs of the other party conceding; *compensation,* in which one party rewards the other for making a concession; *logrolling,* in which each party concedes on issues of low priority; and *bridging,* in which new options are developed that satisfy both parties (Pruitt, 1991a).

How would you classify the tactics involved in the policy used by the Italian government in the following example? In response to a wave of terrorism in the 1970s, Italy enacted a "repentant terrorist" law that allowed law enforcement officials to offer terrorists greatly reduced sentences and protection from reprisals for providing testimony against other members of their groups (Hayes, 1991). Terrorists who did not provide testimony against their groups were severely punished. When more than one member of a group was captured, they were isolated from one another and they were told they could get a reduced sentence by testifying against the others. However, if an individual did not give testimony and other members did, that individual would receive a stiff sentence. If none of the members gave testimony the government's case would be weakened and the members could all go free or receive light sentences.

From the perspective of the government, getting testimony in exchange for giving a reduced sentence involves cost cutting, since the government is reducing the costs to the terrorists of making concessions. From the perspective of the terrorists, getting a reduced sentence in exchange for giving testimony is a form of compensation, since a reduced sentence is a reward for making a concession. In this instance both sides get something they want. However, in the process, the terrorists must violate the trust their group has placed in them, so the choice to give testimony involves a loss for them as well. The policy works, despite this cost, because the government can back up its request with the use of a contentious threat tactic—a stiff sentence—which increases the costs of not giving testimony. This policy was found to be most effective when the members of the terrorist groups did not trust each other very much to begin with.

Problem solving is typically the dominant strategy used during mediation, the next topic of discussion.

Mediation

Mediation, the use of third parties to resolve disputes, is often an effective technique of conflict resolution (Pruitt & Kressel, 1985; Wall & Lynn, 1993). In many cases mediation is superior to resolving disputes by courtroom adjudication (McEwen & Maiman, 1981, 1989; Pearson & Theones, 1984, 1989; Roehl & Cook, 1985, 1989, but for an exception see Vidmar, 1985) and to resolving disputes through arbitration, in which a third party decides the dispute (Shapiro & Brett, 1993). Mediation is often less costly than adjudication (Pearson & Thoennes, 1984). In addition, compliance with mediated disputes and user satisfaction with mediation tend to be quite high (often over 75%) (Pearson & Theonnes, 1984; Roehl & Cook, 1985).

The role of the mediator includes setting agendas, gaining acceptance from the parties, controlling communication between the parties, identifying the issues or diagnosing the problems, meeting separately with the parties when necessary, suggesting solutions, encouraging problem solving, ''selling solutions,'' and sometimes threatening the parties with binding arbitration. Although not all mediation is the same, it typically proceeds through three stages: (1) *Setting the stage,* which involves clarifying ground rules and gathering information; (2) *Problem solving,* which involves posing issues and generating solutions; and (3) *Achieving a workable solution,* which can involve pressing the parties to reach an agreement (Pruitt, Welton, Fry, McGillicuddy, Castrianno, & Zubek, 1989).

Mediators who have a friendly manner and who have control over the process of the negotiations have been found to be the most successful (Prein, 1984; Tyler, 1987). Fair and impartial mediators generally create more satisfactory solutions to disputes (Shapiro & Brett, 1993), but impartiality is not crucial to the success of some types of mediation (Bercovitch, 1989). In fact, disputants sometimes prefer a mediator who is partial to one side because this mediator has special knowledge of that side or a capacity to work with that side. For instance, the United States selected Algeria to serve as a mediator when it successfully negotiated with Iran for the release of the captured American diplomats in 1980. Algeria was not selected because it was impartial, but because the U.S. government believed that the Algerians had the needed connections to high officials in the Iranian government and would be trusted by them (Zartman & Touval, 1985). Also, since Algeria hoped to improve its own relations with the United States, it had a stake in achieving a solution satisfactory to the United States.

Mediation tends to be most effective when the disputants are committed to finding a solution; when the issues involve concrete issues such as property or wages rather than general principles (e.g., honor); and when the parties are relatively equal in power (Bercovitch, 1989; Carnevale & Pruitt, 1992; Pruitt, McGillicuddy, Welton, & Fry, 1989). It is interesting to note that mediation is more effective when it is backed by the threat of arbitration than when there is no threat of arbitration (McGillicuddy, Welton, & Pruitt, 1987).

Mediation is most needed in intense disputes where there are high levels of conflict and hostility, although these are also the disputes that are most difficult to settle (Bercovitch, 1989; Kressel & Pruitt, 1989). In intense disputes, the most active mediators tend to be the most successful, while in less intense disputes, limited intervention by the mediator is often most effective. Specifically it has been found that in high-intensity disputes active, forceful mediator behavior, including posing problems to be solved and using pressure tactics, is most effective (Bercovitch, 1989; Donohue, 1989; Lim & Carnevale, 1990; Zubek, Pruitt, Peirce, & Iocolano, 1989).

Intergroup Workshops

A special case of mediation involves the use of small workshops consisting of members of the opposing sides to a dispute—not to resolve disputes, but to foster mutual understanding. Groups of researchers from Harvard, Yale, and London have pioneered this approach (Burton, 1972, 1987; Doob, 1974; Kelman, 1990; Kelman & Cohen, 1986; Rouhana & Kelman, 1994). They bring together members of the conflicting parties with a group leader from a third party. The participants are usually not the group leaders or their direct advisers (i.e., the president or cabinet members) but influential members of the group (e.g., prominent businesspeople or community leaders). During the *first stage* of their meetings they define the conflict. During the *second stage* they discuss the nature of conflict in general and their own conflict in particular. During the *third stage* they discuss options for resolving the conflict. Finally, during the *fourth stage* they attempt a solution, gather more information, redefine the conflict or suggest new options.

One such workshop brought together influential members of previously warring factions in Nicaragua to discuss human rights issues of mutual concern (Brenes, 1992). The participants found that issues such as the expropriation of land from large landowners by campesinos could be reduced to the bare essentials—in this case a sense of economic security on the one side and survival on the other. Both groups agreed that property rights exist and constitute an important element of identity, and this agreement on property rights was used as a basis for framing solutions to this problem.

The group leader attempts to present the conflict as a problem to be solved, not a contest to be won. He or she not only fosters a norm of analytical processing concerning the various aspects of the conflict but also encourages participants to express their feelings, hopes, and fears. The participants are encouraged to engage in role taking so they can consider the views of both sides when discussing solutions. The ultimate goal is to feed new ideas and changed perceptions into the decision-making processes within each group.

Workshops of the type just described have now been used to facilitate the resolution of a wide variety of conflicts. A particularly interesting workshop has been conducted with Blacks and Whites in South Africa (Kamfer & Venter, 1994), using members of these two groups who worked for the same large corporation. The goal of this workshop was to enable the two groups to work together effectively, despite the ethnic diversity that existed in the workplace. Mixed groups of about 25 people met for two days to discuss intergroup relations. People started by giving their names and several of their group identities (e.g., Black, female, Protestant). Then the group facilitator ''blurred'' these categories by asking people to stand in a box if they belonged to the groups mentioned (e.g., women, firstborn child, born in Pretoria). This made it clear that there were many crosscutting categories that brought different people together, in addition to the ''official'' racial designations of the government that served to divide them. In other exercises the participants anonymously wrote down the stereotypes they had of various groups, and then members of the stereotyped groups discussed how the stereotypes made them feel. Later, group members recalled instances in which they had been discriminated against. Toward the end of the workshop the participants were asked to discuss aspects of their groups in which they took pride and to discuss the meaning of belonging to certain superordinate groups (e.g., being a South African). Finally, the participants discussed techniques of dealing with everyday racial conflict situations and how to apply these techniques in their jobs and lives. Thus, the workshops taught the participants about stereotyping, discrimination, and some of the positive and negative aspects of group identity, along with techniques of conflict resolution.

Taken together, the studies on negotiation, mediation, and workshops make a very important point. Not all conflicts have destructive outcomes. It is also possible to deal with conflicts in constructive ways (Deutsch, 1994; Fisher, 1994; Ross, 1993; Rubin, 1994). For instance, one recent laboratory study found that intergroup negotiations can reduce prejudice (Thompson, 1993). A practical example is provided by a workshop conducted to facilitate resolution of the conflict between Turkish and Greek Cypriots by the Canadian Institute for International Peace and Security (Fisher, 1994). The workshop dealt with the needs and fears each side was experiencing and assisted them in providing assurances to each other to assuage those fears. The parties reached a consensus on the desired qualities of a renewed relationship. The participants reported that the workshops increased understanding and mutual empathy.

Based on his experiences conducting workshops for Israelis and Palestinians, Kelman (1978, 1987) has developed a set of prescriptions that facilitate constructive conflict resolution.

Each side should:

1. Acquire insight into the perspective of the other side.
2. Believe that there is someone to talk to and something to talk about.
3. Distinguish between the dreams and the operational programs of the other side.
4. Be persuaded that mutual concessions will create a new situation.
5. Be persuaded that structural changes conducive to a stable solution can take place.
6. Be responsive to psychological needs and concerns of the other side.

Although there is little hard empirical evidence on these factors, it has been suggested that addressing them can produce a more complex and subtle view of the other side, aid in identifying destructive interpretations of the actions of the other side, and facilitate the design of effective solutions (Ross, 1993).

Unilateral De-escalation

> Escalation and de-escalation . . . bear an intimate relation to the process of negotiation. It seems perfectly clear that the political policy of tension escalation, calculated or otherwise, can only hamper or even render impossible successful negotiation. It creates an atmosphere of resentment and distrust in which honest dealing cannot be expected. . . . Calculated de-escalation, on the other hand, is explicitly designed to create and maintain an atmosphere of mutual trust within which agreements of increasing significance become possible. (Osgood, 1966, pp. 29–30)

Intense conflicts often run the risk of escalating into violent confrontations. Misunderstandings abound, communication is poor or non-existent, mistrust, hostility, and stress levels are high, and hopes for resolution are dim. Is open conflict inevitable under these conditions? Not according to advocates of the Graduated and Reciprocated Initiatives in Tension-reduction (GRIT) strategy (Lindskold, 1986; Osgood, 1959, 1962, 1966). This strategy involves a series of steps that are designed to produce GRIT. This approach assumes that under some circumstances intense conflicts can be de-escalated through the use of unilateral concessions.

As outlined by Lindskold (1986), the preliminary steps necessary to initiate GRIT include: a general statement of intentions by one side to reduce tension through subsequent acts, a public announcement of the unilateral de-escalation in advance, and an invitation to the other side to reciprocate the de-escalation. After laying this groundwork, the initiator unilaterally implements the first de-escalation without requiring reciprocation. The initiator may then continue to make de-escalating moves, even in the absence of reciprocation. These initiatives are supposed to be unambiguous and open to verification by the other side. These conciliatory behaviors are intended to establish the credibility of the initiator. To avoid a skeptical response, the de-escalating move should involve some risk and place the initiator in a vulnerable position. The initiating party should also make it clear that it retains the capacity to retaliate. If the other side responds, the initiator must choose whether or not to match the size of the response in its subsequent de-escalations. The ultimate goal is to defuse the conflict through bilateral de-escalating. Unilateral de-escalation is used as a strategy to achieve this goal.

Experimental evidence is largely supportive of all of these points (reviewed by Lindskold, 1986). To illustrate this approach consider the following situation (known as the prisoner's dilemma), which is an experimental analogue to the Italian "repentant terrorist" law.

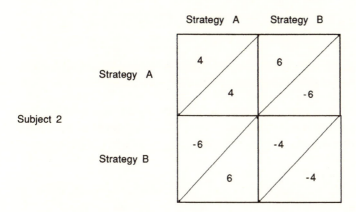

Note: The numbers above the diagonal are the payoffs for Subject 1 and the numbers below the diagonal are the payoffs for Subject 2.

FIGURE 6.3
The prisoner's dilemma.

Two people are asked to participate in a decision-making game in which the object is to accumulate as many points as possible by making strategic choices (figure 6.3). Each person has a choice of two strategies (A or B) and must select a strategy without knowing what strategy the other person has chosen. Imagine you are playing this game against us. If you want to get the highest number of points available, you should choose strategy B, but this will only work if we select strategy A. But if we are also trying to maximize our outcomes by choosing B, all of us lose. If you are willing to settle for a smaller reward, you can choose strategy A, as long as you trust us not to double-cross you by selecting strategy B. In the long run, both sides will be better off if they consistently choose strategy A, but in the short run it always pays better if one side betrays the other to get the high reward.

In studies using the prisoner's dilemma, the subjects make a series of choices and receive feedback on their outcomes after each choice. Research shows that if person 1 consistently chooses strategy A, person 2 takes advantage of 1 by choosing strategy B about 50 percent of the time (Oskamp, 1971). The highest outcomes occur when person 1 starts out with a string of strategy B decisions and then switches to continuous strategy A decisions. Apparently this communicates to person 2 that person 1 is willing to inflict costs on person 2 but would prefer to cooperate with person 2 to ensure continuous modest payoffs. This pattern of results shows a clear parallel to the GRIT idea that once a conflict is underway, one party can gain cooperation from the other if that party starts making consistent concessions (whether they are initially reciprocated or not), provided that it is clear that the first party is willing to retaliate if necessary. The prisoner's dilemma paradigm has also been used to demonstrate that using GRIT strategies increases the quality of future negotiations (Lindskold & Han, 1988). In this study, subjects first played the prisoner's dilemma game against an opponent who either used the GRIT strategy (an initial mixture of strategy choices followed by a written communication that he would engage in continuous cooperation) or was consistently competitive (including lying in a note about his intentions). The subjects then engaged in a bargaining task. Those who had previously had experience with the GRIT partner were better able to maximize their joint outcomes in the bargaining task than those who had experience with competitive partners.

A dramatic example of the use of GRIT occurred during the Cold War when the United States made a unilateral concession to the Soviet Union (Lindskold, 1986). In 1963, after the Cuban missile crisis, President Kennedy announced a "strategy for peace." He said the United States would unilaterally stop all atmospheric testing of nuclear weapons and would not resume it unless the Soviet Union did. The Soviets responded by agreeing to a request by the United States that UN observers be sent to the war-torn nation of Yemen. Next the United States unilaterally agreed to restore full recognition to the Hungarian delegation to the UN (Hungary was then part of the Soviet sphere of influence). A week after the initial speech, Premier Khrushchev announced that he had ordered a halt to the production of Soviet strategic bombers. Very shortly thereafter, the Soviet Union agreed to install a direct telephone line between the White House and the Kremlin that the United States had proposed a year earlier. A series of further reciprocal gestures followed, including the signing of an atmospheric test-ban treaty, approval of direct airline flights between the capitals of the two countries, and a pact not to orbit nuclear weapons. Thus, an initial unilateral de-escalation gesture produced a series of bilateral agreements.

GRIT is most likely to work when both sides are motivated to resolve the conflict peacefully and are in a position to make compromises. Unilateral concessions run the risk of an exploitative response by the other side and it is for this reason that the capacity and willingness to retaliate must be made clear. In GRIT, cooperation is combined with firmness. GRIT works best when the parties are relatively equal in power or when the superior party makes the concessions. When the weaker party makes unilateral concessions it can invite exploitation, but even the weaker party can sometimes achieve a breakthrough in a stalemated conflict by initiating a unilateral concession.

In 1967 Israel and Egypt engaged in a war that was costly to both sides. It was clear to both nations that Israel was militarily superior, but nonetheless Israel continued to fear attacks from Egypt and its other Middle Eastern neighbors. In 1971 Anwar Sadat offered to sign a peace treaty with Israel, if Israel would withdraw from the Sinai Peninsula. This offer was dismissed by Israel, in part because none of its neighbors had ever been willing to talk peace. This stalemate lasted until 1977, when Sadat unilaterally offered to travel to Israel to address its parliament concerning his peace offer. To make such an offer was extremely risky for Sadat personally, and it caused Egypt to lose the support of the Arab world. This conciliatory gesture was accepted by Israel and a peace treaty ensued largely because this act entailed such high costs to Sadat and it was so irrevocable (Lebow & Stein, 1987). This is an instance where the weaker party made a unilateral conciliatory move that was successful in getting the desired response, and where it is likely that a low-cost, reversible gesture would have failed.

Although unilateral concessions are typically made without the intervention of a third party, in some instances a third party induces one of the disputants to make a unilateral concession. A case-study analysis of 20 international disputes found that third-party mediation was an effective way of breaking cycles of mutual competition and coercion (Leng & Wheeler, 1979). Leng (1984) argues that firmness in response to coercion, combined with conciliatory initiatives, can be an effective policy. He argues that during the Cold War, the United States obtained more favorable outcomes when inducements were backed by threats than when it used inducements or threats alone.

The overall conclusion that can be drawn from the literature on negotiation and unilateral de-escalation has been nicely summarized by Patchen (1988):

> [A] successful policy . . . is one that combines a measure of
> firmness and a measure of flexibility, both a willingness to
> vigorously resist coercion by an adversary and a willingness to

reciprocate and sometimes initiate concessions. By words and especially by deeds, it is important to show the adversary that one will not be exploited but also that one is ready to cooperate. The adversary should be convinced that there is little to be gained by coercion and much to be gained by cooperation. (p. 342)

A Methodological Caveat

The research on conflict resolution just discussed rests on a somewhat shaky database. Three types of methods underlie the conclusions offered in this chapter. First, investigators have examined individual case histories or done comparative analyses of case studies of actual conflicts. Second, investigators have run simulations of conflict situations done in the laboratory or by computer. Third, experimentally oriented investigators have conducted laboratory experiments.

A prime concern with all of these types of methods is the issue of generalizability. Case studies are typically not representative and the samples tend to be small. In many instances they involve international conflicts, and the extent to which it is appropriate to generalize the results concerning international conflicts to smaller-scale conflicts is questionable. The correlational nature of the results obtained from these studies makes establishing causality difficult. Simulations, when they are done in the laboratory, are quite artificial and the sample sizes again are often very small. Computer simulations run the risk of not including a sufficient number of relevant variables and of underestimating the complexity of human behavior. Laboratory studies of conflict, such as those involving games, are often as artificial as simulations and frequently examine individuals rather than groups, thus making it difficult to generalize to intergroup conflicts. Laboratory experiments and simulations both tend to be of short duration and cannot involve the full range of contentious, conciliatory, or problem-solving tactics involved in real-world negotiations (e.g., violence cannot be threatened or used). The limitations of these techniques mean that all of the conclusions presented in this chapter should be regarded as somewhat tentative (except this one, of course).

Summary

Intergroup conflict occurs when groups attempt to achieve incompatible goals or when one group attempts to impose its values on another. It has a variety of causes. Intergroup conflicts can be caused by real competition for scarce resources or power, or by real differences in values, beliefs, or norms. Conflict may also come about when one group perceives that it is deprived relative to another group. This type of conflict is more likely when social comparisons are made with more-advantaged outgroups. Feelings of relative deprivation are more likely when the ingroup experiences rising expectations than when its expectations are falling or stationary. In addition, conflict may arise when the basic psychological needs of the group for identity, recognition, security, or participation are denied. Such needs cannot be negotiated away. To resolve need-based conflicts, the needs of both groups must be met. Realistic group conflict, relative deprivation, and unmet needs result in hatred, anger, and ethnocentrism, which may themselves promote conflict by antagonizing the outgroup.

Some conflicts can be managed through deterrence—the use of threats. Deterrence is unlikely to permanently resolve conflicts and often results in hostile or contentious responses. The use of deterrence assumes that groups make rational decisions based largely on avoiding costs, but research suggests that these assumptions may not be valid. For a deterrent designed to instill fear to be effective, the threatened consequences must be seen as inescapable and highly probable, and the threatened group must be capable of making the requested change.

Negotiation and mediation are usually more effective techniques of resolving conflicts than deterrence. Negotiation occurs when the parties to a conflict discuss solutions. In attempting to solve a conflict, the parties may be concerned with their own outcomes and/or with the outcomes of the other party. The most successful form of concession making involves a tit-for-tat strategy. Contentious tactics often elicit contentious responses and this leads them to fail. When contentious tactics fail, they are often followed by attempts at problem solving. The goal of problem-solving tactics is to expand the pie, cut the costs of making concessions, compensate for losses, engage in logrolling, or find bridging solutions.

Mediation occurs when negotiations are facilitated by a third party who sets agendas, identifies issues, diagnoses the problems, suggests solutions, and encourages their acceptance. In some types of mediation, the facilitators need not be impartial. If the conflict is an intense one, the facilitators may have to be active and forceful to succeed. It is helpful if the parties are committed to resolving the conflict, the issues do not involve general principles, and the parties are equal in power. Analytical intergroup workshops designed to increase understanding and generate solutions are often a useful prelude to full-scale negotiations.

In intense conflicts that are stalemated, unilateral de-escalation can sometimes break the impasse. The party utilizing this technique makes it known that it will make a unilateral concession and invites reciprocation. The concession-making party should make it clear that it retains the capacity to retaliate if the other side takes undue advantage of the concession. Unilateral concessions are most likely to succeed if they are made by the stronger party, but they are sometimes successful when made by the weaker party.

REFERENCES

Abe, H., & Wiseman, R. L. (1983). A cross-cultural confirmation of the dimensions of intercultural effectiveness. *International Journal of Intercultural Relations, 7,* 53–67.

Abeles, R. P. (1976). Relative deprivation, rising expectations, and black militancy. *Journal of Social Issues, 32,* 119–138.

Abrams, D., & Hogg, M. A. (1990). *Social identity theory: Constructive and critical advances.* New York: Springer-Verlag.

Ackerman, N., & Jahoda, M. (1950). *Anti-Semitism and emotional disorders: A psycho-analytic interpretation.* New York: Harper.

Adlerfer, C. P. (1982). Problems of changing white males' behavior and beliefs concerning race relations. In P. Goodman & associates (Eds.), *Change in organizations* (pp. 122–165). San Francisco: Jossey-Bass.

Adorno, T. W., Frenkel-Brunswick, E., Levinson, D. J., & Sanford, R. N. (1950). *The authoritarian personality.* New York: Harper.

Ajzen, I., & Fishbein, M. (1977). Attitude-behavior relations: A theoretical analysis and a review of empirical research. *Psychological Bulletin, 84,* 888–918.

Al-Zahrini, S. S. A. (1991). Cross-cultural differences in attributions of responsibility to the self, the family, the ingroup, and the outgroup in the USA and Saudi Arabia. Unpublished doctoral dissertation, University of Michigan. Cited in P. B. Smith & M. H. Bond. (1993). *Social psychology across cultures.* Boston: Allyn & Bacon.

Albert, R. D. (1983). The intercultural sensitizer or culture assimilator: A cognitive approach. In D. Landis & R. W. Brislin (Eds.), *Handbook of intercultural training* (Vol. 2). New York: Pergamon.

Albert, R. D., & Adamopoulos, J. (1980). An attributional approach to culture learning: The culture assimilator. In M. P. Hamnett & R. W. Brislin (Eds.), *Research in culture learning: Language and conceptual studies.* Honolulu: Culture Learning Institute, East-West Center.

Albert, R. D., & Triandis, H. C. (1979). Cross-cultural training: A theoretical framework and some observations. In H. Trueba & C. Barnett-Mizrahi (Eds.), *Bilingual multicultural education and the professional: From theory to practice*. Rowley, MA: Newbury House.

Allen, V. L., & Wilder, D. A. (1975). Categorization, belief similarity, and group discrimination. *Journal of Personality and Social Psychology, 32*, 971–977.

Allport, F. H., et al. (1953). The effects of segregation and the consequences of desegregation: A social science statement. *Minnesota Law Review, 37*, 429–440.

Allport, G. W. (1954). *The nature of prejudice*. Reading, MA: Addison-Wesley.

Amir, Y. (1976). The role of intergroup contact in change of prejudice and race relations. In P. Katz & D. A. Taylor (Eds.), *Towards the elimination of racism* (pp. 245–308). New York: Pergamon.

Anderson, J. R. (1983). *The architecture of cognition*. Cambridge, MA: Harvard University Press.

Archer, D. (1985). Social deviance. In G. Lindzey & E. Aronson (Eds.), *Handbook of social psychology* (3rd ed., Vol. 2, pp. 743–804). New York: Random House.

Armor, D. J. (1980). White flight and the future of desegregation. In W. Stephan & J. Feagin (Eds.), *School desegregation: Past, present, and future*. New York: Plenum.

Armor, D. J. (1988). School busing: A time for change. In P. A. Katz & D. A. Taylor (Eds.), *Eliminating racism: Profiles in controversy* (pp. 259–280). New York: Plenum.

Aronson, E., Blaney, N., Stephan, C., Sikes, J., & Snapp, M. (1978). *The jigsaw classroom*. Beverly Hills, CA: Sage.

Aronson, E., & Thibodeau, R. (1992). The jigsaw classroom: A cooperative strategy for reducing prejudice. In J. Lynch, C. Modgil, & S. Modgil (Eds.), *Cultural diversity in the schools* (Vol. 2, pp. 231–256). London: Falmer Press.

Ashmore, R. D. (1970). The problem of intergroup prejudice. In B. Collins (Ed.), *Social psychology* (pp. 247–297). Reading, MA: Addison-Wesley.

Associated Press. (1993). Schools regressing toward segregation. *Las Cruces Sun News*, Dec. 14, 1993.

Astin, A. (1982). *Minorities in American education*. San Francisco: Jossey-Bass.

Axelrod, R. (1984). *The evolution of cooperation*. New York: Basic Books.

Azar, E. E. (1986). Protracted international conflicts: Ten propositions. In E. E. Azar & R. W. Burton (Eds.), *International conflict resolution: Theory and practice* (pp. 28–39). Boulder, CO: Lynne Reiner Publishers.

Babiker, I. E., Cox, J. L., & Miller, P. M. C. (1980). The measurement of culture distance and its relationship to medical consultation, symptomatology and examination performance of overseas students at Edinburgh University. *Social Psychiatry, 15*, 109–116.

Baker, S. M., & Devine, P. G. (1988). *Faces as primes for stereotype activation*. Paper presented at the Midwestern Psychological Association, Chicago, IL.

Banaji, M. R., Hardin, C., & Rothman, A. J. (1993). Implicit stereotyping in person judgment. *Journal of Personality and Social Psychology, 65,* 272–281.

Bar-Tal, D. (1990). Causes and consequences of delegitimation: Models of conflict and ethnocentrism. *Journal of Social Issues, 46,* 65–82.

Bargh, J. A. (1984). Automatic and conscious processing of social information. In R. S. Wyer, & T. K. Srull (Eds.), *Handbook of social cognition* (pp. 1–44). Hillsdale, NJ: Erlbaum.

Bargh, J. A. (1988). Automatic information processing: Implications for communication and affect. In L. Donophew, H. E. Sypher, & T. E. Higgins (Eds.), *Communication, social cognition and affect* (pp. 9–32). Hillsdale, NJ: Erlbaum.

Barna, L. M. (1983). The stress factor in intercultural relations. In D. Landis & R. W. Brislin (Eds.), *Handbook of intercultural training, Vol II: Issues in training methodology.* New York: Pergamon.

Barnlund, D. C. (1989). *Communicative styles of Japanese and Americans.* Belmont, CA: Wadsworth.

Begley, T. M., & Alker, H. (1982). Anti-busing protests: Attitudes and actions. *Social Psychology Quarterly, 45,* 187–197.

Ben-Yoav, O., & Pruitt, D. G. (1984). Resistance to yielding and the expectation of cooperative future interaction in negotiation. *Journal of Experimental Social Psychology, 20,* 323–353.

Benton, A. A., Kelley, H. H., & Liebling, B. (1972). Effects of extremity of offers and concession rate on the outcomes of bargaining. *Journal of Personality and Social Psychology, 23,* 78–83.

Bercovitch, J. (1989). International dispute resolution: A comparative empirical analysis. In K. Kressel, D. G. Pruitt, & associates (Eds.), *Mediation research: The process and effectiveness of third-party intervention* (pp. 284–299). San Francisco: Jossey-Bass.

Bettencourt, B. A., Brewer, M. B., Rogers-Croak, M., & Miller, N. (1992). Cooperation and the reduction of intergroup bias: The role of reward structure and social orientation. *Journal of Experimental Social Psychology, 28,* 301–319.

Bhawuk, D. P. S. (1990). Cross-cultural orientation programs. In R. W. Brislin (Ed.), *Applied cross-cultural psychology.* Newbury Park, CA: Sage.

Billing, M., & Tajfel, H. (1973). Social categorization and similarity in intergroup behavior. *European Journal of Social Psychology, 3,* 27–52.

Black Enterprise. (1992). Identifying 1990s racism. November 23, p. 49.

Black, J. S., & Mendenhall, M. (1990). Cross-cultural training effectiveness: A review and theoretical framework for future research. *Academy of Management Review, 15,* 113–136.

Blanchard, F. A., Adelman, L., & Cook, S. W. (1975). Effect of group success and failure upon interpersonal attraction in cooperating interracial groups. *Journal of Personality and Social Psychology, 31,* 1020–1030.

Blanchard, F. A., & Cook, S. W. (1976). Effects of helping a less competent member of a cooperating interracial group on the development of interpersonal attraction. *Journal of Personality and Social Psychology, 34,* 1245–1255.

Blanchard, F. A., Weigel, R. H., & Cook, S. W. (1975). The effect of competence of group members upon interpersonal attraction in cooperating interracial groups. *Journal of Personality and Social Psychology, 32,* 519–530.

Blaney, N., Stephan, C., Rosenfield, D., Aronson, E., & Sikes, J. (1977). Interdependence in the classroom: A field study. *Journal of Educational Psychology, 69,* 121–128.

Blumberg, R. G., & Roye, W. J. (1980). *Interracial bonds.* New York: General Hall.

Bobo, L. (1983). Whites' opposition to busing: Symbolic racism or realistic group conflict? *Journal of Personality and Social Psychology, 45,* 1196–1210.

Bobo, L. (1985). *Racial differences in response to the black political movement.* Paper presented at the Annual Meeting of the American Sociological Association, Washington, D.C.

Bobo, L. (1988). Group conflict, prejudice, and the paradox of contemporary racial attitudes. In P. A. Katz & D. A. Taylor (Eds.), *Eliminating racism: Profiles in controversy* (pp. 85–116). New York: Plenum.

Bochner, S. (1982). The social psychology of cross-cultural relations. In S. Bochner (Ed.), *Cultures in contact* (pp. 5–44). New York: Pergamon.

Bodenhausen, G. V. (1988). Stereotypic biases in social decision making and memory: Testing process models for stereotype use. *Journal of Personality and Social Psychology, 55,* 726–737.

Bodenhausen, G. V. (1993). Emotions, arousal, and stereotype judgments: A heuristic model of affect and stereotyping. In D. M. Mackie & D. L. Hamilton (Eds.), *Affect, cognition and stereotyping: Interactive processes in group perception* (pp. 13–37). Orlando, FL: Academic Press.

Bodenhausen, G. V., Kramer, G. P., & Susser, K. (1993). *Happiness and stereotypic thinking in social judgment.* Unpublished manuscript, Michigan State University, East Lansing.

Bodenhausen, G. V., Sheppard, L. A., & Kramer, G. P. (in press). Negative affect and social judgment. *European Journal of Social Psychology.*

Bodenhausen, G. V., & Wyer, R. S., Jr. (1985). Effects of stereotypes on decision making and information-processing strategies. *Journal of Personality and Social Psychology, 48,* 267–282.

Bogardus, E. S. (1925). Measuring social distance. *Journal of Applied Sociology, 9,* 299–308.

Bond, M. H. (1988). Finding the universal dimensions of individual variation in multicultural studies of values: The Rokeach and Chinese value surveys. *Journal of Personality and Social Psychology, 55,* 1009–1015.

Bond, M. H. (1991). Cultural influences on modes of impression management: Implications of the culturally diverse organization. In R. A. Giacolone & P. Rosenfeld (Eds.), *Applied impression management.* Newbury Park, CA: Sage.

Bond, M. H. (1994). Continuing encounters with Hong Kong. In W. J. Lonner & R. Malpass (Eds.), *Psychology and culture.* Boston: Allyn & Bacon.

Bond, M. H., Hewstone, M., Wan, K.-C., & Chiu, C.-K. (1985). Group-serving attributions across intergroup contexts: Cultural differences in the explanation of sex-typed behaviors. *European Journal of Social Psychology, 15,* 435–451.

Bond, M. H., Leung, K., & Wan, K.-C. (1982). How does cultural collectivism operate? The impact of task and maintenance contributions on reward allocation. *Journal of Cross-Cultural Psychology, 13,* 186–200.

Bond, M. H., Wan, K.-C., Leung, K., & Giacolone, R. A. (1985). How are responses to verbal insult related to cultural collectivism and power distance? *Journal of Cross-Cultural Psychology, 16,* 111–127.

Borgida, E., & Omoto, A. M. (1986). *Racial stereotyping and prejudice: The role of personal involvement.* Paper presented at the Annual Meeting of the American Psychological Association, Washington, DC.

Boski, P. (1983). A study of person perception in Nigeria: Ethnicity and self versus other attributions for achievement-related outcomes. *Journal of Cross-Cultural Psychology, 14,* 85–108.

Bower, G. H. (1980). Mood and memory. *American Psychologist, 36,* 129–148.

Boxer, A. H. (1969). *Experts in Asia: An inquiry into Australian technical assistance.* Canberra: Australian National University Press.

Braddock, J. H. II. (1987). *The impact of segregated school experiences on college and major field choices of black high school graduates: Evidence from the high school and beyond survey.* Paper presented at the National Conference on School Desegregation, University of Chicago.

Braddock, J. H. II, Crain, R., & McPartland, J. (1984). A long-term view of desegregation: Some recent studies of graduates as adults. *Phi Delta Kappan, 66,* 259–264.

Braddock, J. H. II, & McPartland, J. (1982). Assessing school desegregation effects: New directions in research. *Research in Sociology of Education and Socialization, 3.*

Braddock, J. H. II, & McPartland, J. (1983). *More evidence on the social-psychological processes that perpetuate minority segregation: The relationship of school desegregation and employment desegregation.* Baltimore: Johns Hopkins University.

Braddock, J. H. II, & McPartland, J. (1987). How minorities continue to be excluded from equal employment opportunities: Research on labor market and institutional barriers. *Journal of Social Issues, 43,* 5–39.

Braddock, J. H. II, & McPartland, J. (1988). The social and academic consequences of school desegregation. *Equity and Choice,* Feb. 5–10, 63–73.

Braddock, J. H. II, McPartland, J., & Trent, W. (1984). *Desegregated schools and desegregated work environments.* Paper presented at the American Educational Research Association.

Bradley, L. A., & Bradley, G. W. (1977). The academic achievement of black students in desegregated schools: A critical review. *Review of Educational Research, 47,* 377–449.

Breckler, S. J., & Wiggins, E. C. (1989). Affect versus evaluation in the structure of attitudes. *Journal of Experimental Social Psychology, 25,* 253–271.

Brein, M., & David, K. H. (1971). Intercultural communication and the adjustment of the sojourner. *Psychological Bulletin, 76,* 215–230.

Brenes, A. (1992). Personal communication. Universidad de Costa Rica, San Jose, Costa Rica.

Brewer, M. B. (1979). In-group bias in the minimal intergroup situation: A cognitive-motivational analysis. *Psychological Bulletin, 86,* 307–324.

Brewer, M. B. (1986). The role of ethnocentrism in intergroup conflict. In S. Worchel & W. G. Austin (Eds.), *Psychology of intergroup relations* (2nd ed.). Chicago: Nelson-Hall.

Brewer, M. B., & Campbell, D. T. (1976). *Ethnocentrism and intergroup attitudes: East African evidence.* New York: Halsted.

Brewer, M. B., Dull, V., & Lui, L. (1981). Perceptions of the elderly: Stereotypes as prototypes. *Journal of Personality and Social Psychology, 46,* 646–670.

Brewer, M. B., Ho, H., Lee, J., & Miller, N. (1987). Social identity and social distance among Hong Kong schoolchildren. *Personality and Social Psychology Bulletin, 13,* 156–165.

Brewer, M. B., & Kramer, R. (1985). The psychology of intergroup attitudes and behavior. *Annual Review of Psychology, 36,* 219–243.

Brewer, M. B., & Miller, N. (1984). Beyond the contact hypothesis: Theoretical perspectives on desegregation. In N. Miller & M. B. Brewer (Eds.), *Groups in contact: The psychology of desegregation* (pp. 281–302). Orlando: Academic Press.

Brewer, M. B., & Miller, N. (1988). Contact and cooperation: When do they work. In P. A. Katz & D. A. Taylor (Eds.), *Eliminating racism: Profiles in controversy* (pp. 315–326). New York: Plenum.

Bridgeman, D. L. (1977). *The influence of cooperative interdependent learning on role taking and moral reasoning: A theoretical and empirical field study with fifth-grade students.* Unpublished doctoral dissertation, University of California, Santa Cruz.

Brigham, J. C. (1971). Ethnic stereotypes. *Psychological Bulletin, 76,* 15–38.

Brislin, R. W. (1981). *Cross-cultural encounters: Face-to-face interaction.* New York: Pergamon.

Brislin, R. W., Cushner, K., Cherrie, C., & Yong, M. (1986). *Intercultural interactions: A practical guide.* Beverly Hills: Sage.

Brislin, R. W., Landis, D., & Brandt, M. E. (1983). Conceptualizations of intercultural behavior and training. In D. Landis & R. W. Brislin (Eds.), *Handbook of intercultural training* (Vol. 1). New York: Pergamon.

Brislin, R. W., & Pedersen, P. (1976). *Cross-cultural orientation programs.* New York: Gardner Press.

Brown, R., & Wade, G. (1987). Superordinate goals and intergroup behavior: The effect of role ambiguity and status on intergroup attitudes and task performance. *European Journal of Social Psychology, 17,* 131–142.

Brown, R. J., & Abrams, D. (1986). The effects of intergroup similarity and goal interdependence on intergroup attitudes and task performance. *Journal of Experimental Social Psychology, 22,* 78–92.

Bruner, J. (1958). Social psychology and perception. In E. E. Maccoby, T. M. Newcomb, & E. L. Hartley (Eds.), *Readings in social psychology*. New York: Holt.

Bruner, J. S. (1973). *Beyond the information given*. New York: Norton.

Burnstein, E., & McCrae, A. U. (1962). Some effects of shared threat and prejudice in racially mixed groups. *Journal of Abnormal and Social Psychology, 64*, 257–260.

Burton, J. W. (1972). Conflict resolution. *International Studies Quarterly, 16*, 41–52.

Burton, J. W. (1986). The procedures of conflict resolution. In E. E. Azar & R. W. Burton (Eds.), *International conflict resolution: Theory and practice* (pp. 92–116). Boulder, CO: Lynne Reiner Publishers.

Burton, J. W. (1987). *Resolving deep-rooted conflict*. Lanham, MD: University Press of America.

Campbell, D. T. (1967). Stereotypes and the perception of group differences. *American Psychologist, 22*, 812–829.

Carnevale, P. J., & Keenan, P. A. (1990). *Decision frame and social goals in integrative bargaining: The likelihood of agreement versus the quality*. Paper presented at the Annual Meeting of the International Association of Conflict Management, Vancouver, BC. Cited in Carnevale, P. J., & Pruitt, D. G. (1992). Negotiation and mediation. *Annual Review of Psychology, 43*, 531–582.

Carnevale, P. J., & Pruitt, D. G. (1992). Negotiation and mediation. *Annual Review of Psychology, 43*, 531–582.

Carter, D. E., Detine, S. L., Spero, J., & Benson, F. W. (1975). Peer acceptance and school related variables in an integrated junior high school. *Journal of Educational Psychology, 67*, 267–273.

Chaiken, S., & Stangor, C. (1987). Attitudes and attitude change. *Annual Review of Psychology, 38*, 575–630.

Chinese Cultural Connection. (1987). Chinese values and the search for culture-free dimensions of culture. *Journal of Cross-Cultural Psychology, 18*, 143–164.

Clark, M. S., & Isen, A. M. (1982). Toward understanding the relationship between feeling states and social behavior. In A. Hastorf & A. M. Isen (Eds.), *Cognitive social psychology* (pp. 73–108). New York: Elsevier North-Holland.

Cohen, E. (1980). Design and redesign of the desegregated school: Problems of status, power, and conflict. In W. G. Stephan & J. Feagin (Eds.), *School desegregation* (pp. 251–280). New York: Plenum.

Cohen, E. (1984). The desegregated school: Problems of status, power and interethnic climate. In N. Miller & M. B. Brewer (Eds.), *Groups in contact* (pp. 77–96). New York: Academic Press.

Cohen, E., & Roper, S. (1972). Modification of interracial interaction disability: An application of status characteristics theory. *American Sociological Review, 37*, 643–657.

Cohen, S. P., & Azar, E. E. (1981). From war to peace: The transition between Egypt and Israel. *Journal of Conflict Resolution, 25*, 87–114.

Cook, S. W. (1962). The systematic study of socially significant events: A strategy for social research. *Journal of Social Issues, 18*, 66–84.

Cook, S. W. (1969). Motives in a conceptual analysis of attitude-related behavior. In W. J. Arnold & D. Levine (Eds.), *Nebraska symposium on motivation* (Vol. 18, pp. 179–236). Lincoln, NE: University of Nebraska Press.

Cook, S. W. (1979). Social science and school desegregation: Did we mislead the Supreme Court? *Personality and Social Psychology Bulletin, 5,* 420–437.

Cook, S. W. (1984). The 1954 social science statement and school desegregation: A reply to Gerard. *American Psychologist, 39,* 819–832.

Cook, S. W. (1985). Experimenting on social issues: The case of school desegregation. *American Psychologist, 40,* 452–460.

Costrich, N. J., Feinstein, L., Kidder, L., Marachek, J., & Pascale, L. (1975). When stereotypes hurt: Three studies of penalties for sex-role reversal. *Journal of Experimental Social Psychology, 11,* 520–530.

Crain, R. (1970). School integration and occupational achievement of Negroes. *American Journal of Sociology, 75,* 593–606.

Crain, R., & Mahard, R. (1978a). Desegregation and black achievement: A review of the research. *Law and Contemporary Problems, 42,* 17–56.

Crain, R., & Mahard, R. (1978b). School racial composition and black college attendance and achievement test performance. *Sociology of Education, 51,* 81–101.

Crain, R., & Straus, J. (1986). *School desegregation and black occupational attainments: Results from a long-term experiment.* Unpublished report. Baltimore: Johns Hopkins University.

Crain, R., & Weisman, C. (1972). *Discrimination, personality and achievement.* New York: Seminar Press.

Crain, R. L., Hawes, J. A., Miller, R. L., & Peichert, J. A. (1985). *Finding niches: Desegregated students 16 years later.* Report R3243-NIE. Santa Monica, CA: The Rand Corporation.

Crocker, J., Fiske, S. T., & Taylor, S. E. (1984). Schematic bases of belief change. In R. Eiser (Ed.), *Attitude judgment* (pp. 197–226). New York: Springer.

Crocker, J., Hannah, D. B., & Weber, R. (1983). Person memory and causal attributions. *Journal of Personality and Social Psychology, 44,* 55–66.

Crocker, J., & Major, B. (1989). Social stigma and self-esteem: The self-protective properties of stigma. *Psychological Review, 96,* 608–630.

Crocker, J., Voelkl, K., Testa, M., & Major, B. (1991). Social stigma: The affective consequences of attributional ambiguity. *Journal of Personality and Social Psychology, 60,* 218–228.

Crosby, F. (1982). *Relative deprivation and working women.* New York: Oxford University Press.

Crosby, F. J., Pufall, A., Snyder, R. S., O'Connell, M., & Whalen, P. (1989). The denial of personal disadvantage among you, me, and all the other ostriches. In M. Crawford & M. Gentry (Eds.), *Gender and thought: Psychological perspectives.* New York: Springer-Verlag.

Darley, J. M., Fleming, J. H., Hilton, J. L., & Swann, W. B., Jr. (1986). *Dispelling negative expectancies: The impact of interaction goals and target characteristics on the expectation confirmation process.* Unpublished manuscript, Princeton University.

Darley, J. M., & Gross, P. H. (1983). A hypothesis-confirming bias in labeling effects. *Journal of Personality and Social Psychology, 44,* 20–43.

Deaux, K., & Lewis, L. L. (1984). Structure of gender stereotypes: Interrelationships among components and gender label. *Journal of Personality and Social Psychology, 46,* 991–1004.

deCallieres, F. (1716, reissued in 1976). *On the matter of negotiating with princes.* Notre Dame, IN: Notre Dame University Press.

de Heusch, L. (1964). Massacres colletif ua Rwanda. *Synthesis, 19,* 416–426.

Desforges, D. M., Lord, C. G., Ramsey, S. L., Mason, J. A., VanLeeuven, M. D., West, S. C., & Lepper, M. R. (1991). Effects of structured cooperative contact on changing negative attitudes toward stigmatized social groups. *Journal of Personality and Social Psychology, 60,* 531–544.

deTocqueville, A. (1856, reissued in 1955). *The old regime and the French revolution.* New York: Harper Bros.

Deutsch, M. (1949). A theory of cooperation and competition. *Human Relations, 2,* 129–152.

Deutsch, M. (1994). Constructive conflict resolution: Principles, training and research. *Journal of Social Issues, 50,* 13–32.

Devine, P. G. (1989). Sterotypes and prejudice: Their automatic and controlled components. *Journal of Personality and Social Psychology, 56,* 5–18.

Devine, P. G., & Baker, S. M. (1991). Measurement of racial subtyping. *Personality and Social Psychology Bulletin, 17,* 44–50.

Devine, P. G., Hirt, E. R., & Gehrke, E. M. (1990). Diagnostic and confirmation strategies in trait hypothesis testing. *Journal of Personality and Social Psychology, 58,* 952–963.

Devine, P. G., Monteith, M. J., Zuwerink, J. R., & Elliot, A. J. (1991). Prejudice with and without compunction. *Journal of Personality and Social Psychology, 60,* 817–830.

DeVries, D. L., & Edwards, K. J. (1974). Student teams and learning games: Their effects on cross-race and cross-sex interaction. *Journal of Educational Psychology, 66,* 741–749.

DeVries, D. L., & Slavin, R. E. (1978). Teams-games-tournament (TGT): Review of 10 classroom experiments. *Journal of Research and Development in Education, 12,* 28–38.

Diehl, M. (1989). Justice and discrimination between minimal groups: The limits of equity. *British Journal of Social Psychology, 28,* 227–239.

Dodd, C. H. (1982). *Dynamics of intercultural communication.* Dubuque, IA: Wm. C. Brown.

Doise, W. (1978). *Groups and individuals: Explanations in social psychology.* Cambridge: Cambridge University Press.

Dollard, J., Doob, L., Miller, N. E., Mowrer, O., & Sears, R. (1939). *Frustration and aggression.* New Haven: Yale University Press.

Donnerstein, E. M., & Donnerstein, M. (1972). White rewarding behavior as a function of Black retaliation. *Journal of Personality and Social Psychology, 24,* 327–333.

Donnerstein, E. M., & Donnerstein, M. (1973). Variables in interracial aggression: Potential ingroup censure. *Journal of Personality and Social Psychology, 27,* 143–150.

Donohue, W. A. (1989). Communicative competence in mediators. In K. Kressel, D. G. Pruitt, & associates (Eds.), *Mediation research: The process and effectiveness of third-party intervention* (pp. 322–343). San Francisco: Jossey-Bass.

Doob, L. W. (1974). A Cyprus workshop: An exercise in intervention methodology. *Journal of Social Psychology, 84,* 161–178.

Dovidio, J. F., Evans, N., & Tyler, R. B. (1986). Racial stereotypes: The contents and their cognitive representation. *Journal of Experimental Social Psychology, 22,* 22–37.

Dovidio, J. F., & Gaertner, S. L. (1981). The effects of race, status, and ability on helping behavior. *Social Psychology Quarterly, 44,* 192–203.

Dovidio, J. F., & Gaertner, S. L. (1983a). Race, normative structure, and help-seeking. In B. M. DePaulo, A. Nadler, & J. D. Fisher (Eds.), *New directions in helping* (Vol. 2). New York: Academic Press.

Dovidio, J. F., & Gaertner, S. L. (1983b). The effects of sex, status, and ability on helping behavior. *Journal of Applied Social Psychology, 13,* 191–205.

Dovidio, J. F., & Gaertner, S. L. (1986). Prejudice, discrimination, and racism: Historical and contemporary approaches. In J. F. Dovidio & S. L. Gaertner (Eds.), *Prejudice, discrimination, and racism* (pp. 1–34). New York: Academic Press.

Du Bois, C. (1956). *Foreign students and higher education in the United States.* Washington: American Council on Education.

Duckitt, J. (1992a). *The social psychology of prejudice.* New York: Praeger.

Duckitt, J. (1992b). Psychology and prejudice: A historical analysis and integrative framework. *American Psychologist, 47,* 1182–1193.

Duncan, B. (1976). Differential social perception and attribution of intergroup violence: Testing the lower limits of stereotyping Blacks. *Journal of Personality and Social Psychology, 34,* 590–598.

Dutta, S., Kanungo, R. N., & Freibergs, V. (1972). Retention of affective material: Effects of intensity of affect on retrieval. *Journal of Personality and Social Psychology, 23,* 65–80.

Eagly, A. H., & Chaiken, S. (1992). *The psychology of attitudes.* San Diego, CA: Harcourt Brace Jovanovich.

Elon, A. (1993). The peacemakers. *The New Yorker, 59* (Dec. 20), 77–85.

Epstein, J. A., & Harackiewicz, J. M. (1992). Winning is not enough: The effects of competition and achievement orientation on intrinsic interest. *Personality and Social Psychology Bulletin, 18,* 128–138.

Erber, R. (1991). Affective and semantic priming: Effects of mood on category accessibility and inference. *Journal of Experimental Social Psychology, 27,* 480–498.

Erber, R., & Fiske, S. T. (1984). Outcome dependency and attention to inconsistent information. *Journal of Personality and Social Psychology, 47,* 709–726.

Eshel, S., & Peres, Y. (1973). The integration of a minority group: A causal model. Cited in Amir, Y. (1976). The role of intergroup contact in change of prejudice and race relations. In P. Katz (Ed.), *Towards the elimination of racism* (pp. 245–308). New York: Pergamon.

Esses, V. M., Haddock, G., & Zanna, M. P. (1990). The role of mood in the expression of stereotypes. In M. P. Zanna & J. M. Olson (Eds.), *The psychology of prejudice: The Ontario symposium* (Vol. 7). Hillsdale: Erlbaum.

Farley, R. (1985). Three steps forward and two back? Recent changes in the social and economic status of blacks. In R. D. Alba (Ed.), *Ethnicity and race in the U.S.A.* Boston: Routledge & Kegan Paul.

Fazio, R. H. (1986). How do attitudes guide behavior? In R. M. Sorrentino & E. T. Higgins (Eds.), *The handbook of motivation and cognition: Foundations of social behavior.* New York: Guilford.

Fazio, R. H., Effrein, E. A., & Falender, V. J. (1981). Self-perceptions following social interaction. *Journal of Personality and Social Psychology, 41,* 232–242.

Feagin, J. R. (1992). The continuing significance of racism: Discrimination against Black students in White colleges. *Journal of Black Studies, 22,* 546–578.

Feirabend, I., & Feirabend, R. (1972). Systematic conditions of political aggression: An application of frustration-aggression theory. In I. Feirabend, R. Feirabend, & T. Gurr (Eds.), *Anger, violence, and politics.* Englewood Cliffs, NJ: Prentice-Hall.

Festinger, L. (1954). A theory of social comparison processes. *Human Relations, 7,* 114–140.

Fischer, H., & Trier, U. P. (1962). *The relationship between German Swiss and West Swiss: A sociopsychological research.* Bern: Hans Huber. Cited in Iwao, S., & Triandis, H. C. (1993). Validity of auto- and heterostereotypes among Japanese and American students. *Journal of Cross-Cultural Psychology, 24,* 428–444.

Fisher, R. (1994). General principles for resolving intergroup conflict. *Journal of Social Issues, 50,* 47–66.

Fiske, S. T. (1982). Schema-triggered affect: Applications to social perception. In M. S. Clark & S. T. Fiske (Eds.), *Affect and cognition* (pp. 55–74). Hillsdale, NJ: Erlbaum.

Fiske, S. T., & Neuberg, S. L. (1989). A continuum of impression formation, from category-based to individuating processes: Influences of information and motivation on attention and interpretation. In M. Zanna (Ed.), *Advances in experimental social psychology* (pp. 1–74). San Diego: Academic Press.

Fiske, S. T., & Pavelchak, M. A. (1986). Category-based versus piecemeal-based affective responses: Developments in schema-triggered affect. In R. M. Sorrentino & E. T. Higgins (Eds.), *The handbook of motivation and cognition: Foundations of social behavior* (pp. 167–203). New York: Guilford Press.

Forgas, J. P., & Bower, G. H. (1986). Mood effects on person-perception judgments. *Journal of Personality and Social Psychology, 53,* 53–60.

Foschi, M., & Takagi, J. (1991). Ethnicity, task outcome, and attributions: A theoretical review and assessment. *Advances in group processes* (Vol. 8, pp. 177–203). New York: JAI Press.

Frey, D., & Gaertner, S. L. (1986). Helping and the avoidance of inappropriate interracial behavior: A strategy that can perpetuate a non-prejudiced self-image. *Journal of Personality and Social Psychology, 50,* 1083–1090.

Fry, W. R., Firestone, I. J., & Williams, D. L. (1983). Negotiation process and outcome of stranger dyad and dating couples: Do lovers lose? *Basic and Applied Social Psychology, 4,* 1–16.

Furnham, A., & Bochner, S. (1982). Social difficulty in a foreign culture: An empirical analysis of culture shock. In S. Bochner (Ed.), *Cultures in contact: Studies in cross-cultural interaction.* Oxford: Pergamon.

Furnham, A., & Bochner, S. (1986). *Cultural shock: Psychological reactions to unfamiliar environments.* New York: Methuen.

Gaertner, S. L. (1973). Helping behavior and discrimination among liberals and conservatives. *Journal of Personality and Social Psychology, 25,* 335–341.

Gaertner, S. L., & Dovidio, J. F. (1977). The subtlety of white racism, arousal, and helping behavior. *Journal of Personality and Social Psychology, 35,* 691–707.

Gaertner, S. L., & Dovidio, J. F. (1986). The aversive form of racism. In J. F. Dovidio & S. L. Gaertner (Eds.), *Prejudice, discrimination, and racism* (pp. 61–90). Orlando, FL: Academic Press.

Gaertner, S. L., Mann, J., Dovidio, J. F., Murrell, A., & Pomare, M. (1990). How does cooperation reduce intergroup bias? *Journal of Personality and Social Psychology, 59,* 692–704.

Gaertner, S. L., Mann, J., Murrell, A., & Dovidio, J. F. (1989). Reducing intergroup bias: The benefits of recategorization. *Journal of Personality and Social Psychology, 57,* 239–249.

Gerard, H. B. (1983). School desegregation: The social science role. *American Psychologist, 38,* 869–877.

Gilbert, D. T., & Hixon, G. (1991). The trouble of thinking: Activation and application of stereotypic beliefs. *Journal of Personality and Social Psychology, 60,* 509–517.

Gilbert, D. T., & Jones, E. E. (1986). Perceiver-induced constraint: Interpretations of self-generated reality. *Journal of Personality and Social Psychology, 50,* 269–280.

Gochenour, T. (1977). The albatross. In D. Batchelder & E. G. Warner (Eds.), *Beyond experience.* Brattleboro, VT: Experiment Press.

Goffman, E. (1963). *Stigma.* Englewood Cliffs, NJ: Prentice-Hall.

Gonzales, A. (1979). *Classroom cooperation and ethnic balance.* Paper presented at the Annual Convention of the American Psychological Association, New York.

Grant, P. R., & Holmes, J. G. (1981). The integration of implicit personality theory, schemas, and stereotype images. *Social Psychology Quarterly, 44,* 107–115.

Green, K. (1981). *Integration and achievement: Preliminary results from a longitudinal study of educational attainment among black students.* Paper presented at the Annual Meeting of the American Educational Research Association.

Greenberg, J., & Rosenfield, D. (1979). Whites' ethnocentrism and their attributions for behavior of Blacks: A motivational analysis. *Journal of Personality, 47,* 643–657.

Greenblatt, S. L., & Willie, C. V. (1980). The serendipitous effects of school desegregation. In W. G. Stephan & J. Feagin (Eds.), *School desegregation* (pp. 51–66). New York: Plenum.

Greenwald, A. (1968). On defining attitude and attitude theory. In A. Greenwald, T. Brock, & T. Ostrom (Eds.), *Psychological foundations of attitudes* (pp. 361–388). New York: Academic Press.

Gudykunst, W. B. (1988). Uncertainty and anxiety. In Y. Y. Kim & W. B. Gudykunst (Eds.), *Theories in intercultural communication.* Newbury Park, CA: Sage.

Gudykunst, W. B., Gao, G. E., Schmidt, K. L., Nishida, T., Bond, M. H., Leung, K., Wang, G., & Barraclough, R. A. (1992). The influence of individualism-collectivism, self-monitoring, and predicted outcome value on communication in ingroup and outgroup relationships. *Journal of Cross-Cultural Psychology, 23,* 196–213.

Gudykunst, W. B., & Hammer, M. R. (1983). Basic training design: Approaches to intercultural training. In D. Landis & R. W. Brislin (Eds.), *Handbook of intercultural training* (Vol. 1). New York: Pergamon.

Gudykunst, W. B., & Hammer, M. R. (1984). Dimensions of intercultural effectiveness: Culture specific or culture general? *International Journal of Intercultural Relations, 8,* 1–10.

Gudykunst, W. B., & Kim, Y. Y. (1984). *Communicating with strangers: An approach to intercultural communication.* New York: Random House.

Gudykunst, W. B., & Kim, Y. Y. (1992). *Communicating with strangers: An approach to intercultural communication* (2nd ed.). New York: McGraw-Hill.

Guimond, S., & Dube-Simard, L. (1983). Relative deprivation theory and the Quebec nationalist movement: The cognition-emotion distinction and the personal-group deprivation issue. *Journal of Personality and Social Psychology, 44,* 526–535.

Gurr, T. R. (1970). *Why men rebel.* Princeton: Princeton University Press.

Hall, E. T. (1976). *Beyond culture.* New York: Doubleday.

Hallinan, M. T., & Smith, S. S. (1985). The effects of classroom composition on students' interracial friendliness. *Social Psychology Quarterly, 48,* 3–16.

Hamill, R., Wilson, T. D., & Nisbett, R. E. (1980). Insensitivity to sample bias: Generalizing from atypical cases. *Journal of Personality and Social Psychology, 39.*

Hamilton, D. L., Sherman, S. J., & Ruvolo, C. M. (1990). Stereotype-based expectancies: Effects on information processing and social behavior. *Journal of Social Issues, 46,* 35–60.

Hammer, M. R., Gudykunst, W. B., & Wiseman, R. I. (1977). Dimensions of intercultural effectiveness. *International Journal of Intercultural Relations, 2,* 382–393.

Hammer, W. C. (1974). Effects of bargaining strategy and pressure to reach agreement in a stalemated negotiation. *Journal of Personality and Social Psychology, 30,* 458–467.

Harding, J., & Hogrefe, R. (1952). Attitudes of white department store employees toward Negro coworkers. *Journal of Social Issues, 8,* 18–28.

Harding, J., Kutner, B., Proshansky, N., & Chein, I. (1954). Prejudice and ethnic relations. In G. Lindzey (Ed.), *Handbook of social psychology* (Vol. 2, pp. 1021–1061). Cambridge: Addison-Wesley.

Harnett, D. L., & Vincelette, J. P. (1978). Strategic influences on bargaining effectiveness. In H. Sauermann (Ed.), *Contributions to experimental economics.* Cited in Carnevale, P. J., & Pruitt, D. G. (1992). Negotiation and mediation. *Annual Review of Psychology, 43,* 531–582.

Harrington, H. J., & Miller, N. (1992). Research and theory in intergroup relations: Issues of consensus and controversy. In J. Lynch, C. Modgil, & S. Modgil (Eds.), *Cultural diversity in the schools* (Vol. 2, pp. 159–178). London: Falmer Press.

Harris, M. J., Milich, R., Corbitt, E. M., Hoover, D. W., & Brady, M. (1992). Self-fulfilling effects of stigmatizing information on children's social interactions. *Journal of Personality and Social Psychology, 63,* 41–50.

Haslam, S. A., & Turner, J. C. (1992). Context-dependent variation in social stereotyping 2: The relationship between frame of reference, self-categorization, and accentuation. *European Journal of Social Psychology, 22,* 251–277.

Haslam, S. A., Turner, J. C., Oakes, P. J., McGarty, C., & Hayes, B. K. (1992). Context-dependent variation in social stereotyping 1: The effects of intergroup relations as mediated by social change and frame of reference. *European Journal of Social Psychology, 12,* 3–20.

Hastie, R., & Kumar, A. P. (1979). Person memory: Personality traits as organizing principles in memory for behaviors. *Journal of Personality and Social Psychology, 37,* 25–38.

Hastie, R., & Park, B. (1986). The relationship between memory and judgment depends on whether the judgment task is memory-based or on-line. *Psychological Review, 93,* 258–268.

Hauserman, N., Walen, S. R., & Behling, M. (1973). Reinforced racial integration in the first grade: A study of generalization. *Journal of Applied Behavioral Analysis, 6,* 193–200.

Hayes, R. E. (1991). Negotiations with terrorists. In Kremenyuk, V. A. (Ed.), *International negotiation* (pp. 364–378). San Francisco: Jossey-Bass.

Hemsley, G. D., & Marmurek, H. V. C. (1982). Person memory: The processing of consistent and inconsistent person information. *Personality and Social Psychology Bulletin, 8,* 433–438.

Hendricks, M., & Bootzin, R. (1976). Race and sex as stimuli for negative affect and physical avoidance. *Journal of Social Psychology, 98,* 111–120.

Hepworth, J. T., & West, S. G. (1988). Lynchings and the economy: A time-series reanalysis of Hovland and Sears (1940). *Journal of Personality and Social Psychology, 55,* 239–247.

Hertz-Lazarowitz, R., & Miller, N. (1992). *Interaction in cooperative groups.* New York: Cambridge University Press.

Hertz-Lazarowitz, R., Sapir, C., & Sharan, S. (1982). The effects of two cooperative learning methods and traditional teaching on the achievement and social relations of pupils in mixed ethnic junior high school classes. Cited in Schwarzwald, J., & Amir, Y. (1984). Interethnic relations and education: An Israeli perspective. In N. Miller & M. Brewer (Eds.), *Groups in contact: The psychology of desegregation* (pp. 53–76). Orlando, FL: Academic Press.

Hewstone, M., Bond, M. H., & Wan, C.-K. (1983). Social facts and social attributions: The exploration of intergroup differences in Hong Kong. *Social Cognition, 2,* 142–157.

Hewstone, M., & Brown, R. (1986). Contact is not enough: An intergroup perspective on the contact hypothesis. In M. Hewstone & R. Brown (Eds.), *Contact and conflict in intergroup encounters.* Oxford: Basil Blackwell.

Hewstone, M., Islam, M. R., & Judd, C. M. (1993). Models of crossed categorization and intergroup relations. *Journal of Personality and Social Psychology, 64,* 779–793.

Hewstone, M., & Jaspars, H. (1982). Intergroup relations and attribution processes. In H. Tajfel (Ed.), *Social identity and intergroup relations.* Cambridge: Cambridge University Press.

Hewstone, M., & Ward, C. (1985). Ethnocentrism and causal attribution in Southeast Asia. *Journal of Personality and Social Psychology, 48,* 614–623.

Higgins, E. T., & King, G. (1981). Accessibility of social constructs: Information processsing consequences of individual and contextual variables. In N. Cantor & J. F. Kihlstrom (Eds.), *Personality, cognition, and social interaction* (pp. 69–122). Hillsdale, NJ: Erlbaum.

Higgins, E. T., & Rholes, W. S. (1978). ''Saying is believing'': Effects of message modification on memory and liking for the person described. *Journal of Experimental Social Psychology, 14,* 363–378.

Higgins, E. T., Rholes, W. S., & Jones, C. R. (1977). Category accessibility and impression formation. *Journal of Experimental Social Psychology, 13,* 141–154.

Hilton, J. L., & Darley, J. M. (1985). Constructing other persons: A limit of the effect. *Journal of Experimental Social Psychology, 21,* 1–18.

Hilton, J. L., & vonHippel, W. (1990). The role of consistency in the judgment of stereotype-relevant behaviors. *Personality and Social Psychology Bulletin, 16,* 430–448.

Hoffman, E. (1985). The effects of race-ratio composition on the frequency of organizational communication. *Social Psychology Quarterly, 48,* 17–26.

Hofstede, G. (1980). *Culture's consequences.* Beverly Hills, CA: Sage.

Hofstede, G. (1984). *Culture's consequences.* Beverly Hills, CA: Sage.

Hofstede, G., & Bond, M. (1984). Hofstede's culture dimensions. *Journal of Cross-Cultural Psychology, 15,* 417–433.

Hogg, M. A., & Abrams, D. (1988). *Social identification: A social psychology of intergroup relations and group processes.* New York: Routledge.

Hogg, M. A., & Abrams, D. (1990). Social motivation, self-esteem, and social identity. In D. Abrams & M. A. Hogg (Eds.), *Social identity theory: Constructive and critical advances*. New York: Springer-Verlag.

Hogg, M. A., & McGarty, C. (1990). Self-categorization and social identity. In D. Abrams & M. A. Hogg (Eds.), *Social identity theory: Constructive and critical advances*. New York: Springer-Verlag.

Hogg, M. A., & Sutherland, J. (1991). Self-esteem and intergroup discrimination in the minimal group paradigm. *British Journal of Social Psychology, 30,* 51–62.

Hogg, M. A., & Turner, J. C. (1985a). Interpersonal attraction, social identification, and psychological group formation. *European Journal of Social Psychology, 15,* 51–66.

Hogg, M. A., & Turner, J. C. (1985b). When liking begets solidarity: An experiment on the role of interpersonal attraction in psychological group formation. *British Journal of Social Psychology, 24,* 267–281.

Hogg, M. A., & Turner, J. C. (1987). Intergroup behavior, self-stereotyping, and the salience of social categories. *British Journal of Social Psychology, 26,* 325–340.

Hogg, M. A., Turner, J. C., Nascimento-Schulze, C., & Spriggs, D. (1986). Social categorization, intergroup behavior, and self-esteem: Two experiments. *Revista de Psicologia Social, 1,* 23–37.

Holloway, S. D., Kashiwagi, K., Hess, R. D., & Azuma, H. (1986). Causal attributions by Japanese and American mothers and children about performance in mathematics. *International Journal of Psychology, 21,* 269–286.

Homans, G. C. (1961). *Social behavior: Its elementary forms.* New York: Harcourt, Brace, & World.

Hornstein, H. A. (1965). Effects of different magnitudes of threats and magnitude of punishment upon interpersonal bargaining. *Journal of Experimental Social Psychology, 1,* 282–293.

Inkeles, A., & Levinson, J. (1969). National character: The study of modal personality and sociocultural systems. In G. Lindzey & E. Aronson (Eds.), *Handbook of social psychology* (Vol. 4). Reading, MA: Addison-Wesley.

Isen, A. M. (1982). Some perspectives on cognitive social psychology. In A. H. Hastorf & A. M. Isen (Eds.), *Cognitive social psychology* (pp. 1–31). New York: Elsevier.

Isen, A. M. (1984). Toward understanding the role of affect in cognition. In R. S. Wyer & T. K. Srull (Eds.), *Handbook of social cognition* (Vol. 2, pp. 179–236). Hillsdale, NJ: Erlbaum.

Islam, M. R., & Hewstone, M. (1993). Intergroup attribution and affective consequences in minority and majority groups. *Journal of Personality and Social Psychology, 64,* 936–950.

Iwao, S., & Triandis, H. C. (1993). Validity of auto- and heterostereotypes among Japanese and American students. *Journal of Cross-Cultural Psychology, 24,* 428–444.

Jackman, M. R., & Crane, M. (1986). "Some of my best friends are Black . . .": Interracial friendship and Whites' racial attitudes. *Public Opinion Quarterly, 50,* 459–486.

Jackson, L. A., & Cash, T. F. (1985). Components of gender stereotypes and their implications for stereotype and nonstereotype judgments. *Personality and Social Psychology Bulletin, 11,* 326–344.

Jackson, L. A., MacCoun, R. J., & Kerr, N. L. (1987). Stereotypes and nonstereotype judgments. *Personality and Social Psychology Bulletin, 13,* 45–52.

Jacobson, C. K. (1985). Resistance to affirmative action: Self-interest or racism? *Journal of Conflict Resolution, 29,* 306–329.

James, W. (1890). *The principles of psychology.* New York: Holt.

Janis, I. L. (1986). Problems of international crisis management in the nuclear age. *Journal of Social Issues, 42,* 201–220.

Janis, I. L., & Mann, L. (1977). *Decision-making: A psychological analysis of choice, conflict, and commitment.* New York: Free Press.

Jervis, R., Lebow, R. N., & Stein, J. G. (1985). *Psychology and deterrence.* Baltimore, MD: Johns Hopkins University Press.

John, O. P., Hampson, S. E., & Goldberg, L. R. (1991). The basic level in personality-trait hierarchies: Studies of trait use and accessibility in different contexts. *Journal of Personality and Social Psychology, 60,* 348–361.

Johnson, D. W., & Johnson, R. T. (1992a). Positive interdependence: Key to effective cooperation. In R. Hertz-Lazarowitz & N. Miller (Eds.), *Interaction in cooperative groups* (pp. 174–199). New York: Cambridge University Press.

Johnson, D. W., & Johnson, R. T. (1992b). Social interdependence and cross-ethnic relationships. In J. Lynch, C. Modgil, & S. Modgil (Eds.), *Cultural diversity in the schools* (Vol. 2, pp. 179–190). London: Falmer Press.

Johnson, D. W., Johnson, R., & Maruyama, G. (1984). Goal interdependence and interpersonal attraction in heterogeneous classrooms. In N. Miller & M. B. Brewer (Eds.), *Groups in contact* (pp. 187–213). New York: Academic Press.

Johnston, L., & Hewstone, M. (1992). Cognitive models of stereotype change. *Journal of Experimental Social Psychology, 28,* 360–386.

Jonas, K., & Hewstone, M. (1986). The assessment of national stereotypes: A methodological study. *Journal of Social Psychology, 126,* 745–754.

Jones, J. (1972). *Prejudice and racism.* Reading, MA: Addison-Wesley.

Jost, J. T., & Banaji, M. R. (in press). The role of stereotyping in system-justification and the production of false consciousness. *British Journal of Social Psychology.*

Judd, C. M., & Park, B. (1988). Out-group homogeneity: Judgments of variability at the individual and group levels. *Journal of Personality and Social Psychology, 54,* 779–788.

Kamfer, L., & Venter, J. L. (1994). First evaluation of a stereotype reduction workshop. *South African Journal of Psychology, 24,* 13–20.

Kanter, R. M. (1977). *Men and women of the corporation.* New York: Basic Books.

Karlins, M., Coffman, T. L., & Walters, G. (1969). On the fading of social stereotypes: Studies in three generations of college students. *Journal of Abnormal and Social Psychology, 13,* 1–16.

Kashima, Y., & Triandis, H. C. (1986). The self-serving bias in attributions as a coping strategy: A cross-cultural study. *Journal of Cross-cultural Psychology, 17,* 83–98.

Katz, D. (1965). Nationalism and strategies of international conflict resolution. In H. C. Kelman (Ed.), *International behavior: A social-psychological analysis.* New York: Holt, Rinehart, & Winston.

Katz, D., & Braly, K. N. (1933). Racial stereotypes among 100 college students. *Journal of Abnormal and Social Psychology, 28,* 280–290.

Katz, I., Glass, D. C., & Cohen, S. (1973). Ambivalence, guilt, and the scapegoating of minority group victims. *Journal of Experimental Social Psychology, 9,* 423–436.

Katz, I., Glass, D. C., Lucido, D. J., & Farber, J. (1979). Harm-doing and victim's racial or orthopedic stigma as determinants of helping behavior. *Journal of Personality, 47,* 430–464.

Katz, I., & Hass, R. G. (1988). Racial ambivalence and American value conflict: Correlational and priming studies of dual cognitive structures. *Journal of Personality and Social Psychology, 55,* 893–905.

Katz, I., Hass, R. G., & Wackenhut, J. (1986). Racial ambivalence, value duality, and behavior. In J. F. Dovidio & S. L. Gaertner (Eds.), *Prejudice, discrimination, and racism.* New York: Academic Press.

Katz, I., Wackenhut, J., & Glass, D. C. (1986). An ambivalence-amplification theory of behavior toward the stigmatized. In S. Worchel & W. G. Austin (Eds.), *Psychology of intergroup relations* (2nd ed., pp. 103–117). Chicago: Nelson-Hall.

Katz, P. A., & Taylor, D. A. (1988). *Eliminating racism: Profiles in controversy.* New York: Plenum.

Kelley, H. H. (1952). Two functions of reference groups. In G. E. Swanson, T. M. Newcomb, & E. L. Hartley (Eds.), *Readings in social psychology* (2nd ed). New York: Holt, Rinehart, & Winston.

Kelley, H. H. (1967). Attribution theory in social psychology. In D. Levine (Ed.), *Nebraska symposium on motivation* (Vol. 15). Lincoln, NE: University of Nebraska Press.

Kelly, C. (1989). Political identity and perceived intragroup homogeneity. *British Journal of Social Psychology, 28,* 239–250.

Kelman, H., & Pettigrew, T. (1959). How to understand prejudice. *Commentary, 28,* 436–441.

Kelman, H. C. (1978). Israelis and Palestinians: Psychological prerequisites for mutual acceptance. *International Security, 3,* 162–186.

Kelman, H. C. (1987). The political psychology of the Arab-Israeli conflict: How can we overcome the barriers to a negotiated solution? *Political Psychology, 8,* 347–363.

Kelman, H. C. (1990). Interactive problem-solving: A social psychological approach to conflict resolution. In J. Burton & F. Dukes (Eds.), *Conflict: Readings in management and resolution* (pp. 199–215). New York: St. Martin's Press.

Kelman, H. C., & Cohen, S. P. (1986). Resolution of international conflict: An interactional approach. In S. Worchel & W. G. Austin (Eds.), *Psychology of intergroup relations* (pp. 323–432). Chicago: Nelson Hall.

Kim, Y. (1977). Inter-ethnic and intra-ethnic communication. In N. Jain (Ed.), *International and intercultural communication annual* (Vol. 4). Falls Church, VA: Speech Communication Association.

Kim, Y. (1979). Toward an interactive theory of communication-acculturation. In N. Jain (Ed.), *Communication yearbook 3.* New Brunswick: Transaction.

Kinder, D. R. (1986). The continuing American dilemma: White resistance to racial change 40 years after Myrdal. *Journal of Social Issues, 42,* 151–172.

Kinder, D. R., & Sears, D. O. (1981). Prejudice and politics: Symbolic racism versus racial threats to the good life. *Journal of Personality and Social Psychology, 40,* 414–431.

Kitayama, S., & Markus, H. R. (1992). *Construal of the self as a cultural frame: Implications for internationalizing psychology.* Paper presented at a symposium on internationalization and higher education, Ann Arbor, MI.

Kitayama, S., Markus, H. R., & Kurokawa, M. (1991). *Culture, self, and emotion: The structure and frequency of emotional experience.* Paper presented at the Society for Psychological Anthropology, Chicago, IL.

Kluckhohn, F., & Strodtbeck, F. L. (1961). *Variations in value orientation.* Evanston: Row, Peterson.

Kluegel, J. R. (1990). Trends in whites' explanations of the black-white gap in SES. *American Sociological Review, 55,* 512–525.

Kluger, R. (1976). *Simple justice.* New York: Knopf.

Kraemer, A. J. (1974). *The development of cultural self-awareness: Design of a program of instruction.* HumRRO Prof. Paper 27–29. Alexandria, VA: Human Resource Research Organization.

Kressel, K., & Pruitt, D. G. (1989). Conclusion: A research perspective on the mediation of social conflict. In K. Kressel, D. G. Pruitt, and associates (Eds.), *Mediation research* (pp. 394–434). San Francisco: Jossey-Bass.

Krol, R. A. (1980). A meta-analysis of comparative research on the effects of desegregation on academic achievement. *The Urban Review, 12,* 211–224.

Krueger, J., & Rothbart, M. (1988). Use of categorical and individuating information in making inferences about personality. *Journal of Personality and Social Psychology, 55,* 187–195.

Krueger, J., Rothbart, M., & Sriram, N. (1989). Category learning and change: Differences in sensitivity to information that enhances or reduces intercategory distinctions. *Journal of Personality and Social Psychology, 56,* 866–875.

Kruglanski, A. W. (1989). *Lay epistemics and human knowledge: Cognitive and motivational bases.* New York: Plenum.

Kulik, J. (1983). Confirmatory attribution and the perpetuation of social beliefs. *Journal of Personality and Social Psychology, 44,* 1171–1181.

Kume, T. (1985). Managerial attitudes toward decision-making: North America and Japan. In W. B. Gudykunst, L. P. Stewart, & S. Ting-Toomey (Eds.), *Communication, culture, and organizational processes.* Beverly Hills: Sage.

Kuper, L. (1977). *The pity of it all.* Minneapolis, MN: University of Minnesota Press.

Laber, J. (1993). Bosnia: Questions about rape. *The New York Review of Books, XL*(6), 3–6.

Lalonde, R. N. (1992). The dynamics of group differentiation in the face of defeat. *Personality and Social Psychology Bulletin, 18,* 336–342.

Landis, D., & Brislin, R. W. (Eds.). (1983). *Handbook of intercultural training* (Vol. 1). New York: Pergamon.

Landis, D., Brislin, R. W., & Hulgus, J. F. (1985). Attributional training versus contact in acculturative learning: A laboratory study. *Journal of Applied Social Psychology, 15,* 466–482.

Langer, E. J., Bashner, R. S., & Chanowitz, B. (1985). Decreasing prejudice by increasing discrimination. *Journal of Personality and Social Psychology, 49,* 113–120.

Lebow, R. N., & Stein, J. G. (1987). Beyond deterrence. *Journal of Conflict Resolution, 43,* 5–71.

Lee, Y.-T., & Ottani, V. (1993). Determinants of in-group and out-group perceptions of heterogeneity: An investigation of Sino-American stereotypes. *Journal of Cross-Cultural Psychology, 24,* 298–318.

Lemyre, L., & Smith, P. M. (1985). Intergroup discrimination and self-esteem in the minimal group paradigm. *Journal of Personality and Social Psychology, 49,* 660–670.

Leng, R. J. (1984). Reagan and the Russians: Crisis bargaining beliefs and the historical record. *American Political Science Review, 78,* 338–355.

Leng, R. J., & Wheeler, H. G. (1979). Influence strategies, success, and war. *Journal of Conflict Resolution, 23,* 655–684.

Lerner, M. J. (1980). *Belief in a just world: A fundamental delusion.* New York: Plenum.

Lerner, M. J., & Miller, D. T. (1978). Just world research and the attribution process. *Psychological Bulletin, 85,* 1030–1051.

LeVine, R. A., & Campbell, D. T. (1972). *Ethnocentrism: Theories of conflict, ethnic attitudes, and group behavior.* New York: Wiley.

Lewin, K. (1951). *Field theory in social science: Selected theoretical papers.* New York: Harper & Row.

Lim, R. G., & Carnevale, P. J. (1990). Contingencies in mediation disputes. *Journal of Personality and Social Psychology, 58,* 259–272.

Lindskold, S. (1986). GRIT: Reducing distrust through carefully introduced conciliation. In S. Worchel & W. G. Austin (Eds.), *Psychology of intergroup relations* (pp. 305–323). Chicago: Nelson-Hall.

Lindskold, S., & Han, G. (1988). GRIT as a foundation for integrative bargaining. *Personality and Social Psychology Bulletin, 14,* 335–345.

Link, P. (1994). The old man's new China. *New York Review of Books, 41,* 31–36.

Linville, P. W. (1982). The complexity-extremity effect and age-based stereotyping. *Journal of Personality and Social Psychology, 42,* 192–211.

Linville, P. W., Fischer, G. W., & Salovey, P., (1989). Perceived distributions of the characteristics of in-group and out-group members: Empirical evidence and a computer simulation. *Journal of Personality and Social Psychology, 57,* 165–188.

Linville, P. W., Salovey, P., & Fischer, G. W. (1986). Stereotyping and perceived distributions of social characteristics: An application to ingroup-outgroup perception. In J. Dovidio & S. L. Gaertner (Eds.), *Prejudice, discrimination, and racism.* New York: Academic Press.

Lippman, W. (1922). *Public opinion.* New York: Harcourt Brace.

Locksley, A., Borgida, E., Brekke, N., & Hepburn, C. A. (1980). Sex stereotypes and social judgment. *Journal of Personality and Social Psychology, 39,* 821–831.

Locksley, A., Hepburn, C., & Ortiz, V. (1982). Social stereotypes and the judgment of individuals: An instance of the base-rate fallacy. *Journal of Experimental Social Psychology, 18,* 23–42.

Lofland, L. H. (1973). *A world of strangers.* New York: Basic Books.

Longshore, D. (1982). School racial composition and blacks' attitudes toward desegregation: The problem of control in desegregated schools. *Social Science Quarterly, 63,* 674–687.

Lord, C. G., Lepper, M. R., & Preston, E. (1984). Considering the opposite: A corrective strategy for social judgment. *Journal of Personality and Social Psychology, 47,* 1231–1243.

Lucker, G. W., Rosenfield, D., Aronson, E., & Sikes, J. (1977). Performance in the interdependent classroom. *American Educational Research Journal, 13,* 115–123.

Maass, A., Salvi, D., Acuri, L., & Semin, G. (1989). Language use in intergroup contexts: The linguistic intergroup bias. *Journal of Personality and Social Psychology, 57,* 981–993.

Mackie, D. M., Allison, S. T., Worth, L. T., & Asuncion, A. G. (1992). Social decision making processes: The generalization of outcome-biased counter-stereotypic inferences. *Journal of Experimental Social Psychology, 28,* 23–42.

Mackie, D. M., & Hamilton, D. L. (Eds.). (1993). *Affect, cognition, and stereotyping.* New York: Academic Press.

Mackie, D. M., Hamilton, D. L., Schroth, H. A., Carlisle, C. J., Gersho, B. F., Meneses, L. M., Nedler, B. F., & Reichel, L. D. (1989). The effects of induced mood on expectancy-based illusory correlations. *Journal of Experimental Social Psychology, 25,* 524–544.

Major, B., Cozarelli, C., Testa, M., & McFarlin, D. B. (1988). Self-verification versus expectancy-confirmation in social interaction: The impact of self-focus. *Personality and Social Psychology Bulletin, 14,* 346–359.

Markus, H. R., & Kitayama, S. (1991). Culture and the self: Implications for cognition, emotion, and motivation. *Psychological Review, 98,* 224–253.

Martin, C. L. (1987). A ratio measure of stereotyping. *Journal of Personality and Social Psychology, 52,* 489–499.

Martin, J. N. (1984). Intercultural reentry: Conceptualization and directions for future research. *International Journal of Intercultural Relations, 8,* 1–22.

Marx, K. (1843/1964). *Das capital.* New York: International.

Masson, C. N., & Verkuyten, M. (1993). Prejudice, ethnicity, contact and ethnic group preferences among Dutch young adolescents. *Journal of Applied Social Psychology, 23,* 156–168.

Matsumoto, D., Kudoh, T., Scherer, K., & Wallbott, H. (1988). Antecedents of and reactions to emotions in the United States and Japan. *Journal of Cross-Cultural Psychology, 19,* 267–286.

Mayer, J. D. (1989). How mood influences cognition. In N. E. Sharkey (Ed.), *Advances in cognitive science* (Vol. 1, pp. 290–313). New York: Wiley.

Mayer, J. D., Gayle, M., Meehan, M. E., & Haarman, A. (1990). Toward better specification of the mood-consistency effect in recall. *Journal of Experimental Social Psychology, 26,* 465–480.

Mayer, J. D., & Salovey, P. (1988). Personality moderates: The interaction of mood and cognition. In K. Fiedler & J. Forgas (Eds.), *Affect, cognition and social behavior* (pp. 87–99). Toronto: Hogrefe.

McArthur, L. Z. (1981). Judging a book by its cover: A cognitive analysis of the relationship between physical appearance and stereotyping. In H. Hastorf & A. Isen (Eds.), *Cognitive social psychology.* New York: Elsevier North-Holland.

McArthur, L. Z., & Post, D. L. (1977). Figural emphasis and person perception. *Journal of Experimental Social Psychology, 13,* 520–535.

McArthur, L. Z., & Soloman, L. K. (1978). Perceptions of an aggressive encounter as a function of the victim's salience and the perceiver's arousal. *Journal of Experimental Social Psychology, 13,* 520–535.

McCauley, C., & Stitt, C. L. (1978). An individual and quantitative measure of stereotypes. *Journal of Personality and Social Psychology, 36,* 929–940.

McCauley, C., Stitt, C. L., & Segall, M. (1980). Stereotyping: From prejudice to prediction. *Psychological Bulletin, 87,* 195–208.

McClendon, M. J. (1974). Interracial contact and the reduction of prejudice. *Sociological Focus, 7,* 47–65.

McClintock, C. G. (1972). Social motivation—A set of propositions. *Behavioral Science, 17,* 438–454.

McConahay, J., & Hawley, W. (1976). *Attitudes of Louisville and Jefferson County citizens toward busing for public school desegregation.* Unpublished report. Durham, NC: Duke University.

McEwen, C. A., & Maiman, R. J. (1981). Small claims mediation in Maine: An empirical assessment. *Maine Law Review, 33,* 237–268.

McEwen, C. A., & Maiman, R. J. (1989). Mediation in small claims court: Consensual processes and outcomes. In K. Kressel, D. G. Pruitt, & associates (Eds.), *Mediation research: The process and effectiveness of third-party intervention* (pp. 53–67). San Francisco: Jossey-Bass.

McGillicuddy, N. B., Welton, G. L., & Pruitt, D. G. (1987). Third-party intervention: A field experiment comparing three different methods. *Journal of Personality and Social Psychology, 53,* 104–112.

Merton, R. K. (1948). The self-fulfilling prophecy. *Antioch Review, 8,* 193–210.

Messick, D. M., & Mackie, D. M. (1989). Intergroup relations. *Annual Review of Psychology, 40,* 45–81.

Miller, J. G. (1984). Culture and the development of everyday social explanation. *Journal of Personality and Social Psychology, 46,* 961–978.

Miller, N., & Brewer, M. B. (Eds.). (1984). *Groups in contact: The psychology of desegregation.* Orlando, FL: Academic Press.

Miller, N., & Brewer, M. B. (1986). Categorization effects on ingroup and outgroup perception. In J. Dovidio & S. L. Gaertner (Eds.), *Prejudice, discrimination, and racism.* New York: Academic Press.

Miller, N., Brewer, M. B., & Edwards, K. (1985). Cooperative interaction in desegregated settings: A laboratory analogue. *Journal of Social Issues, 41,* 63–81.

Miller, N., & Davidson-Podgorny, G. (1987). Theoretical models of intergroup relations and the use of cooperative teams as an intervention for desegregated settings. In C. Hendrick (Ed.), *Group processes and intergroup relations, 9,* 41–67.

Miller, N., & Harrington, H. J. (1990). A model of category salience for intergroup relations: Empirical tests of the relevant variables. In P. J. D. Drenth, J. A. Sargeant, & R. J. Takens (Eds.), *European perspectives in psychology* (Vol. 3, pp. 205–220). New York: John Wiley & Sons.

Miller, N., & Harrington, H. J. (1992). Social categorization and intergroup acceptance: Principles for the design and development of cooperative learning teams. In R. Hertz-Lazarowitz & N. Miller (Eds.), *Interaction in cooperative groups* (pp. 203–227). New York: Cambridge University Press.

Minard, R. D. (1952). Race relations in the Pocahontas coal field. *Journal of Social Issues, 8,* 29–44.

Monteith, M. J. (1993). Self-regulation of prejudiced responses: Implications for progress in prejudice-reduction efforts. *Journal of Personality and Social Psychology, 65,* 469–485.

Monteith, M. J., Devine, P. G., & Zuwerink, J. R. (1993). Self-directed versus other-directed affect as a consequence of prejudice-related discrepancies. *Journal of Personality and Social Psychology, 64,* 198–210.

Morganthau, T. (1992). At the brink of disaster. *Newsweek,* Oct. 25, pp. 22–25.

Mullen, B., & Hu, L. (1989). Perceptions of ingroup and outgroup variability: A meta-analytic integration. *Basic and Applied Social Psychology, 10,* 233–252.

Mummendey, A., & Schreiber, H. J. (1983). Better or just different? Positive social identity by discrimination against or by differentiation from outgroups. *European Journal of Social Psychology, 13,* 389–398.

Mummendey, A., & Schreiber, H. J. (1984). "Different" just means "better": Some obvious and some hidden pathways to ingroup favoritism. *British Journal of Social Psychology, 23,* 363–368.

Mummendey, A., & Simon, B. (1989). Better or different? III: The impact of importance of comparison dimension and relative ingroup size upon intergroup discrimination. *British Journal of Social Psychology, 28,* 1–16.

Mummendey, A., Simon, B., Dietze, C., Grunert, M., Haeger, G., Kessler, S., Lettgen, S., & Schaferhoff, S. (1992). Categorization is not enough: Intergroup discrimination in negative outcome situations. *Journal of Experimental Social Psychology, 28,* 125–144.

Myrdal, G. (1944). *An American dilemma: The Negro problem and modern democracy.* New York: Random House.

Neidenthal, P. M. (1990). Implicit perception of affective information. *Journal of Experimental Social Psychology, 26,* 505–527.

Neuberg, S. L. (1989). The goal of forming accurate impressions during social interactions: Attenuating the impact of negative expectancies. *Journal of Personality and Social Psychology, 56,* 374–386.

Neuberg, S. L., Judice, T. N., Virdin, L. M., & Carillo, M. A. (1993). Perceiver self-presentation goals as moderators of expectancy influences: Ingratiation and disconfirmation of negative expectancies. *Journal of Personality and Social Psychology, 64,* 409–420.

Newcomb, T., Turner, R., & Converse, E. (1965). *Social psychology.* New York: Holt, Rinehart, & Winston.

Newsweek. (1991). Race on campus: Failing the test? May 6, pp. 26–27.

Ng, S. H. (1981). Equity theory and the allocation of rewards between groups. *European Journal of Social Psychology, 11,* 439–444.

Ng, S. H. (1985). Biases in reward allocation resulting from personal status, group status, and allocation procedure. *Australian Journal of Social Psychology, 37,* 297–307.

Norvel, N., & Worchel, S. (1981). A re-examination of the relation between equal-status contact and intergroup attraction. *Journal of Personality and Social Psychology, 41,* 902–908.

Oakes, P. J., & Turner, J. C. (1980). Social categorization and intergroup behavior: Does minimal intergroup discrimination make social identity more positive? *European Journal of Social Psychology, 10,* 295–301.

Oakes, P. J., Turner, J. C., & Haslam, S. A. (1991). Perceiving people as group members: The role of fit in the salience of social categorizations. *British Journal of Social Psychology, 30,* 125–144.

Oberg, C. (1960). Cultural shock: Adjustment to new cultural environments. *Practical Anthropology, 7,* 177–182.

Olson, J. M., & Zanna, M. P. (1993). Attitudes and attitude change. *Annual Review of Psychology, 44,* 117–154.

Olzak, S. (1992). *The dynamics of ethnic competition and conflict.* Stanford: Stanford University Press.

Orfield, G. (1980). School desegregation and residential segregation: A social science statement. In W. Stephan & J. Feagin (Eds.), *School desegregation: Past, present, and future.* New York: Plenum.

Osgood, C. E. (1959). Suggestions for winning the real war with communism. *Journal of Conflict Resolution, 3,* 295–325.

Osgood, C. E. (1962). *An alternative to war or surrender.* Urbana: University of Illinois Press.

Osgood, C. E. (1966). *Perspective in foreign policy.* Palo Alto, CA: Pacific Books.

Oskamp, S. (1971). Effects of programmed strategies on cooperation in prisoner's dilemma and other mixed-motive games. *Journal of Conflict Resolution, 15,* 225–259.

Paige, R. M. (1983). Cultures in contact: On intercultural relations among American and foreign students in the U.S. university context. In D. Landis & R. W. Brislin (Eds.), *Handbook of intercultural training* (Vol. 3). New York: Pergamon.

Paige, R. M. (1990). International students: Cross-cultural psychological perspectives. In R. W. Brislin (Ed.), *Applied cross-cultural psychology.* Newbury Park, CA: Sage.

Park, B., & Hastie, R. (1987). The perception of variability in category development: Instance- versus abstraction-based stereotypes. *Journal of Personality and Social Psychology, 53,* 621–635.

Park, B., & Judd, C. M. (1990). Measures and models of perceived group variability. *Journal of Personality and Social Psychology, 59,* 173–191.

Park, B., Judd, C. M., & Ryan, C. S. (1991). Social categorization and the representation of variability information. *European Review of Social Psychology, 2,* 211–245.

Park, B., & Rothbart, M. (1982). Perception of outgroup homogeneity and levels of social categorization: Memory for the subordinate attributes of ingroup and outgroup members. *Journal of Personality and Social Psychology, 42,* 1050–1068.

Parrish, T. S., & Fleetwood, R. S. (1975). Amount of conditioning and subsequent change in racial attitudes of children. *Perceptual and Motor Skills, 40,* 79–86.

Parsons, M. A. (1986). Attitude changes following desegregation in New Castle County, Delaware. In R. L. Green (Ed.), *Metropolitan desegregation.* New York: Plenum.

Patchen, M. (1988). *Resolving disputes between nations: Coercion or conciliation.* Durham, NC: Duke University Press.

Peabody, D. (1985). *National characteristics.* Cambridge: Cambridge University Press.

Pearce, D. (1980). *Breaking down barriers: New evidence on the impact of metropolitan school desegregation on housing patterns.* Washington, DC: National Institute of Education.

Pearce, W. B., & Kang, K. (1988). Conceptual migrations. In Y. Kim & W. Gudykunst (Eds.), *Cross-cultural adaptation.* Newbury Park, CA: Sage.

Pearson, J., & Theones, N. (1984). Mediating and litigating custody disputes: A longitudinal evaluation. *Family Law Quarterly, 17,* 497–524.

Pearson, J., & Theones, N. (1989). Divorce mediation: Reflections on a decade of research. In K. Kressel, D. G. Pruitt, & associates (Eds.), *Mediation research: The process and effectiveness of third-party intervention* (pp. 9–31). San Francisco: Jossey-Bass.

Perdue, C. W., Dovidio, J. F., Gurtman, M. B., & Tyler, R. B. (1990). "Us" and "them": Social categorization and the process of intergroup bias. *Journal of Personality and Social Psychology, 59,* 475–486.

Perdue, C. W., & Gurtman, M. B. (1990). Evidence of the automaticity of ageism. *Journal of Experimental Social Psychology, 26,* 199–216.

Perry, G. A. (1973). *A better chance: Evaluation of student attitudes and academic performance, 1964–1972.* Boston: A Better Chance.

Pettigrew, T. F. (1969). Racially separate or together? *Journal of Social Issues, 25,* 43–69.

Pettigrew, T. F. (1975). *Racial discrimination in the United States.* New York: Harper & Row.

Pettigrew, T. F. (1979a). Racial change and social policy. *Annals, 441,* 114–131.

Pettigrew, T. F. (1979b). The ultimate attribution error: Extending Allport's cognitive analysis of prejudice. *Personality and Social Psychology Bulletin, 5,* 461–476.

Pettigrew, T. F. (1986). The intergroup contact hypothesis reconsidered. In M. Hewstone & R. Brown (Eds.), *Contact and conflict in intergroup encounters* (pp. 169–195). London: Basil Blackwell.

Posner, M. I., & Snyder, C. R. R. (1975). Attention and cognitive control. In R. L. Solso (Ed.), *Information processing and cognition* (pp. 55–86). Hillsdale, NJ: Erlbaum.

Pratto, F., & Bargh, J. A. (1991). Stereotyping based on apparently individuating information: Trait and global components of sex stereotypes under attention overload. *Journal of Experimental Psychology, 27,* 26–47.

Prein, H. (1984). A contingency approach for conflict intervention. *Group Organizational Studies, 9,* 81–102.

Preston, J. W., & Robinson, J. D. (1976). Equal status contact and the modification of racial prejudice: A re-examination of the contact hypothesis. *Social Forces, 54,* 911–924.

Pruitt, D. G. (1991a). Strategic choice in negotiation. In J. W. Breslin & J. Z. Rubin (Eds.), *Negotiation theory and practice.* Cambridge, MA: Program on Negotiation Books.

Pruitt, D. G. (1991b). Strategy in negotiation. In V. A. Kremenyuk (Ed.), *International negotiation: Analyses, approaches, and issues.* San Francisco: Jossey-Bass.

Pruitt, D. G., Carnevale, P. J., Ben-Yoav, O., Nochajski, T. H., & Van Slyck, M. (1983). Incentives for cooperation in integrative bargaining. In R. Tietz (Ed.), *Aspiration levels in bargaining and economic decision making* (pp. 22–34). Berlin: Springer.

Pruitt, D. G., & Kressel, K. (1985). The mediation of social conflict. *Journal of Social Issues, 41,* 1–10.

Pruitt, D. G., McGillicuddy, N. B., Welton, G. L., & Fry, W. R. (1989). Process of mediation in dispute settlement. In K. Kressel, D. G. Pruitt, & associates (Eds.), *Mediation research: The process and effectiveness of third-party intervention.* San Francisco: Jossey-Bass.

Pruitt, D. G., & Rubin, J. Z. (1986). *Social conflict: Escalation, stalemate, and settlement.* New York: Random House.

Pruitt, D. G., Welton, G. L., Fry, W. R., McGillicuddy, N. B., Castrianno, L., & Zubek, J. M. (1989). The process of mediation: Caucusing, control, and problem-solving. In M. A. Rahim (Ed.), *Managing conflict: An interdisciplinary approach.* New York: Praeger.

Quattrone, G. A. (1986). On the perception of a group's variability. In S. Worchel & W. G. Austin (Eds.), *Psychology of intergroup relations.* Chicago: Nelson-Hall.

Rabbie, J. M., & Horowitz, M. (1969). Arousal of ingroup-outgroup bias by a chance win or loss. *Journal of Personality and Social Psychology, 13,* 269–277.

Rabbie, J. M., Schot, J. C., & Visser, L. (1989). Social identity theory: A conceptual and empirical critique from the perspective of a behavioral interaction model. *European Journal of Social Psychology, 19,* 171–202.

Ramirez, M. (1967). Identification with Mexican family values and authoritarianism in Mexican-Americans. *Journal of Social Psychology, 73,* 3–11.

Randolph, G., Landis, D., & Tzeng, O. C. S. (1977). The effects of time and practice upon cultural assimilator training. *International Journal of Intercultural Relations, 1,* 105–119.

Rasinski, K. A., Crocker, J., & Hastie, R. (1985). Another look at sex stereotypes and social judgments: An analysis of the social perceiver's use of subjective probabilities. *Journal of Personality and Social Psychology, 49,* 327–337.

Reskin, B. F., & Padavic, I. (1988). Supervisors as gatekeepers: Male supervisors' responses to women's integration in plant jobs. *Social Problems, 35,* 536–551.

Rhuly, S. (1976). *Orientations to intercultural communication.* Chicago: Science Research Associates.

Rime, B., Philippot, P., & Cisamolo, D. (1990). Social schemata of peripheral changes in emotion. *Journal of Personality and Social Psychology, 59,* 38–49.

Riordan, C. (1978). Equal-status interracial contact: A review and revision of the concept. *International Journal of Intercultural Relations, 2,* 161–185.

Robinson, J. W., Jr., & Preston, J. D. (1976). Equal-status contact and modification of racial prejudice: A re-examination of the contact hypothesis. *Social Forces, 54,* 911–924.

Roehl, J. A., & Cook, R. F. (1985). Issues in mediation: Obstacles and possibilities. *Journal of Social Issues, 41,* 161–178.

Roehl, J. A., & Cook, R. F. (1989). Mediation in interpersonal disputes: Effectiveness and limitations. In K. Kressel, D. G. Pruitt, & associates (Eds.), *Mediation research: The process and effectiveness of third-party intervention* (pp. 31–52). San Francisco: Jossey-Bass.

Rogers, E. M. (1983). *Diffusion of innovations.* New York: Free Press.

Rokeach, M. (1971). Long-range experimental modification of values, attitudes and behavior. *American Psychologist, 26,* 453–459.

Rosati, J. A., Carroll, D. J., & Coate, R. A. (1990). A critical assessment of the power of human needs in world society. In J. Burton & F. Dukes (Eds.), *Conflict: Readings in management and resolution* (pp. 156–179). New York: St. Martin's Press.

Rosch, E. (1978). Principles of categorization. In E. Rosch & B. B. Loyd (Eds.), *Cognition and categorization* (pp. 87–116). Hillsdale, NJ: Erlbaum.

Rose, R. (1990). Northern Ireland: The irreducible conflict. In J. V. Montville (Ed.), *Conflict and peacemaking in multiethnic societies* (pp. 133–150). Lexington, MA: D. C. Heath.

Rosenberg, S. (1986). Self-esteem research: A phenomenological corrective. In J. Prager, D. Longshore, & M. Seeman (Eds.), *School desegregation research: New approaches to situational analyses.* New York: Plenum.

Rosenfield, D., Stephan, W. G., & Lucker, G. W. (1981). Attraction to competent and incompetent members of cooperative and competitive groups. *Journal of Applied Social Psychology, 11,* 416–433.

Ross, L. (1977). The intuitive psychologist and his shortcomings: Distortions in the attribution process. In L. Berkowitz (Ed.), *Advances in experimental social psychology* (Vol. 10). New York: Academic Press.

Ross, M. H. (1991). The role of evolution in ethnocentric conflict and its management. *Journal of Social Issues, 47,* 167–185.

Ross, M. H. (1993). *The management of conflict.* New Haven: Yale University Press.

Rossell, C. H. (1978). School desegregation and community social change. *Law and Contemporary Problems, 42,* 133–183.

Rothbart, M., Evans, M., & Fulero, S. (1979). Recall of confirming events: Memory processes and the maintainance of social stereotypes. *Journal of Experimental Social Psychology, 15,* 343–355.

Rothbart, M., & Hallmark, W. (1988). Ingroup-outgroup differences in the perceived efficacy of coercion and conciliation in resolving social conflict. *Journal of Personality and Social Psychology, 55,* 248–257.

Rothbart, M., & John, O. P. (1985). Social categorization and behavioral episodes: A cognitive analysis of the effects of intergroup contact. *Journal of Social Issues, 41,* 81–104.

Rothbart, M., & Lewis, S. (1988). Inferring category attributes from examplar attributes: Geometric shapes and social categories. *Journal of Personality and Social Psychology, 55,* 861–872.

Rouhana, N. N., & Kelman, H. C. (1994). Promoting joint thinking in international conflicts: An Israeli-Palestinian continuing workshop. *Journal of Social Issues, 50,* 157–178.

Rubin, J. Z. (1994). Models of conflict management. *Journal of Social Issues, 50,* 33–46.

Rubin, J. Z., Pruitt, D. G., & Kim, S. H. (1994). *Social conflict: Escalation, stalemate, and settlement.* New York: McGraw-Hill.

Rudmin, F. W. (1994). Property. In W. J. Lonner & R. Malpass (Eds.), *Psychology and culture.* Boston: Allyn & Bacon.

Rumelhart, D. E., Hinton, G. E., & McClelland, J. L. (1986). A general framework for parallel distributed processing. In D. E. Rumelhart, J. L. McClelland, & the PDP research group. *Parallel distributed processing* (pp. 45–76). Cambridge, MA: MIT Press.

Runciman, W. G. (1966). *Relative deprivation and equal justice: A study of attitudes to social inequality in twentieth-century England.* Berkeley, CA: University of California Press.

Ruscher, J. B., & Fiske, S. T. (1990). Interpersonal competition can cause individuating processes. *Journal of Personality and Social Psychology, 58,* 832–843.

Ryan, W. (1971). *Blaming the victim.* New York: Vintage.

Sachdev, I., & Bourhis, R. Y. (1987). Status differentials and intergroup behavior. *European Journal of Social Psychology, 17,* 277–293.

Sachdev, I., & Bourhis, R. Y. (1991). Power and status differentials in minority and majority group relations. *European Journal of Social Psychology, 21,* 1–24.

Sagar, H. A., & Schofield, J. W. (1980). Racial and behavioral cues in black and white children's perceptions of ambiguously aggressive acts. *Journal of Personality and Social Psychology, 39,* 590–598.

Samovar, L. A., Porter, R. E., & Jain, N. E. (1981). *Understanding intercultural communication.* Belmont, CA: Wadsworth.

Sande, G. N., Goethals, G. R., Ferrari, L., & Worth, L. T. (1989). Value-guided attributions: Maintaining the moral self-image and the diabolical enemy-image. *Journal of Social Issues, 45,* 91–118.

Sappington, A. A. (1976). Effects of desensitization of white prejudice to blacks upon subjects' stereotypes of blacks. *Perceptual and Motor Skills, 43,* 938.

Schaller, M. (1991). Social categorization and the formation of group stereotypes: Further evidence for biased information processing in the perception of group-behavior correlations. *European Journal of Social Psychology, 21,* 25–35.

Schelling, T. (1960). *The strategy of conflict.* Cambridge: Harvard University Press.

Schofield, J. (1991). School desegregation and intergroup relations: A review of the literature. *Review of Education, 17,* 335–409.

Schuman, H., & Harding, J. (1963). Sympathetic identification with the underdog. *Public Opinion Quarterly, 90,* 675–695.

Schuman, H., Steeh, C., & Bobo, L. (1985). *Racial attitudes in America.* Cambridge: Harvard University Press.

Schwartz, S. H., & Bilsky, W. (1987). Towards a psychological structure of human values. *Journal of Personality and Social Psychology, 53,* 550–562.

Schwartz, S. H., & Bilsky, W. (1990). Toward a theory of the universal content and structure of values: Extensions and cross-cultural replications. *Journal of Personality and Social Psychology, 58,* 878–891.

Schwarzwald, J., & Amir, Y. (1984). Interethnic relations and education: An Israeli perspective. In N. Miller & M. B. Brewer (Eds.), *Groups in contact: The psychology of desegregation* (pp. 53–76). Orlando, FL: Academic Press.

Sears, D. O. (1986). Symbolic racism. In P. A. Katz & D. A. Taylor (Eds.), *Eliminating racism: Profiles in controversy.* New York: Plenum.

Sears, D. O., & Allen, H. M., Jr. (1984). The trajectory of local desegregation controversies and whites' opposition to busing. In N. Miller & M. B. Brewer (Eds.), *Groups in contact: The psychology of desegregation.* New York: Academic Press.

Sears, D. O., & Citrin, J. (1985). *Tax revolt: Something for nothing in California.* Cambridge: Harvard University Press.

Sears, D. O., & Funk, C. L. (1991). The role of self-interest in social and political attitudes. In M. Zanna (Ed.), *Advances in experimental social psychology* (Vol. 24, pp. 1–99). Orlando, FL: Academic Press.

Sears, D. O., & Huddy, L. (1990). On the origins of political disunity among women. In L. A. Tilly & P. Gurin (Eds.), *Women, politics, and change* (pp. 249–277). New York: Russell Sage.

Sears, D. O., & Kinder, D. R. (1971). Racial tensions and voting in Los Angeles. In W. Z. Hirsch (Ed.), *Los Angeles: Viability and prospects for metropolitan leadership.* New York: Praeger.

Sears, D. O., & Kinder, D. R. (1985). Whites' opposition to busing: On conceptualizing and operationalizing group conflict. *Journal of Personality and Social Psychology, 48,* 1141–1147.

Sears, D. O., & Lau, R. R. (1983). Inducing apparently self-interested political preferences. *American Journal of Political Science, 27,* 223–252.

Sears, D. O., Lau, R. R., Tyler, T. R., & Allen, H. M., Jr. (1980). Self-interest vs. symbolic politics in policy attitudes and presidential voting. *American Political Science Review, 74,* 670–684.

Secord, P. E., & Backman, C. W. (1964). *Social psychology.* New York: McGraw-Hill.

Selltiz, C., & Cook, S. W. (1962). Factors influencing attitudes of foreign students toward the host country. *Journal of Social Issues, 18,* 7–23.

Shapiro, D. L., & Brett, J. M. (1993). Comparing three processes underlying judgments of procedural justice: A field study of mediation and arbitration. *Journal of Personality and Social Psychology, 65,* 1167–1177.

Sharan, S., & Shachar, H. (1988). *Language and learning in the cooperative classroom.* New York: Springer.

Shaw, R. P., & Wong, Y. (1989). *The genetic seeds of warfare: Evolution, nationalism, and patriotism.* Boston: Unwin & Hyman.

Sherif, M., Harvey, O. J., White, B. J., Hood, W. R., & Sherif, C. W. (1961). *Intergroup conflict and cooperation: The robbers' cave experiment.* Norman: University of Oklahoma Press.

Sherif, M., & Sherif, C. W. (1956). *An outline of social psychology* (2nd ed.). New York: Harper and Row.

Sherif, M., & Sherif, C. W. (1967). Attitude as the individual's own categories: The social judgment-involvement approach to attitude and attitude change. In C. W. Sherif & M. Sherif (Eds.), *Attitude, ego-involvement and change.* New York: Wiley.

Shirts, G. (1973). *BAFA-BAFA: A cross-cultural simulation.* Del Mar, CA: Simile 11.

Shweder, R. A., & Bourne, E. J. (1982). Does the concept of the person vary cross-culturally? In A. J. Marsella & G. M. White (Eds.), *Cultural conceptions of mental health and therapy* (pp. 97–137). London: D. Reidel.

Simmons, R. G. (1978). Blacks and high self-esteem: A puzzle. *Social Psychology, 41,* 57–67.

Simon, B., & Brown, R. (1987). Perceived intragroup homogeneity in minority-majority contexts. *Journal of Personality and Social Psychology, 53,* 703–711.

Simon, B., Mlicki, P., Johnston, L., Caetano, A., Warowicki, M., van Knippenberg, A., & Deridder, R. (1990). The effects of ingroup and outgroup homogeneity on ingroup favoritism, stereotyping, and overestimation of relative ingroup size. *European Journal of Social Psychology, 20,* 519–523.

Simon, B., & Pettigrew, T. F. (1990). Social identity and perceived group homogeneity: Evidence for the ingroup homogeneity effect. *European Journal of Social Psychology, 20,* 269–286.

Simpson, G. E., & Yinger, J. M. (1985). *Racial and cultural minorities: An analysis of prejudice and discrimination* (5th ed.). New York: Plenum.

Skov, R. B., & Sherman, S. J. (1986). Information-gathering processes: Diagnosticity, hypothesis-confirmatory strategies, and perceived hypothesis confirmation. *Journal of Experimental Social Psychology, 22,* 93–121.

Skowronski, J. J., Carlston, D. E., & Isham, J. T. (1993). Implicit versus explicit impression formation: The differing effects of overt labeling and covert priming on memory and impressions. *Journal of Experimental Social Psychology, 29,* 17–41.

Slavin, R. E. (1978). Student teams and achievement divisions. *Journal of Research and Development in Education, 12,* 381–387.

Slavin, R. E. (1985). Cooperative learning: Applying contact theory in desegregated schools. *Journal of Social Issues, 41,* 45–62.

Slavin, R. E. (1990). *Cooperative learning: Theory, research, and practice.* Englewood Cliffs, NJ: Prentice-Hall.

Slavin, R. E. (1992a). When and why does cooperative learning increase achievement: Theoretical and empirical perspectives. In R. Hertz-Lazarowitz & N. Miller (Eds.), *Interaction in cooperative groups* (pp. 145–173). New York: Cambridge University Press.

Slavin, R. E. (1992b). Cooperative learning: Applying contact theory in the schools. In J. Lynch, C. Modgil, & S. Modgil (Eds.), *Cultural diversity in the schools* (Vol. 2, pp. 333–348). London: Falmer Press.

Smalley, W. B. (1963). Culture shock, language shock, and the shock of self-discovery. *Practical Anthropology, 10,* 49–56.

Smith, D. L., Pruitt, D. G., & Carnevale, P. J. (1982). Matching and mismatching: The effect of own limit, other's toughness, and time pressure on concession rate in negotiation. *Journal of Personality and Social Psychology, 42,* 876–883.

Smith, E. E., Shoben, E. J., & Rips, L. J. (1974). Structure and process in semantic memory. *Psychological Review, 81,* 214–241.

Smith, E. R. (1990). Content and process specificity in the effects of prior experiences. In T. K. Srull & R. S. Wyer (Eds.), *Advances in social cognition* (Vol. 3, pp. 1–59). Hillsdale, NJ: Lawrence Erlbaum.

Smith, E. R., & Lerner, M. (1986). Development of automatism of social judgments. *Journal of Personality and Social Psychology, 50,* 246–259.

Smith, E. R., & Zarate, M. A. (1990). Exemplar and prototype use in social categorization. *Social Cognition, 8,* 243–262.

Smith, P. B., & Bond, M. H. (1993). *Social psychology across cultures.* Boston: Allyn and Bacon.

Smock, P. J., & Wilson, F. D. (1991). Desegregation and the stability of White enrollments: A school level analysis, 1968–1984. *Sociology of Education, 64,* 278–292.

Sniderman, P. M., & Tetlock, P. E. (1986a). Symbolic racism: Problems of motive attribution in political analysis. *Journal of Social Issues, 42,* 129–150.

Sniderman, P. M., & Tetlock, P. E. (1986b). Reflections on American racism. *Journal of Social Issues, 42,* 173–188.

Snyder, M. (1984). When belief creates reality. In L. Berkowitz (Ed.), *Advances in experimental social psychology* (Vol. 18, pp. 247–305). Orlando, FL: Academic Press.

Snyder, M. (1992). Motivational foundations of behavioral confirmation. In M. Zanna (Ed.), *Advances in experimental social psychology* (Vol. 25, pp. 67–114). Orlando, FL: Academic Press.

Snyder, M., & Haugen, J. A. (1994). Why does behavioral confirmation occur? A functional perspective on the role of the perceiver. *Journal of Experimental Social Psychology, 30,* 218–246.

Snyder, M., & Swann, W. B. (1978). Hypothesis-testing in social interaction. *Journal of Personality and Social Psychology, 36,* 1202–1212.

Snyder, M., Tanke, E. D., & Berscheid, E. (1977). Social perception and interpersonal behavior: On the self-fulfilling nature of social stereotypes. *Journal of Personality and Social Psychology, 35,* 656–666.

Snyder, M., & White, P. (1981). Testing hypotheses about other people: Strategies of verification and falsification. *Personality and Social Psychology Bulletin, 7,* 39–43.

Snyder, M. L., Stephan, W. G., & Rosenfield, D. (1978). Attributional egotism. In J. Harvey, W. Ickes, & R. Kidd (Eds.), *New directions in attributional research* (Vol. 2, pp. 91–120). New York: Wiley.

Spaulding, S., & Flack, M. (1976). *The world's students in the United States*. New York: Praeger.

Spears, R., & Manstead, S. R. (1988). The social context of stereotyping and differentiation. *European Journal of Social Psychology, 19,* 101–121.

Spence, J. T., & Helmreich, R. L. (1978). *Masculinity and femininity*. Austin, TX: University of Texas Press.

Spickard, P. R. (1992). The illogic of American racial categories. In M. P. P. Root (Ed.), *Racially mixed people in America* (pp. 12–23). Newbury Park, CA: Sage.

Srull, T. K. (1981). Person memory: Some tests of associative storage and retrieval models. *Journal of Experimental Psychology: Human Learning and Memory, 7,* 440–463.

Srull, T. K., Lichtenstein, M., & Rothbart, M. (1985). Associative storage and retrieval processes in person memory. *Journal of Experimental Psychology: Learning, Memory, and Cognition, 11,* 316–345.

St. John, N. (1975). *School desegregation: Outcomes for children*. New York: Wiley.

Stangor, C. (1986). *Response biases and individual construct accessibility: Alternative measures of gender stereotypes*. Unpublished manuscript, New York University.

Stangor, C., & Duan, C. (1991). Effects of multiple task demands upon memory for information about social groups. *Journal of Experimental and Social Psychology, 27,* 357–378.

Stangor, C., Lynch, L., Duan, C., & Glass, B. (1992). Categorization of individuals on the basis of multiple social features. *Journal of Personality and Social Psychology, 62,* 207–218.

Stangor, C., & McMillan, D. (1992). Memory for expectancy-congruent and expectancy-incongruent information: A review of the social and social developmental literatures. *Psychological Bulletin, 111,* 42–61.

Stephan, C. W. (1992). Intergroup anxiety and intergroup interaction. In J. Lynch, D. Modgil, & S. Modgil (Eds.), *Cultural diversity and the schools: Prejudice, polemic or progress?* London: Falmer Press.

Stephan, C. W., & Stephan, W. G. (1992). Reducing intercultural anxiety through intercultural contact. *International Journal of Intercultural Relations, 16,* 89–106.

Stephan, W. G. (1977). Cognitive differentiation in intergroup perception. *Sociometry, 40,* 50–58.

Stephan, W. G. (1978). School desegregation: An evaluation of predictions made in *Brown vs. The Board of Education*. *Psychological Bulletin, 85,* 217–238.

Stephan, W. G. (1983). Intergroup relations. In D. Perlman & P. C. Cozby (Eds.), *Social psychology*. New York: Holt, Rinehart, & Winston.

Stephan, W. G. (1985). Intergroup relations. In G. Lindzey & E. Aronson (Eds.), *Handbook of social psychology* (Vol. 3, pp. 599–658). New York: Addison-Wesley.

Stephan, W. G. (1986). Effects of school desegregation: An evaluation 30 years after *Brown*. In L. Saxe & M. Saks (Eds.), *Advances in applied social psychology* (Vol. 4). New York: Academic Press.

Stephan, W. G. (1987). The contact hypothesis in intergroup relations. In C. Hendrick (Ed.), *Group processes and intergroup relations*. Beverly Hills: Sage.

Stephan, W. G. (1991). School desegregation: Short-term and long-term effects. In H. J. Knopke, R. J. Norrell, & R. W. Rogers (Eds.), *Opening doors: Perspective on race relations in contemporary America* (pp. 100–118). Tuscaloosa: University of Alabama Press.

Stephan, W. G., Ageyev, V., Coates-Shrider, L., Stephan, C. W., & Abalakina, M. (1994). On the relationship between stereotypes and prejudice: An international study. *Personality and Social Psychology Bulletin, 20,* 277–284.

Stephan, W. G., Ageyev, V. S., Stephan, C. W., Abalakina, M., Stefanenko, T., & Coates-Shrider, L. (1993). Soviet and American stereotypes: A comparison of methods. *Social Psychology Quarterly, 56,* 54–64.

Stephan, W. G., & Rosenfield, D. (1978a). The effects of desegregation on race relations and self-esteem. *Journal of Educational Psychology, 70,* 670–679.

Stephan, W. G., & Rosenfield, D. (1978b). The effects of desegregation on racial attitudes. *Journal of Personality and Social Psychology, 36,* 795–804.

Stephan, W. G., & Rosenfield, D. (1979). Black self-rejection: Another look. *Journal of Educational Psychology, 70,* 708–716.

Stephan, W. G., & Rosenfield, D. (1982). Racial and ethnic stereotypes. In A. Miller (Ed.), *In the eye of the beholder* (pp. 92–136). New York: Praeger.

Stephan, W. G., & Stephan, C. W. (1984). The role of ignorance in intergroup relations. In N. Miller & M. B. Brewer (Eds.), *Groups in contact: The psychology of desegregation* (pp. 229–257). New York: Academic Press.

Stephan, W. G., & Stephan, C. W. (1985). Intergroup anxiety. *Journal of Social Issues, 41,* 157–175.

Stephan, W. G., & Stephan, C. W. (1989a). Antecedents of intergroup anxiety in Asian-Americans and Hispanic-Americans. *International Journal of Intercultural Relations, 13,* 203–216.

Stephan, W. G., & Stephan, C. W. (1989b). Emotional reactions to interracial achievement outcomes. *Journal of Applied Social Psychology, 19,* 608–621.

Stephan, W. G., & Stephan, C. W. (1993). Cognition and affect in stereotyping: Parallel interactive networks. In D. M. Mackie & D. L. Hamilton (Eds.), *Affect, cognition and stereotyping: Interactive processes in group perception* (pp. 111–136). Orlando, FL: Academic Press.

Stephan, W. G., Stephan, C. W., & Cabezas de Vargas, M. (in press). Emotional expression in Costa Rica and the United States. *Journal of Cross-Cultural Psychology.*

Stephan, W. G., Stephan, C. W., Wenzel, B., & Cornelius, J. (1991). Intergroup interaction and self-disclosure. *Journal of Applied Social Psychology, 21,* 1370–1378.

Stern, L. D., Marrs, S., Cole, E., & Millar, M. G. (1984). Processing time and recall of inconsistent and consistent behaviors of individuals and groups. *Journal of Personality and Social Psychology, 47,* 253–262.

Stevenson, H. W., Stigler, J. W., Lee, S. Y., Lucker, G. W., Kitamura, S., & Hsu, C. C. (1985). Cognitive performance and academic achievement of Japanese, Chinese, and American children. *Child Development, 56,* 713–734.

Stewart, E. (1966). The simulation of cultural differences. *Journal of Communication, 16,* 291–304.

Stewart, E., Danielian, J., & Foster, R. (1969). *Simulating intercultural communication through role playing.* Arlington: HUMRRO Technical Report 69–7.

Streufert, S., & Streufert, S. C. (1986). The development of internation conflict. In S. Worchel & W. G. Austin (Eds.), *Psychology of intergroup relations* (pp. 134–152). Chicago: Nelson-Hall.

Stroessner, S. J., Hamilton, D. L., & Mackie, D. M. (1992). Affect and stereotyping: The effect of induced mood on distinctiveness-based illusory correlation. *Journal of Personality and Social Psychology, 62,* 564–576.

Stroessner, S. J., & Mackie, D. M. (1991). Affect and perceived group variability: Implications for stereotyping and prejudice. In D. M. Mackie & D. L. Hamilton (Eds.), *Affect, cognition and stereotyping: Interactive processes in group perception* (pp. 63–86). Orlando, FL: Academic Press.

Sumner, W. G. (1906). *Folkways.* Boston: Ginn.

Swann, W. B., Jr., & Ely, R. J. (1984). A battle of wills: Self-verification versus behavioral confirmation. *Journal of Personality and Social Psychology, 46,* 1287–1302.

Swowronski, J. J., Carlston, D. E., & Isham, J. T. (1993). Implicit versus explicit impression formation: The differing effects of overt labeling and covert priming on memory and impressions. *Journal of Experimental Social Psychology, 29,* 17–41.

Tajfel, H. (Ed.). (1978). *Differentiation between social groups: Studies in the social psychology of intergroup relations.* London: Academic Press.

Tajfel, H. (1981). *Human groups and social categories: Studies in social psychology.* Cambridge: Cambridge University Press.

Tajfel, H. (1982). *Social identity and intergroup relations.* Cambridge: Cambridge University Press.

Tajfel, H., Billig, M., Bundy, R. P., & Flament, C. (1971). Social categorization and intergroup behavior. *European Journal of Social Psychology, 1,* 149–178.

Tajfel, H., & Turner, J. C. (1979). An integrative theory of intergroup conflict. In S. Worchel & W. G. Austin (Eds.), *Psychology of intergroup relations.* Monterey, CA: Brooks-Cole.

Tajfel, H., & Turner, J. C. (1986). The social identity theory of intergroup behavior. In S. Worchel & W. G. Austin (Eds.), *Psychology of intergroup relations* (2nd ed.). Chicago: Nelson-Hall.

Taylor, D. M., & Jaggi, V. (1974). Ethnocentrism and causal attribution in a South Indian context. *Journal of Cross-Cultural Psychology, 5,* 162–171.

Taylor, D. M., & Moghaddam, F. M. (1987). *Theories of intergroup relations.* New York: Praeger.

Taylor, D. M., & Porter, L. E. (1994). A multicultural view of stereotyping. In W. J. Lonner & R. Malpass (Eds.), *Psychology and culture.* Boston: Allyn & Bacon.

Thomas, W. I., & Thomas, D. S. (1928). *The child in America.* New York: Alfred A. Knopf.

Thompson, L. (1993). The impact of negotiation on intergroup relations. *Journal of Experimental Social Psychology, 29,* 304–325.

Ting-Toomey, S. (1985). Toward a theory of conflict and culture. In W. B. Gudykunst, L. P. Stewart, & S. Ting-Toomey (Eds.), *Communication, culture, and organizational processes*. Beverly Hills: Sage.

Ting-Toomey, S. (1988). A face-negotiation theory. In Y. Kim & W. B. Gudykunst (Eds.), *Theory in intercultural communication*. Newbury Park, CA: Sage.

Triandis, H. C. (1972). *The analysis of subjective culture*. New York: John Wiley & Sons.

Triandis, H. C. (1975). Culture training, cognitive complexity, and interpersonal attitudes. In R. W. Brislin, S. Bochner, & W. J. Lonner (Eds.), *Cross-cultural perspectives on learning*. New York: Wiley.

Triandis, H. C. (1976). *Interpersonal behavior*. Monterey, CA: Brooks/Cole.

Triandis, H. C. (1977). Subjective culture and interpersonal relations across cultures. *Annals of the New York Academy of Sciences, 285,* 418–434.

Triandis, H. C. (1983). Essentials of studying cultures. In D. Landis & R. W. Brislin (Eds.), *Handbook of intercultural training* (Vol. 1). New York: Pergamon.

Triandis, H. C. (1990). Theoretical concepts that are applicable to the analysis of ethnocentrism. In R. W. Brislin (Ed.), *Applied cross-cultural psychology*. Newbury Park, CA: Sage.

Triandis, H. C. (1994). *Culture and social behavior*. New York: McGraw-Hill.

Triandis, H. C., Brislin, R. W., & Hui, C. H. (1988). Cross-cultural training across the individualism-collectivism divide. *International Journal of Intercultural Relations, 12,* 269–289.

Triandis, H. C., Lisansky, J., Setiadi, B., Chang, B., Marin, G., & Betancourt, H. (1982). Stereotyping among Hispanics and Anglos. *Journal of Cross-Cultural Psychology, 13,* 409–426.

Triandis, H. C., McCusker, C., & Hui, C. H. (1990). Multimethod probes of individualism and collectivism. *Journal of Personality and Social Psychology, 59,* 1006–1020.

Triandis, H. C., & Vassiliou, V. (1967). Frequency of contact and stereotyping. *Journal of Personality and Social Psychology, 7,* 316–328.

Trifonovich, G. (1977). On cross-cultural techniques. In R. Brislin (Ed.), *Culture learning: Concepts, applications, and research*. Honolulu, HI: University of Hawaii Press.

Trope, Y., & Bassok, M. (1983). Information-gathering strategies in hypothesis-testing. *Journal of Experimental Social Psychology, 52,* 560–576.

Turner, J. C. (1978). Social categorization and social discrimination in the minimal group paradigm. In H. Tajfel (Ed.), *Differentiation between social groups: Studies in the social psychology of intergroup relations*. London: Academic Press.

Turner, J. C. (1981). The experimental social psychology of intergroup behaviour. In J. Turner & H. Giles (Eds.), *Intergroup behaviour*. Oxford: Blackwell.

Turner, J. C. (1985). Social categorization and the self-concept: A social cognitive theory of group behavior. In E. J. Lawler (Ed.), *Advances in group processes: Theory and research* (Vol. 2). Greenwich, CT: JAI Press.

Turner, J. C., Brown, R. J., & Tajfel, H. (1979). Social comparison and group interest in ingroup favoritism. *European Journal of Social Psychology, 9,* 187–204.

Turner, J. C., Hogg, M. A., Oakes, P. J., Reicher, S. D., & Wetherell, M. S. (1987). *Rediscovering the social group: A self-categorization theory.* New York: Basil Blackwell.

Tyler, T. R. (1987). The psychology of disputant concerns in mediation. *Negotiation Journal, 3,* 367–374.

U.S. Commission on Civil Rights. (1967). *Racial isolation in the schools.* Washington, DC: U.S. Government Printing Office.

U.S. Commission on Civil Rights. (1987). *The new evidence on school desegregation.* Washington, DC: U.S. Government Printing Office.

Vanbeselaere, N. (1991). The different effects of simple and crossed categorizations: A result of the category differentiation process or of differential category salience? *European Review of Social Psychology, 2,* 247–278.

van den Berghe, P. L. (1967). *Race and racism.* New York: Wiley.

van den Berghe, P. L. (1981). *The ethnic phenomenon.* New York: Elsevier.

Vanneman, R., & Pettigrew, T. (1982). Race and relative deprivation in the urban United States. *Race, 13,* 461–486.

Vidmar, N. (1985). An assessment of mediation in small claims court. *Journal of Social Issues, 41,* 127–144.

Vitz, P. C., & Kite, W. R. (1970). Factors affecting conflict and negotiation within an alliance. *Journal of Experimental Social Psychology, 5,* 233–247.

Vivian, J., Brown, R., & Hewstone, M. J. (1994). Intergroup contact: Theoretical and empirical developments. In R. Ben-Ari & Y. Rich (Eds.), *Understanding and enhancing education for diverse students: An international perspective.* Tel-Aviv: Bar-Ilan University Press.

Wagner, U., & Schonbach, P. (1984). Links between educational status and prejudice: Ethnic attitudes in West Germany. In M. B. Brewer & N. Miller (Eds.), *Groups in contact: The psychology of desegregation* (pp. 29–52). New York: Academic Press.

Wall, J. A., Jr. (1977). Intergroup bargaining: Effects of opposing constituents' stance, opposing representatives' bargaining, and representatives' locus of control. *Journal of Conflict Resolution, 21,* 459–474.

Wall, J. A., Jr., & Lynn, A. (1993). Mediation. *Journal of Conflict Resolution, 37,* 160–194.

Walster, E., Walster, G. W., & Berscheid, E. (1978). *Equity: Theory and research.* Boston: Allyn & Bacon.

Watson, G. (1947). *Action for unity.* New York: Harper.

Weber, R., & Crocker, J. (1983). Cognitive processing in the revision of stereotypic beliefs. *Journal of Personality and Social Psychology, 45,* 961–977.

Webster, S. W. (1961). The influence of interracial contact on social acceptance in a newly desegregated school. *Journal of Educational Psychology, 45,* 292–296.

Weigel, R. H., & Howes, P. W. (1985). Conceptions of racial prejudice. *Journal of Social Issues, 41,* 117–138.

Weigel, R. H., Wiser, P. L., & Cook, S. W. (1975). The impact of cooperative learning experiences on cross-ethnic relations and helping. *Journal of Social Issues, 31,* 219–244.

Weinberg, M. (1983). *The search for quality integrated education.* Westport, CT: Greenwood Press.

Wetherell, M. S. (1982). Cross-cultural studies of minimal groups. In H. Tajfel (Ed.), *Social identity and intergroup relations.* Cambridge: Cambridge University Press.

Wicker, A. (1969). Attitudes vs. actions: The relationship of verbal and overt behavioral responses to attitude objects. *Journal of Social Issues, 25,* 41–78.

Wilder, D. A. (1986). Social categorization: Implications for creation and reduction of intergroup bias. In L. Berkowitz (Ed.), *Advances in experimental social psychology* (Vol. 19). Orlando, FL: Academic Press.

Wilder, D. A., & Allen, V. L. (1978). Group membership and preference for information about others. *Personality and Social Psychology Bulletin, 4,* 106–110.

Wilder, D. A., & Shapiro, P. (1991). Facilitation of outgroup stereotypes by enhanced ingroup identity. *Journal of Personality and Social Psychology, 27,* 431–452.

Williams, R. M., Jr. (1947). *The reduction of intergroup tensions.* New York: Social Science Research Council.

Williams, R. M., Jr. (1964). *Strangers next door.* Englewood Cliffs, NJ: Prentice-Hall.

Williams, R. M., Jr. (1977). *Mutual accommodation: Ethnic conflict and cooperation.* Minneapolis: University of Minnesota Press.

Wilson, F. D. (1985). The impact of school desegregation on White public school enrollment. *Sociology of Education, 58,* 137–153.

Wilson, K. L. (1979). The effects of integration and class on black educational attainment. *Sociology of Education, 52,* 84–98.

Woodmansee, J., & Cook, S. W. (1967). Dimensions of verbal racial attitudes: Their identification and measurement. *Journal of Personality and Social Psychology, 7,* 240–250.

Worchel, S. (1986). The role of cooperation in reducing intergroup conflict. In S. Worchel & W. G. Austin (Eds.), *Psychology of intergroup relations.* Chicago: Nelson-Hall.

Word, C., Zanna, M. P., & Cooper, J. (1974). The nonverbal mediation of self-fulfilling prophecies in interracial interaction. *Journal of Experimental Social Psychology, 10,* 109–120.

Wortman, P. M., King, C., & Bryant, F. B. (1982). *Meta-analyses of quasi-experiments: School desegregation and Black achievement.* Ann Arbor, MI: Institute for Social Research.

Wyer, R. S., Jr., & Martin, L. L. (1986). Person memory: The role of traits, group stereotypes, and specific behaviors in the cognitive representation of persons. *Journal of Personality and Social Psychology, 50,* 661–675.

Zanna, M., Crosby, F., & Lowenstein, G. (1987). Male reference groups and discontent among female professionals. In B. A. Gutek & L. Larwood (Eds.), *Women's career development.* Newbury Park, CA: Sage.

Zartman, I. W., & Touval, S. (1985). International mediation: Conflict resolution and power politics. *Journal of Social Issues, 41,* 27–45.

Ziegler, S. (1981). The effectiveness of cooperative learning teams for increasing cross-ethnic friendship: Additional evidence. *Human Organization, 40,* 264–268.

Zubek, J. M., Pruitt, D. G., Peirce, R. S., & Iocolano, A. (1989). Mediator and disputant characteristics in behavior as they effect the outcome of community negotiations. Summarized in Carnevale, P. J., & Pruitt, D. G. (1992). Negotiation and mediation. *Annual Review of Psychology, 43,* 531–582.

INDEX

Abalakina, M., 5–7, 14, 123, 124
Abe, H., 133
Abeles, R. P., 148
Abrams, D., 64, 101, 102, 106, 198
Abstraction model, social identity
 theory, 98–99
Accentuation, 104–105
Achievement, and school desegregation,
 77–78, 80, 82
Ackerman, N., 34, 35
Acuri, L., 24
Adamopoulos, S., 134
Adelman, L., 64
Adlerfer, C. P., 68
Adorno, T. W., 35
Affect, and stereotyping, 17–18
African Americans
 and prejudice, 33–34, 40, 41–53,
  56–57
 school desegregation, 74–84
 shift in conflicts in United States,
  144
 slavery of, 9–10
 stereotyping of, 9–10, 12, 90
Ageyev, V., 5–7, 14, 123, 124
Ajzen, I., 34
Albert, R. D., 134, 135
Alker, H., 149
Allen, H. M., Jr., 51, 52
Allen, V. L., 20, 92
Allison, S. T., 28
Allport, F. H., 62, 63, 74
Allport, G. W., 1, 9, 34, 52, 62, 63,
 109, 124

Al-Zahrini, S. S. A., 126
America, individualistic culture of,
 119–122
Amir, Y., 66, 79
Anderson, J. R., 13
Anxiety, intergroup, 128–130
Arab-Israeli conflict, 141–142, 150, 169
Archer, D., 47
Armor, D. J., 81, 82
Aronson, E., 64, 66, 68, 85
Ashmore, R. D., 71
Associated Press, 77
Associative network models
 nodes of, 13–14, 15, 16, 17
 of stereotypes, 13–26
Astin, A., 80, 81
Asuncion, A. G., 28
Attitudes, definitions of, 34–35
Attitude surveys, of prejudice, 40
Attributional training programs, in
 intercultural communication,
 134–135
Attributions
 biases, and intercultural relations,
  124–125
 collectivist vs. individualistic
  cultures, 125
 ultimate attribution error, 12, 13
Authority
 in contact hypothesis, 68–69
 impact on intergroup relations, 68
Autostereotypes, 123
Aversive racism theory, 48–50
Axelrod, R., 158

Mutually assured destruction (MAD), 152, 159
Myrdal, G., 42

Nascimento-Schulze, C., 101
Nationalism, and social identity, 108
Native Americans, and hantavirus, 156
Nedler, B. F., 26
Needs
    conflict and deprivation of basic needs, 149–152
    sociobiological theory of, 151
Negotiation, 156–162
    compromise in, 157
    concessions in, 157–158
    contending in, 159–160
    definition of, 156, 157
    dual concern model, 156–157
    and motivation, 156–157
    problem solving in, 160–162
Neidenthal, P. M., 18
Neuberg, S. L., 17, 28, 29
Newcomb, T., 34
Newsweek, 33
Ng, S. H., 101, 102
Nisbeth, R. E., 25
Nishida, T., 120
Nochajski, T. H., 157
Nonviolence, Gandhian, 160
Northern Ireland, 143
Norvel, N., 65

Oakes, P. J., 90, 94, 100–107
Oberg, C., 130
O'Connell, M., 102
Olson, J. M., 35
Olzak, S., 40, 145
Omoto, A. M., 28
Orfield, G., 81
Ortiz, V., 67
Osgood, C. E., 166
Oskamp, S., 167
Ottani, V., 126
Outgroup homogeneity, 94–99

Padavic, I., 24
Paige, R. M., 130, 132
Park, B., 97–100, 112
Parrish, T. S., 71
Parsons, M. A., 78
Pascale, L., 24
Patchen, M., 158, 169

Pavelchak, M. A., 17
Peabody, D., 122, 123
Peace Corps training, 137
Pearce, D., 81
Pearce, W. B., 118
Pearson, J., 162
Pedersen, P., 70, 132, 133, 135, 137, 138
Peichert, J. A., 80
Peirce, R. S., 160, 163
Percentage method, measurement of stereotypes, 5
Perdue, C. W., 17
Peres, Y., 70
Perry, G. A., 80
Persian Gulf War, 104
Personal identity, nature of, 90
Personalization, and improvement of intergroup relations, 109–111
Pettigrew, T., 34, 147
Pettigrew, T. F., 12, 30, 62, 65, 77, 80, 82, 83, 100
Pomare, M., 30, 86, 111, 112
Porter, L. E., 124
Porter, R. E., 117, 132
Posner, M. I., 17
Post, D. L., 27
Pratto, F., 28
Prein, H., 162
Prejudice
    definitions of, 34
    measurement of, 40
    realistic group conflict theory of, 39–40, 56–57
    and school desegregation, 78–79
    social psychology explanations of, 35–39
Preston, E., 28
Preston, J. W., 65
Prisoner's dilemma, 167–168
Problem solving
    in conflict resolution, 160–162
    methods of, 161
Proshansky, N., 63
Pruitt, D. G., 156, 157, 159–163
Psychological needs
    conflict and deprivation of basic needs, 149–152
    sociobiological theory of, 151
Pufall, A., 102

Quattrone, G. A., 94

Rabbie, J. M., 92, 102
Racism
    aversive racism theory of, 48–50
    compunction theory of, 52–54
    covert racism theory, 41–43, 54–56
    definition of, 35
    examples of, in United States, 35–36
    formulation of theories of, 41–42
    future view of, 57–58
    new racism concept, 42
    response amplification theory of,
      44–47
    symbolic racism theory of, 50–52
Ramirez, M., 126
Ramsey, S. L., 65
Randolph, G., 70
Rasinski, K. A., 25
Realistic group conflict theory, 144–145
    basic premise of, 144
    ethnic competition theory, 145
    of intergroup conflict, 144–145
    as predictive tool, 144
    of racism, 39–40, 56–57, 93
Recategorization, and improvement of
    intergroup relations, 111–112
Reentry shock, 132
Reichel, L. D., 26
Reicher, S. D., 90, 94, 100, 102, 106,
    107
Relative deprivation theory, 145–149
    egoistic relative deprivation, 147
    experience of relative deprivation,
      145–146
    fraternal deprivation, 147
    of intergroup conflict, 145–149
    perception of equity in, 146
    situations leading to relative
      deprivation, 148–149
    and social exchange theory, 146
Reskin, B. F., 24
Response amplification theory, of
    racism, 44–47
Rholes, W. S., 18, 22
Rhuly, S., 138, 139
Riordan, C., 65, 66
Rips, L. J., 14
Robbers Cave study, 84
Robinson, J. D., 65
Roehl, J. A., 162
Rogers, E. M., 132, 153
Rogers-Croak, M., 68
Rokeach, M., 70

Role-playing, in intercultural
    communication training, 135
Roper, S., 29, 65, 70
Rosati, J. A., 149, 151
Rosch, E., 8
Rose, R., 143
Rosenberg, S., 78
Rosenfield, D., 9, 11, 12, 64, 65, 68, 70,
    78, 85, 87, 124
Ross, L., 124
Ross, M. H., 151, 165
Rossell, C. H., 78, 81, 82
Rothbart, M., 22, 23, 28, 67, 69, 86, 97,
    98, 109, 112, 160, 209
Rothman, A. J., 15, 16
Rouhana, N. N., 163
Roye, W. J., 68
Rubin, J. Z., 157, 161, 165
Rudmin, F. W., 116
Rumelhart, D. E., 13
Runciman, W. G., 147
Ruscher, J. B., 71
Ruvolo, C. M., 22
Rwanda civil war, 1–3
Ryan, C. S., 98, 99, 100
Ryan, W., 36

Sachdev, I., 101
Sadat, Anwar, 169
Sagar, H. A., 22, 37
St. John, N., 77, 78
Salovey, P., 18, 96, 97, 98
Salvi, D., 24
Samovar, L. A., 117, 132
Sande, G. N., 128
Sandinistas, 160–161
Sanford, R. N., 35
Sapir, C., 86
Sappington, A. A., 71
Schaferhoff, S., 93, 101
Schaller, M., 106
Schelling, T., 159
Scherer, K., 120
Schmidt, K. L., 120
Schofield, J., 70, 82
Schofield, J. W., 22, 37
Schonbach, P., 70
School desegregation, 74–84
    abandonment of policy, 82
    long-term effects of, 79–81
    pace of, 77
    short-term effects of, 77–79